D0832595

Pitt Press Series

EURIPIDES

THE ALCESTIS

CAMBRIDGE UNIVERSITY PRESS
London: FETTER LANE, E.C.
C. F. CLAY, Manager

Edinburgh: 100, PRINCES STREET
Berlin: A. ASHER AND CO.
Leipzig: F. A. BROCKHAUS
New York: G. P. PUTNAM'S SONS
Bombay and Calcutta: MACMILLAN AND CO., Ltd.

All rights reserved

EURIPIDES

THE ALCESTIS

EDITED BY

W. S. HADLEY, M.A.

FELLOW AND TUTOR OF PEMBROKE COLLEGE, CAMBRIDGE

CAMBRIDGE:
AT THE UNIVERSITY PRESS
1912

First Edition 1896
Reprinted 1901, 1912

PREFACE.

IN preparing the text of the Alcestis I have always had
before me the editions of Kirchhoff (ed. maj. Berlin,
1855, with full critical apparatus: ed. min. Berlin, 1867)
and Prinz (Leipzig, 1879): in cases of difficulty I have
endeavoured to the best of my ability to form an inde-
pendent judgment of my own. In matters of orthography
I have followed Prinz. With regard to the commentary, I
find it hard to particularize my obligations: the list of
scholars who have contributed to the knowledge of Euri-
pides from Valckenaer onwards is a long one: perhaps to
Monk (whose edition admirably sums up the results of the
scholarship of his day) I am indebted more than to any
other: that store of annotations which, gradually growing
up round a text, is from time to time digested in an edition
and becomes the common stock of scholars, must form the
basis of all future work: and in the Alcestis we owe that
store to Monk. Where I have taken anything from more
modern editions I have been careful to acknowledge
my indebtedness; the work on Euripides of Nauck and
Wilamowitz-Moellendorff should be specially mentioned.
Passing on to works of reference, I should like to express
my obligations to Professor Jebb's editions of the Plays

of Sophocles, Schwartz's *Scholia in Euripidem*, Haigh's *Attic Theatre*, Rutherford's *New Phrynichus*, Veitch's *Irregular Greek Verbs*, Meisterhans' *Grammatik der Attischen Inschriften* (2nd ed.), Ellendt-Genthe's *Lexicon Sophocleum* and Beck's Index to Euripides. Grammatical references are in the main to Goodwin's *Moods and Tenses* (revised edition, 1889), and to the same scholar's *Greek Grammar*. I have also referred to Hadley's *Greek Grammar*, and Thompson's *Greek Syntax*. I have purposely abstained from quoting isolated passages from Browning's great translation: it must be read and re-read as a whole. An excellent translation is also to be found in the first volume of Mr Way's *Euripides in English verse*. The study of the play in Dr Verrall's *Euripides the Rationalist* is full of interest.

Finally I must express my grateful thanks to Mr R. A. Neil who has read the proof-sheets and helped me throughout with his valuable advice. For the index I am indebted to the kindness of my friend Mr Hugo Sharpley of Corpus Christi College, Oxford.

TABLE OF CONTENTS.

INTRODUCTION.

AT the end of March or beginning of April in the year
438 B.C. the Athenians were celebrating the City Dionysia.
The festivities, under the direction of the archon eponymus,
extended over five or six days and included performances of
tragedies, comedies and dithyrambs, besides gorgeous proces-
sions through the streets of Athens, hymns and dances at the
statues of the gods in the agora, and solemn sacrifices to the
mystic deity Dionysus, to whose honour all the majestic
pageantry of that brilliant week was dedicated, by whose di-
vinity were hallowed all who took a part, even the humblest,
in the celebration.   In his theatre[1] to the S.E. of the Acropolis

---

[1] It is necessary to state here the modern theory based on the
excavations of Dr Dörpfeld and the German School of Archaeology
at Athens.   It is held that in the fifth century B.C. there was no perma-
nent stone theatre, the earliest existing remains of such a building
dating only from the latter half of the fourth century: that there was
nothing more than a circular orchestra, with a temporary erection on
the side remote from the spectators, representing perhaps a temple or
palace front with a large door in the middle, from which emerged the
principal actors, the rest, with the chorus, entering from the broad
πάροδοι which also gave access to the θέατρον proper, i.e. the audi-
torium : that actors and chorus all performed in the orchestra on the
same level, the actors being distinguished by the superior height im-
parted to their figures by the cothurnus : the sitting accommodation
provided would be benches only.   A modified view is that the stone

were performed the dramas which themselves were the literary outcome of the rude dance and chorus of his earlier worship: for three successive days at dawn the Athenian population thronged the vast spaces of the building, which, commenced 40 or 50 years before, was not to be fully completed for more than a century to come, and sat contented though unfed throughout the day on the unbacked stone seats, with the sun streaming in their faces, though the rocks of the Acropolis behind them warded off the chill north winds of the early spring, listening patiently while tragedies, comedies and dithyrambs were performed for the glory of the god and the satisfaction of the Athenians; ever critical to detect and prompt to punish with jeers or stones any offence against metre, sense, or morals, though it may be admitted that their appreciation of the latter was directed rather by convention than conviction. Such was the audience which at the Dionysia of 438 on one morning listened to a suite of four plays by their favourite Sophocles, to whom finally was awarded the ivy garland of victory: on another to the Cressae, Alcmaeon, Telephus and Alcestis of the younger poet, Euripides, who 17 years before had first contended for the prize of tragedy and was still for another thirty years to 'draw men as they are,' finally winning after his death that first place in the affections of his countrymen, which had been grudged him when alive. The name of the third author selected

theatre was there in the time of Euripides, but that the stage was a temporary wooden structure erected on the occasion of the dramatic contests. According to the latter view it will be noted that actors and chorus perform on different levels, and not, as Dr Dörpfeld would have us believe, commingled in the orchestra. I have thought it best to follow the old-fashioned tradition in the text, as certainty has by no means been attained in this most debated question. The aspect and surroundings of the theatre of Lycurgus have been described, in the belief that its arrangements superseded something of kindred character to themselves. (The English reader may consult Prof. Jebb's article 'Theatrum' in the *Dictionary of Greek and Roman Antiquities*, 3rd ed., 1891; and Miss Harrison's *Mythology and Monuments of Ancient Athens*, pp. 271—295, where Dr Dörpfeld's theory is given at length.)

by the archon for the honour of providing 'new tragedies' has not been preserved.

The scene is one which we may pause to contemplate. Gently rising, tier above tier, from the level of the orchestra in ever widening semicircles, are the seats which accommodate the fifteen or twenty thousand spectators, men women and boys, who gather in bright holiday dresses with garlands on their heads to take part in the great yearly festival: the vast auditorium, in shape resembling a horse-shoe, is intersected by 14 gangways which run upwards from the ground-level, crossing the broad passages ($\delta\iota\alpha\zeta\acute{\omega}\mu\alpha\tau\alpha$) which divide the theatre longitudinally. Prominent in the orchestra stand the statue of the god, which has been brought over-night in torch-lit procession by the ephebi from the neighbouring temple of Dionysus Eleuthereus, and his altar ($\theta\upsilon\mu\acute{\epsilon}\lambda\eta$), round which will go the circling dances of the chorus: for his priest is reserved the throne of honour in the centre of the front row, richly carved, while the remaining marble stalls are inscribed for the most part with the names of the other priests and religious dignitaries for whose use they are set aside: for some rows back extend the seats reserved for the archons and strategi, for the ambassadors of foreign states, for the sons of citizens who have fallen in battle while fighting for their country, for the ten judges appointed by lot, one for each tribe, from a preliminary list of persons carefully selected for their capacity to judge of literary merit, with the votes of five of whom, drawn at random by the archon from the urn in which the chosen ten have placed the tablets containing their several verdicts, rests the momentous decision of the prize. But the right of $\pi\rho o\epsilon\delta\rho\acute{\iota}\alpha$ belongs to few; the mass of Athenians must sit where chance or strength may bring them: high and low, clean and unclean, side by side; the rich man who brings cushions and carpets to soften the stern Peiraic limestone, and the poor man whose entrance fee even of two obols is the gift of a wise state, which thus provides education for her needier sons: the very inmates of the prisons, liberated for the day, are spectators of the scene upon the stage, where fate works out the punishment of sin. A particular block of seats is however set apart for the Council;

and men women and youths each have their appointed quarter. Nature's distinctions are allowed, but Democracy will permit few others.

All eyes are turned in eager expectation to the circular orchestra below, bounded by the marble thrones, and to the long narrow stage behind it raised some 6 or 8 feet above its level. In the orchestra already the tribute of the allies, talent upon talent, has been piled and then carried to the city treasury, striking witness to the supremacy of Athens in the world of action, as the plays soon to follow are of her unrivalled sovereignty in art and literature : distinguished citizens have been presented with the crowns with which a grateful country rewards their services : the orphan sons of those who have fallen for Athens, now grown to manhood, have paraded in full armour, the gift of the state, in the presence of the citizens who have reared them in their fathers' place, before embarking on the careers which henceforth will depend upon their own exertions : the hush of expectancy falls on the vast audience as the herald proclaims εἴσαγε τὸν χορόν.

Euripides is the poet whom the lot bids to provide the morning's tragedies : his chosen theme is woman, woman's power for good and ill, a subject of unfading interest to the poet of humanity. In the Cressae he paints Atreus' erring wife Aerope ; her guilty intrigue with Thyestes and the bloody vengeance of her husband, whence is born the curse that is to dog the house for generations ; γαμεῖτε νῦν γαμεῖτε cries the indignant Atreus in warning to the world, κᾆτα θνῄσκετε | ἢ φαρμάκοισιν ἐκ γυναικὸς ἢ δόλοις. In the Alcmaeon is a double picture ; the injured wife Alphesiboea daring all things, death even at the hands of the father whom she has defied, to aid the husband who has deserted and deceived her ; and Callirrhoe, the supplantress, whose vanity and greed have driven the weak Alcmaeon to his last deceit and death not undeserved : γυναῖκα καὶ ὠφέλειαν | καὶ νόσον ἀνδρὶ φέρειν μεγίσταν | ἐδίδαξα τῶμῷ λόγῳ : thus moralises the poet speaking through the chorus. In the Telephus the main interest, it is true, lies in the fortunes of Heracles' hapless son, from whom the play receives its name : still there is Clytaemnestra, hating her husband and prompting the Mysian king in his extremity to seize Orestes, the issue of her union with the detested Agamemnon, as surety for his life; ἀπέπτυσ' ἐχθροῦ φωτὸς ἔχθιστον τέκος: these are the words of a wife and mother. According to the established custom of the Attic stage three tragedies were followed by a satyric drama, which, representing in a humorous light the characters whose fortunes had provided the pathos of the tragedies, served to relieve the tension of the spectators' feelings, thus fulfilling the same purpose as the comic interludes in our own Elizabethan dramas. But it is by no mere farce that Euripides here proceeds to lighten the possibly gloomy reflexions of his audience; it is by the picture of a faithful woman, willing to die that she may ransom from death a husband whose weakness serves only to bring into stronger relief her own unselfish heroism, and save her children from the sad lot of the fatherless. Humorous elements in the play there are, which will be noted in their place, but they are not of the essence of the poet's conception; and it is to one of those innovations, which Euripides, if he saw good cause, never feared to make, that we owe the most 'loved' of the women who moved upon the ancient stage.

But let us now take our seat with the audience, and look on as the fourth of the morning's plays is unfolded before the unwearied Athenians. Facing the spectators and raised some eight feet above the level of the orchestra, for which it forms a background, is the stage: its depth probably does not exceed ten feet: the scene, painted on moveable canvas and fixed to the permanent stone-work of the stage buildings, is in two pieces; the upper representing the sky, the lower, set forward a foot or two in front of the upper, depicting Admetus' palace front at Pherae: three doors open on to the stage, one, in the centre, splendidly ornate, as befits the state entrance of a Thessalian prince's home; and two smaller doors leading to guest-chambers or the like: before the palace stand statues of tutelary gods, perhaps too a pillar-shaped monument in honour of Apollo of the Highways. Presently there appears upon the stage, easily discernible even from the distant parts of the great theatre, a majestic figure, robed in a high-girt long-sleeved tunic of bright colour, over which is thrown a brilliant mantle; the tragic mask with its lofty brow indicates dignity and repose; a cothurnus of great thickness adds height and impressiveness to the appearance of a character, whom the audience at once recognise from the bow he bears to be the god Apollo. He narrates his experience, during a recent banishment from heaven, of the generous hospitality of Admetus, and sadly announces that the day has come when fate demands the life of Alcestis, freely offered once as ransom for that of her husband. Soon he descries the Death-god coming in search of his victim: very striking is the contrast offered by the two deities upon the stage, one of the aether, the other of the Styx. The fresh arrival (who perhaps appears upon the stage from beneath, by means of the so-called Charon's steps) is clad in none of the well-known conventional dresses of the stage: in his hand he bears a sword: his sombre black-winged figure and hideous mask, with dark shaggy hair and beard, betoken the hated nether power now as ever at strife with the bright god of life, with whom he wrangles for the life of her whom he has come to consecrate with his sacrificial sword. Apollo's pleading is vain, and both leave the stage, Thanatos to execute his gloomy mission, his rival uttering veiled prophecies of the coming of Heracles to frustrate the Death-god's schemes. So ends the prologue (1—76).

Now through the opening into the orchestra on the right of the spectators (for by time-honoured convention persons supposed to be living near enter from the western side, travellers from a distance by the eastern approach, that is on the left hand of the spectators as they sit looking south) march in the Chorus of Pheraean citizens; clad in ordinary Greek dress, three abreast and five deep, fifteen in all, with military precision they enter, preceded by the flute-player, singing in recitative the opening anapaests of the parodos (77—85). 'Why this silence at Admetus' hospitable door? Can the worst have already happened?' Then separating into two divisions they discuss in lyrical duet the sad fortunes of their master's house. 'Would that Asclepios, god of healing, might appear and restore, as erst he did, the dead to life' (86—135). In the formation in which they made their entrance they take up a position facing the stage, with their backs to the audience, as the Coryphaeus, who stands third in the file nearest to the spectators, announces the coming of a handmaiden from the palace who will tell the news (136, 137). Wearing one of the low-browed masks which convention assigned to attendants, and thin-soled buskins, which imparted little if any increase of height to the figure, the maid enters, and first in conversation with the Coryphaeus (138—151), afterwards in a set ῥῆσις (152—198), gives a description of her mistress' desperate condition, with a pathetic account of her farewell to home and household. To an enquiry of the Coryphaeus as to Admetus' behaviour in this calamity (199, 200), the attendant replies that he is stricken with helpless grief, and that in obedience to his wife's earnest wish he is now supporting her from the palace to look for the last time on the light of day (201—212). She then leaves the stage to announce to her master the sympathetic visit of the Chorus, who again take up their mournful duet, as in two divisions they move with sad gestures round the altar of Dionysus (213—243).

At this point Alcestis appears, borne up in her husband's arms. She is clad in robes befitting a princess of high rank; a sweeping tunic of queenly purple and mantle of white with purple border, a diadem surmounting the lofty brow of her mask, contrast with the sombre garb and close-cut hair of her sorrowing husband: accompanying them are their two children and a number of attendants, all clad in black; they wear masks expressive of profound sadness: wife and husband give vent to their emotion in lines of broken lyrical metre (244—272), till after a few anapaests indicative of an attempt at self-control from Admetus (273—279), Alcestis, mastering by a supreme effort both weakness, grief, and natural fears of death, begins a speech of farewell to her husband and children: him she begs, or rather bids, for their children's sake to abstain from a second marriage; but for her son and daughter she has the outpouring of a mother's love and fears (280—325). Admetus replies with vows of life-long fidelity to her memory; for her sake he will hate father and mother; did they not refuse the death which was their duty, nay, their privilege, thus forcing it on his young wife, whose loss is so sore a sorrow? He will stop all form of revelry; he will have a marble image of his wife placed in their bridal chamber; had he Orpheus' voice he would descend beneath the earth and win her back to life and love; but alas! he has not; still when his turn comes at last to die he will be buried in the same coffin with her, and rejoin her in the home, which she is to prepare for him below (328—368). A few hurried lines of prayer and promise, a brief farewell, and Alcestis falls lifeless in her husband's arms: βέβηκεν, οὐκέτ' ἔστιν Ἀδμήτου γυνή is the sad announcement of the Coryphaeus as he gazes upwards from the orchestra on the woeful scene (369—392). Child and father join in lamentation for their loss, while the leader of the Chorus endeavours to administer such consolation as proverbial philosophy can bestow. Admetus, after bidding the Chorus to the funeral, preparations for which it seems he has had in hand, with sad foreknowledge, for some time, gives orders for general mourning among his subjects, and slowly quits the stage with his retinue, his children, and the body of his fair young wife (393—434).

The conclusion of the act is marked by the performance of the first stasimon, an ode sung by the entire Chorus (who now turn to face the audience) in unison, with the most careful and distinct enunciation, so that the whole of the audience may clearly hear and understand each word. The music (the character of which was wont to vary with the theme) is no doubt set in the pathetic Mixo-Lydian mode. As they sing, the choreutae perform the solemn tragic dance called *emmeleia*, accompanying their movements with gestures appropriate to the words of the ode. They bewail the untimely fate of their young queen and foretell her fame in time to come, when her self-sacrifice shall be the theme of song at festivals in every Grecian land. 'Light may the earth lie on thee, lady; happy the man, to whose lot falls a wife like thee' (435—475).

At the conclusion of their song, there appears on the stage above a figure well-known to the Attic playgoer: clad in a lion's

skin and grasping his mighty club, Heracles enters, seeking a
lodging on his way to the far north to accomplish his eighth
labour for his hard task-master Eurystheus : briefly he tells the
object of his journey to the wondering Chorus, who dilate on
the perils of his enterprise. 'It is my destiny, and never shall
it be said that Alcmena's son turned coward,' is the hero's
answer, as he enquires for his old friend Admetus. The latter
re-appears upon the stage, and in answer to Heracles' questions
as to the reason of his mourning, explains that a lady who has
been entrusted to his keeping is but lately dead. Heracles,
albeit hardly satisfied, acquiesces in this answer and prepares
to proceed further on his way in quest of lodging, but the hos-
pitable Admetus constrains him, somewhat against his will, to
remain. 'The guest-chambers are in a distant wing : mourner
and feaster will not meet.' An attendant, at his lord's bidding,
conducts the hungry hero through one of the side-doors to the
chambers which are to be prepared for his reception. To the
expostulating Chorus Admetus, as he quits the stage, replies
that the duties of hospitality are paramount : had he revealed
his real trouble Heracles would without doubt have sought
entertainment elsewhere (476—567). The Chorus now perform
the second stasimon, celebrating the hospitality of their prince,
which won for him the friendship of Apollo : hence his wealth of
flocks and herds, and wide expanse of tilth and pasturage, ex-
tending from the far hills of Epirus to the Aegean. 'Hospitable
to a fault is he : he does not suffer Heracles to pass his door,
although his heart is breaking : still it may be that his is the
truest wisdom : heaven will reward the virtuous' (568—605).

The next act opens with the appearance of Admetus and the
funeral procession on their way to the place of burial without the
city wall, close beside the Larissa road. The solemn cortége
halts that the Chorus may address a sad farewell to their young
mistress, and join the mournful procession which escorts her as
she is carried shoulder-high to her last rest by a band of retain-
ers on the funeral couch on which she has been laid out ; but an
interruption is caused by the unwelcome arrival of Admetus' aged
father, Pheres, with gifts for the dead : he makes his offering and

speaks the set phrases of farewell before his indignant son breaks out with passionate revilings against a father, who, though old, though blest with a noble son, and owing a debt of gratitude to him for consistent kindly treatment, can still, by refusing to sacrifice the few years that yet remain to him, condemn to a widowed life his only child. 'Though your son breathes, childless live and childless die: never will I do aught to cheer the declining years of my miscalled parents' (606—672). But Admetus' outburst is more than answered by the scorn, with which Pheres brutally exposes his son's selfish and unmanly conduct; his stinging rebukes ring in Admetus' ears, and though for the present he may in unseemly contest answer his father insult for insult, sneer for sneer, yet the old man's coarse and tasteless gibes have the stronger case, and will bear fruit in the awakening of Admetus to a sense of his own worthlessness.

The sentiment of this scene is not lofty, but neither Admetus nor Pheres are lofty characters: they are however very human, and the audience welcomes in this, the substitute for a satyric play, a scene of real life as a relief from the heroics, sometimes forced and bombastic, of the legitimate drama (675—740). As Pheres retires, the Chorus with tender respect bid farewell to their dead queen, and mounting the steps which afford communication between orchestra and stage join in the funeral procession as it winds slowly out of the spectators' sight (741—746).

Both stage and orchestra are now vacant: upon the former appears the attendant to whose charge the entertainment of Heracles has been entrusted. Bitterly he complains of the rude merriment of the guest, whose arrival has prevented him from sharing with the other servants in the last tributes of love and sorrow to his mistress. Soon he is followed by the boisterous demi-god himself, merry indeed, but not in the intoxicated state the mortified henchman would have us believe: the hero briefly lays down the rule of life his own hard experience has taught: 'rest and taste good things while you may; sufficient unto the day is the evil thereof, and much there will be of it.' Resentment loosens the tongue hitherto bound by Admetus' command, and gradually the truth comes to Heracles' astounded ears: shame for his own levity, admiration for his host's hospitable insistence, not unmingled with a touch of regret that he has not been thought worthy to share in his friend's sorrow, urge him to instant action: what matter one labour more or less? He will e'en risk a bout with Death, bring back the departed wife, and restore happiness to the desolate home (747—860).

Admetus and the Chorus now return after performing Alcestis' funeral obsequies: the Chorus descend to their accustomed place in the orchestra and from there, while they execute a solemn and mournful dance, join with Admetus, who cannot bring himself to enter his desolate home, in singing a lyrical duologue, mingling sympathy and consolation with the bereaved husband's passionate outbursts of grief and self-reproach. Admetus at last, controlling his emotion, makes a set declaration to the Chorus of his shame and repentance, which, first stirred by his father's reproaches, have by this time worked a change in his self-centred and self-satisfied nature: as he quits the stage, we feel at last some sympathy with the weak king who, ever prosperous till now, and fed on flattery from his youth up, has been conscious of his own wish to do his duty and proudly sure that he has done it: one blast of real sorrow has scattered the cloud of self-importance which has thus far obscured his vision; we shall no longer grudge the blessing, which the gods are about to grant to one who, with many faults of weakness, has many of the virtues which both gods and men love (861—961).

The subject of the third stasimon, which the Chorus now perform, is the dread might of that altarless Deity, whom no prayers may turn, whose features no heaven-inspired statuary has ever revealed to men, Necessity: to her strokes even gods must bow. Not without consolation however are they: Alcestis, the mortal woman, indeed is gone, but in her stead a sainted and immortal Alcestis shall receive at her tomb, now become a shrine, the benedictions and the prayers of reverent passers-by (962—1005). Well-placed and accordant with the 'irony' of Attic drama is this hymn, which celebrates the immutability of Fate's decree just as the reversal of her fiat is to be announced.

Heracles returns: whence comes he? who the muffled

maiden at his side? He has, he tells us, been competing at some games, which he found in progress, as he resumed his northward journey: victorious of course, he is bringing his prize to his kindly host (who, by the way, should not so cruelly have concealed his sorrow from a friend) with the request that, as some compensation for the slight, he will keep the maiden in his house till he return again. Admetus, still as ever weak of will, protests he cannot, begs he may not—and consents. 'Into your own hand only,' insists Heracles, 'will I deliver her; no servant's hand, not even mine own, shall lead her into your palace.' Again protests, again prayers, again submission. Note the art with which the king's weak nature is still used by the poet to lend effectiveness to this the last scene of all. Sorely constrained and with averted head Admetus receives in his obedient but unwilling hand the maiden's. The hero's task is done. 'Look' he cries: and wife and husband are again united.

There is no curtain in the theatre of Dionysus to fall on this touching scene, but as actors and Chorus quit orchestra and stage, there is a tear in many an eye as the tumult of cheering from twenty thousand throats rises skyward; and when the archon draws from the brazen urn the five momentous votes, many a spectator feels that second is not the place deserved by the poet of the Telephus and the Alcestis.

In any appreciation of the play as a whole, in any endeavour to grasp the intention and meaning of the poet's characterization, a critic, after acknowledging the surpassing and unchallenged beauty of the creation which gives the play its name, is at once met by the problem which has puzzled many and annoyed most, the problem of the true reading of the characters of Admetus and Heracles and, in a minor degree, of Pheres. Should he with some boldly assert that all is well—that to a Greek audience Admetus' hospitality at large excuses his selfishness at home, that Heracles' beneficent labours on behalf of humanity bid us overlook his occasionally immoderate diet, that Pheres, mean and cynical, acts as a foil to the brighter character of his son?

Or with others should he admit the imperfect drawing and

peccant taste of the poet who allows upon the stage the miserable contentions of a brutal father with a contemptible son, and the unlovely revellings of a tipsy demi-god, yet for Alcestis' sake pardon her repulsive relatives and coarse deliverer, and console himself with the reflection that after all the play was not a tragedy, but took the place in the tetralogy of a satyric drama, a form of composition wherein Athenian taste was sadly lax: and that, so far from being discontented with minor characters, we should be grateful to meet so lovely a creation as Alcestis in so unlikely a quarter?

Or should he with Dr Verrall[1] maintain that the play is a delicate thrust at the state religion, that Alcestis never dies at all, but merely becomes entranced through the natural fear of a pious believer at the moment foretold for her decease by Apollo of Delphi, that hollow deity, in whose predictions never-theless both she and her husband and all save the wandering soldier of fortune Heracles, whose religion is of the smallest, have implicit faith: that placed, to all appearance dead, in the family mausoleum with indecent haste by her shamefaced husband, who fears lest a public funeral should call attention to his cowardly love of life, she is escorted back by Heracles in so matter-of-fact a manner as inevitably to suggest to the quick Athenian that she has never been dead at all, and that Apollo of Delphi and the Apolline religion with its legends and marvels are mere imposture: that, unpleasant as are Admetus, Pheres and Heracles, they are characters proper to the purpose of the apostle Euripides, sworn foe to the jobbery and immo-rality of Delphi, the Savonarola, or perhaps rather the Erasmus, of ancient Athens?

For myself I cannot regard any of these readings as satis-factory. No amount of hospitality could make a hero of Ad-metus, and Euripides is at such pains to draw the rest of the king's character, his selfishness, his weakness, his egotism, that he could not have wished us to ignore the larger part of the picture: nor again do I feel that the scenes usually condemned stand in need of defence against the second class of critics;

---

[1] *Euripides the Rationalist*, pp. 1—128.

to me they are natural and appropriate, and though that appro-
priateness depends in some measure on the fact of the quasi-
satyric nature of the play, I should not call upon that fact to
bear the main weight of the justification of the scenes in
question.

Dr Verrall's *tour de force* remains: its cleverness is rivalled
by its inconclusiveness: detailed criticism would be unsuited to
this place, and I would only say that it is from Dr Verrall's
point of view, and none other, and in an atmosphere of Dr
Verrall's compounding, and none other, that hints, coincidences,
contradictions assume the appearance of evidence for the pur-
pose of his brief. Standing at such a distance as we do from
Euripides and his Athenians, from Alcestis and her audience,
we may discern from one point of view contrasts and parallels,
lights and shades, which from another fade from sight. If we
start with a firm conviction that Euripides' self-imposed mission
was to assault and undermine the Apolline religion, then we can
with full enjoyment enter into Dr Verrall's subtle arguments,
gaze with interest on the hints torn from their hiding-places by
his strong hand, appreciate contradictions hitherto unsuspected,
and finally agree with Dr Verrall's own Athenian that Apollo
has had a bad time of it: but I fear I must confess myself a
'visitor from Acarnania.' Wit and ingenuity are spread broad-
cast over 'Euripides the Rationalist': the intellectual unrest
and brilliant subjectivity which produced it remind one of the
'Rationalist' himself. A work of Dr Verrall on Euripides is
always noteworthy: it shows the capacity of both.

To put my own view briefly, it is that Euripides thus early
in his career took the opportunity offered by the demand for a
play of less tragic material as a relief from the tenser interest
of the three preceding plays, to produce a drama of the de-
scription best suited to his genius, a drama of manners: bound
as he was by the strait conventions of the contemporary Attic
stage, in tragedy he was always working under irksome restric-
tions, and it was in the next century that Menander, drawing
inspiration from his great predecessor, developed, on gentler
lines may be, high comedy from what would have been in

his master's hand, had the times permitted, romantic drama. No one can deny that Admetus, Pheres, Heracles are all human types of ordinary experience : weakness, tinged with selfishness, yet not entirely unamiable ; a stronger nature, saturated with selfishness, yet content to observe the forms of decency until exasperated ; and the hard-hitting (hard-drinking too) thoughtless generous 'man of his hands,' apt to commit a fault, quick to repair it—surely these are types not unfitted for a dramatist. Skilfully too are the characters of each utilised for the conduct of the action. Why the scene with Pheres, it may be asked? Because without it the play could not proceed : what will put the real truth before the infatuated Admetus and rouse his better nature to recognize his paltry conduct? What but the brutal plain-speaking of his angered father? Retort he may for the moment, but the verbal echoes of his father's taunts in his confession of shame and penitence to the Chorus tell us that the poet intended us to note the effect those taunts have had. How could we tolerate the bestowal of so great a boon as the restoration of a beloved wife on the Admetus of the earlier part of the play? Not till he sees things as they are, not till he has proclaimed his own unworthiness in the first manly words the poet gives to him (935—961), do we sympathize with his grief nor grudge him the good fortune which is to be his. How skilfully too, with how firm a hand, does Euripides paint the now repentant king : still, as before, weak of will, yielding point by point to the insistent Heracles, and by that very weakness furnishing the poet with natural and effective stages in the conduct of the beautiful restoration-scene, with which the drama closes. Does the poet need an apologist? Indeed I think not.

Ὑπόθεσις Ἀλκήστιδος Δικαιάρχου.

Ἀπόλλων ᾐτήσατο παρὰ τῶν Μοιρῶν ὅπως ὁ Ἄδμητος
τελευτᾶν μέλλων παράσχῃ τὸν ὑπὲρ ἑαυτοῦ ἑκόντα τεθνηξόμενον,
ἵνα ἴσον τῷ προτέρῳ χρόνον ζήσῃ. καὶ δὴ Ἄλκηστις ἡ γυνὴ
τοῦ Ἀδμήτου ἐπέδωκεν ἑαυτήν, οὐδετέρου τῶν γονέων ἐθελή-
5 σαντος ὑπὲρ τοῦ παιδὸς ἀποθανεῖν. μετ᾽ οὐ πολὺ δὲ τῆς
συμφορᾶς ταύτης γενομένης Ἡρακλῆς παραγενόμενος καὶ μαθὼν
παρά τινος θεράποντος τὰ περὶ τὴν Ἄλκηστιν ἐπορεύθη ἐπὶ τὸν
τάφον καὶ τὸν Θάνατον ἀποστῆναι ποιήσας ἐσθῆτι καλύπτει τὴν
γυναῖκα, τὸν δὲ Ἄδμητον ἠξίου λαβόντα αὐτὴν τηρεῖν. εἰλη-
10 φέναι δὲ αὐτὴν πάλης ἆθλον ἔλεγε. μὴ βουλομένου δὲ ἐκείνου
ἔδειξεν ἣν ἐπένθει.

[Ἀριστοφάνους γραμματικοῦ ὑπόθεσις.]

Ἄλκηστις ἡ Πελίου θυγάτηρ ὑπομείνασα ὑπὲρ τοῦ ἰδίου
ἀνδρὸς τελευτῆσαι, Ἡρακλέους ἐπιδημήσαντος ἐν τῇ Θετταλίᾳ
15 διασῴζεται, βιασαμένου τοὺς χθονίους θεοὺς καὶ ἀφελομένου τὴν
γυναῖκα. παρ᾽ οὐδετέρῳ κεῖται ἡ μυθοποιία. τὸ δρᾶμα ἐποιήθη
ιζ᾽. ἐδιδάχθη ἐπὶ Γλαυκίνου ἄρχοντος ὀλυμπιάδος πέ᾽ ἔτει
δευτέρῳ. πρῶτος ἦν Σοφοκλῆς, δεύτερος Εὐριπίδης Κρήσσαις,
Ἀλκμαίωνι τῷ διὰ Ψωφῖδος, Τηλέφῳ, Ἀλκήστιδι. εἰσιδ*
20 ἐχορήγει. τὸ δὲ δρᾶμα κωμικωτέραν ἔχει τὴν καταστροφήν.
ἡ μὲν σκηνὴ τοῦ δράματος ὑπόκειται ἐν Φεραῖς μιᾷ πόλει τῆς
Θετταλίας. συνέστηκε δὲ ὁ χορὸς ἔκ τινων πρεσβυτῶν ἐντοπίων,
οἳ καὶ παραγίνονται συμπαθήσοντες τῇ Ἀλκήστιδος συμφορᾷ.
προλογίζει ὁ Ἀπόλλων. τὸ δὲ δρᾶμά ἐστι σατυρικώτερον ὅτι
25 εἰς χαρὰν καὶ ἡδονὴν καταστρέφει. παρὰ τῶν γραμματικῶν
ἐκβάλλεται ὡς ἀνοίκεια τῆς τραγικῆς ποιήσεως ὅ τε Ὀρέστης
καὶ ἡ Ἄλκηστις, ὡς ἐκ συμφορᾶς μὲν ἀρχόμενα, εἰς εὐδαιμονίαν
δὲ καὶ χαρὰν λήξαντα, ἅ ἐστι μᾶλλον κωμῳδίας ἐχόμενα.

ΤΑ ΤΟΥ ΔΡΑΜΑΤΟΣ ΠΡΟΣΩΠΑ.

ΑΠΟΛΛΩΝ.

ΘΑΝΑΤΟΣ.

ΧΟΡΟΣ ΠΡΕΣΒΥΤΩΝ ΦΕΡΑΙΩΝ.

ΘΕΡΑΠΑΙΝΑ.

ΑΛΚΗΣΤΙΣ.

ΑΔΜΗΤΟΣ.

ΕΥΜΗΛΟΣ.

ΗΡΑΚΛΗΣ.

ΦΕΡΗΣ.

ΘΕΡΑΠΩΝ.

IT is usually held that the Alcestis was played by two actors, with the help of an extra performer, who was not regarded as a ὑποκριτὴς proper, to take the character of Eumelus: this being a child's part could not of course be played by one of the regular actors. If this view is correct, the Protagonist would represent Apollo, Alcestis, Pheres and Heracles, a fourfold rôle sufficiently diversified to try the powers of Polus himself, the Deuteragonist taking the parts of Thanatos, Admetus, and the two servants. In the scene between Heracles and the servant, the latter must leave the stage as Heracles is speaking lines 837—860, that he may change his mask and costume and re-appear as Admetus at 861. As Alcestis is silent in the last scene, her part would be taken there by a supernumerary. At the same time we should remember that three was the number of actors usually employed, and the fact that the Alcestis *could* be played by two is no proof that it *was*. Doubtless three actors were required for the tragedies produced along with the Alcestis.

ΕΥΡΙΠΙΔΟΥ ΑΛΚΗΣΤΙΣ.

ΑΠΟΛΛΩΝ.

'Ω δώματ' 'Αδμήτει', ἐν οἷς ἔτλην ἐγὼ
θῆσσαν τράπεζαν αἰνέσαι θεός περ ὤν.
Ζεὺς γὰρ κατακτὰς παῖδα τὸν ἐμὸν αἴτιος
'Ασκληπιόν, στέρνοισιν ἐμβαλὼν φλόγα·
οὗ δὴ χολωθεὶς τέκτονας Δίου πυρὸς   5
κτείνω Κύκλωπας· καί με θητεύειν πατὴρ
θνητῷ παρ' ἀνδρὶ τῶνδ' ἄποιν' ἠνάγκασεν.
ἐλθὼν δὲ γαῖαν τήνδ' ἐβουφόρβουν ξένῳ,
καὶ τόνδ' ἔσῳζον οἶκον ἐς τόδ' ἡμέρας.
ὁσίου γὰρ ἀνδρὸς ὅσιος ὢν ἐτύγχανον,   10
παιδὸς Φέρητος, ὃν θανεῖν ἐρρυσάμην,
Μοίρας δολώσας· ᾔνεσαν δέ μοι θεαὶ
'Άδμητον ἅδην τὸν παραυτίκ' ἐκφυγεῖν,
ἄλλον διαλλάξαντα τοῖς κάτω νεκρόν.
πάντας δ' ἐλέγξας καὶ διεξελθὼν φίλους,   15
πατέρα γεραιάν θ' ἥ σφ' ἔτικτε μητέρα,
οὐχ ηὗρε πλὴν γυναικὸς ὅστις ἤθελε
θανεῖν πρὸ κείνου μηδ' ἔτ' εἰσορᾶν φάος,
ἢ νῦν κατ' οἴκους ἐν χεροῖν βαστάζεται
ψυχορραγοῦσα· τῇδε γὰρ σφ' ἐν ἡμέρᾳ   20
θανεῖν πέπρωται καὶ μεταστῆναι βίου.
ἐγὼ δέ, μὴ μίασμά μ' ἐν δόμοις κίχῃ,

λείπω μελάθρων τῶνδε φιλτάτην στέγην.
ἤδη δὲ τόνδε Θάνατον εἰσορῶ πέλας,
ἱερέα θανόντων, ὅς νιν εἰς Ἅιδου δόμους   25
μέλλει κατάξειν· σύμμετρος δ᾽ ἀφίκετο,
φρουρῶν τόδ᾽ ἦμαρ ᾧ θανεῖν αὐτὴν χρεών.

ΘΑΝΑΤΟΣ.

ἆ ἆ·
τί σὺ πρὸς μελάθροις; τί σὺ τῇδε πολεῖς,
Φοῖβ᾽; ἀδικεῖς αὖ τιμὰς ἐνέρων   30
ἀφοριζόμενος καὶ καταπαύων.
οὐκ ἤρκεσέ σοι μόρον Ἀδμήτου
διακωλῦσαι, Μοίρας δολίῳ
σφήλαντι τέχνῃ; νῦν δ᾽ ἐπὶ τῇδ᾽ αὖ
χέρα τοξήρη φρουρεῖς ὁπλίσας,   35
ἣ τόδ᾽ ὑπέστη πόσιν ἐκλύσασ᾽
αὐτὴ προθανεῖν Πελίου παῖς;
ΑΠ. θάρσει· δίκην τοι καὶ λόγους κεδνοὺς ἔχω.
ΘΑ. τί δῆτα τόξων ἔργον, εἰ δίκην ἔχεις;
ΑΠ. σύνηθες αἰεὶ ταῦτα βαστάζειν ἐμοί.   40
ΘΑ. καὶ τοῖσδέ γ᾽ οἴκοις ἐκδίκως προσωφελεῖν.
ΑΠ. φίλου γὰρ ἀνδρὸς συμφοραῖς βαρύνομαι.
ΘΑ. καὶ νοσφιεῖς με τοῦδε δευτέρου νεκροῦ;
ΑΠ. ἀλλ᾽ οὐδ᾽ ἐκεῖνον πρὸς βίαν σ᾽ ἀφειλόμην.
ΘΑ. πῶς οὖν ὑπὲρ γῆς ἐστι κοὐ κάτω χθονός;   45
ΑΠ. δάμαρτ᾽ ἀμείψας, ἣν σὺ νῦν ἥκεις μέτα.
ΘΑ. κἀπάξομαί γε νερτέραν ὑπὸ χθόνα.
ΑΠ. λαβὼν ἴθ᾽· οὐ γὰρ οἶδ᾽ ἂν εἰ πείσαιμί σε.
ΘΑ. κτείνειν γ᾽ ὃν ἂν χρῇ; τοῦτο γὰρ τετάγμεθα.
ΑΠ. οὔκ, ἀλλὰ τοῖς μέλλουσι θάνατον ἐμβαλεῖν.   50
ΘΑ. ἔχω λόγον δὴ καὶ προθυμίαν σέθεν.

ΑΠ. ἔστ᾽ οὖν ὅπως Ἄλκηστις εἰς γῆρας μόλοι;

ΘΑ. οὐκ ἔστι· τιμαῖς κἀμὲ τέρπεσθαι δόκει.

ΑΠ. οὔτοι πλέον γ᾽ ἂν ἢ μίαν ψυχὴν λάβοις.

ΘΑ. νέων φθινόντων μεῖζον ἄρνυμαι γέρας.   55

ΑΠ. κἂν γραῦς ὄληται, πλουσίως ταφήσεται.

ΘΑ. πρὸς τῶν ἐχόντων, Φοῖβε, τὸν νόμον τιθεῖς.

ΑΠ. πῶς εἶπας; ἀλλ᾽ ἦ καὶ σοφὸς λέληθας ὤν;

ΘΑ. ὠνοῖντ᾽ ἂν οἷς πάρεστι γηραιοὶ θανεῖν.

ΑΠ. οὔκουν δοκεῖ σοι τήνδε μοι δοῦναι χάριν;   60

ΘΑ. οὐ δῆτ᾽· ἐπίστασαι δὲ τοὺς ἐμοὺς τρόπους.

ΑΠ. ἐχθρούς γε θνητοῖς καὶ θεοῖς στυγουμένους.

ΘΑ. οὐκ ἂν δύναιο πάντ᾽ ἔχειν ἃ μή σε δεῖ.

ΑΠ. ἦ μὴν σὺ πείσει καίπερ ὠμὸς ὢν ἄγαν·

τοῖος Φέρητος εἶσι πρὸς δόμους ἀνήρ,   65

Εὐρυσθέως πέμψαντος ἵππειον μέτα

ὄχημα Θρῄκης ἐκ τόπων δυσχειμέρων,

ὃς δὴ ξενωθεὶς τοῖσδ᾽ ἐν Ἀδμήτου δόμοις

βίᾳ γυναῖκα τήνδε σ᾽ ἐξαιρήσεται.

κοὔθ᾽ ἡ παρ᾽ ἡμῶν σοι γενήσεται χάρις   70

δράσεις θ᾽ ὁμοίως ταῦτ᾽, ἀπεχθήσει τ᾽ ἐμοί.

ΘΑ. πόλλ᾽ ἂν σὺ λέξας οὐδὲν ἂν πλέον λάβοις·

ἡ δ᾽ οὖν γυνὴ κάτεισιν εἰς Ἅιδου δόμους.

στείχω δ᾽ ἐπ᾽ αὐτήν, ὡς κατάρξωμαι ξίφει·

ἱερὸς γὰρ οὗτος τῶν κατὰ χθονὸς θεῶν   75

ὅτου τόδ᾽ ἔγχος κρατὸς ἁγνίσῃ τρίχα.

ΧΟΡΟΣ.

τί ποθ᾽ ἡσυχία πρόσθεν μελάθρων;

τί σεσίγηται δόμος Ἀδμήτου;

ἀλλ᾽ οὐδὲ φίλων πέλας ἔστ᾽ οὐδείς,

ὅστις ἂν εἴποι πότερον φθιμένην   80

χρὴ βασίλειαν πενθεῖν, ἢ ζῶσ᾽
ἔτι φῶς λεύσσει Πελίου τόδε παῖς
Ἄλκηστις, ἐμοὶ πᾶσί τ᾽ ἀρίστη
δόξασα γυνὴ
πόσιν εἰς αὑτῆς γεγενῆσθαι.   85

ΗΜΙΧ. κλύει τις ἢ στεναγμὸν ἢ   στρ.
       χειρῶν κτύπον κατὰ στέγας
       ἢ γόον ὡς πεπραγμένων;
ΗΜΙΧ. οὐ μὰν οὐδέ τις ἀμφιπόλων
       στατίζεται ἀμφὶ πύλας.   90
       εἰ γὰρ μετακύμιος ἄτας,
       ὦ Παιάν, φανείης.
ΗΜΙΧ. οὔ τἂν φθιμένης γ᾽ ἐσιώπων.
ΗΜΙΧ. νέκυς ἤδη.
ΗΜΙΧ. οὐ δὴ φροῦδός γ᾽ ἐξ οἴκων.
ΗΜΙΧ. πόθεν; οὐκ αὐχῶ. τί σε θαρσύνει;   95
ΗΜΙΧ. πῶς ἂν ἔρημον τάφον Ἄδμητος

          *   *   *   *   *

       κεδνῆς ἂν ἔπραξε γυναικός;
ΧΟ.   πυλῶν πάροιθε δ᾽ οὐχ ὁρῶ   ἀντ.
       πηγαῖον ὡς νομίζεται
       χέρνιβ᾽ ἐπὶ φθιτῶν πύλαις.   100
ΗΜΙΧ. χαίτα τ᾽ οὔτις ἐπὶ προθύροις
       τομαῖος, ἃ δὴ νεκύων
       πένθει πίτνει· οὐ νεολαία
       δουπεῖ χεὶρ γυναικῶν.
ΗΜΙΧ. καὶ μὴν τόδε κύριον ἦμαρ,   105
ΗΜΙΧ. τί τόδ᾽ αὐδᾷς;
ΗΜΙΧ. ᾧ χρή σφε μολεῖν κατὰ γαίας.
ΗΜΙΧ. ἔθιγες ψυχῆς, ἔθιγες δὲ φρενῶν.
ΗΜΙΧ. χρὴ τῶν ἀγαθῶν διακναιομένων

πενθεῖν ὅστις   110
χρηστὸς ἀπ᾽ ἀρχῆς νενόμισται.

ΗΜΙΧ. ἀλλ᾽ οὐδὲ ναυκληρίαν   στρ.
ἔσθ᾽ ὅποι τις αἴας
στείλας ἢ Λυκίαν
εἴτ᾽ ἐφ᾽ ἕδρας ἀνύδρους   115
Ἀμμωνιάδας
δυστάνου παραλύσει
ψυχάν· μόρος γὰρ ἀπότομος
πλάθει· θεῶν δ᾽ ἐπ᾽ ἐσχάραν
οὐκ ἔχω ἔτι τίνα   120
μηλοθύταν πορευθῶ.

ΗΜΙΧ. μόνος δ᾽ ἄν, εἰ φῶς τόδ᾽ ἦν   ἀντ.
ὄμμασιν δεδορκὼς
Φοίβου παῖς, προλιποῦσ᾽
ἦλθεν ἕδρας σκοτίους   125
Ἅιδα τε πύλας·
δμαθέντας γὰρ ἀνίστη,
πρὶν αὐτὸν εἷλε Διόβολον
πλῆκτρον πυρὸς κεραυνίου.
νῦν δὲ τίν᾽ ἔτι βίου   130
ἐλπίδα προσδέχωμαι;

ΧΟ. πάντα γὰρ ἤδη τετέλεσται βασιλεῦσι,
πάντων δὲ θεῶν ἐπὶ βωμοῖς
αἱμόρραντοι θυσίαι πλήρεις,
οὐδ᾽ ἔστι κακῶν ἄκος οὐδέν.   135
ἀλλ᾽ ἥδ᾽ ὀπαδῶν ἐκ δόμων τις ἔρχεται
δακρυρροοῦσα· τίνα τύχην ἀκούσομαι;
πενθεῖν μέν, εἴ τι δεσπόταισι τυγχάνει,
συγγνωστόν· εἰ δ᾽ ἔτ᾽ ἐστὶν ἔμψυχος γυνὴ
εἴτ᾽ οὖν ὄλωλεν εἰδέναι βουλοίμεθ᾽ ἄν.   140

ΘΕΡΑΠΑΙΝΑ.

καὶ ζῶσαν εἰπεῖν καὶ θανοῦσαν ἔστι σοι.

ΧΟ. καὶ πῶς ἂν αὑτὸς κατθάνοι τε καὶ βλέποι;

ΘΕ. ἤδη προνωπής ἐστι καὶ ψυχορραγεῖ.

ΧΟ. ὦ τλῆμον, οἵας οἷος ὢν ἁμαρτάνεις.

ΘΕ. οὔπω τόδ᾽ οἶδε δεσπότης, πρὶν ἂν πάθῃ.   145

ΧΟ. ἐλπὶς μὲν οὐκέτ᾽ ἐστὶ σῴζεσθαι βίον;

ΘΕ. πεπρωμένη γὰρ ἡμέρα βιάζεται.

ΧΟ. οὔκουν ἐπ᾽ αὐτῇ πράσσεται τὰ πρόσφορα;

ΘΕ. κόσμος γ᾽ ἕτοιμος, ᾧ σφε συνθάψει πόσις.

ΧΟ. ἴστω νυν εὐκλεής γε κατθανουμένη   150
γυνή τ᾽ ἀρίστη τῶν ὑφ᾽ ἡλίῳ μακρῷ.

ΘΕ. πῶς δ᾽ οὐκ ἀρίστη; τίς δ᾽ ἐναντιώσεται;
τί χρὴ γενέσθαι τὴν ὑπερβεβλημένην
γυναῖκα; πῶς δ᾽ ἂν μᾶλλον ἐνδείξαιτό τις
πόσιν προτιμῶσ᾽ ἢ θέλουσ᾽ ὑπερθανεῖν;   155
καὶ ταῦτα μὲν δὴ πᾶσ᾽ ἐπίσταται πόλις·
ἃ δ᾽ ἐν δόμοις ἔδρασε θαυμάσει κλύων.
ἐπεὶ γὰρ ᾔσθεθ᾽ ἡμέραν τὴν κυρίαν
ἥκουσαν, ὕδασι ποταμίοις λευκὸν χρόα
ἐλούσατ᾽, ἐκ δ᾽ ἑλοῦσα κεδρίνων δόμων   160
ἐσθῆτα κόσμον τ᾽ εὐπρεπῶς ἠσκήσατο,
καὶ στᾶσα πρόσθεν ἑστίας κατηύξατο·
δέσποιν᾽, ἐγὼ γὰρ ἔρχομαι κατὰ χθονός,
πανύστατόν σε προσπίτνουσ᾽ αἰτήσομαι,
τέκν᾽ ὀρφανεῦσαι τἀμά, καὶ τῷ μὲν φίλην   165
σύζευξον ἄλοχον, τῇ δὲ γενναῖον πόσιν.
μηδ᾽ ὥσπερ αὐτῶν ἡ τεκοῦσ᾽ ἀπόλλυμαι
θανεῖν ἀώρους παῖδας, ἀλλ᾽ εὐδαίμονας
ἐν γῇ πατρῴᾳ τερπνὸν ἐκπλῆσαι βίον.

πάντας δὲ βωμοὺς οἳ κατ' Ἀδμήτου δόμους 170
προσῆλθε κἀξέστεψε καὶ προσηύξατο,
πτόρθων ἀποσχίζουσα μυρσίνης φόβην,
ἄκλαυστος ἀστένακτος, οὐδὲ τοὐπιὸν
κακὸν μεθίστη χρωτὸς εὐειδῆ φύσιν.
κἄπειτα θάλαμον ἐσπεσοῦσα καὶ λέχος,   175
ἐνταῦθα δὴ 'δάκρυσε καὶ λέγει τάδε·
ὦ λέκτρον, ἔνθα παρθένει' ἔλυσ' ἐγὼ
κορεύματ' ἐκ τοῦδ' ἀνδρός, οὗ θνήσκω πέρι,
χαῖρ'· οὐ γὰρ ἐχθαίρω σ'· ἀπώλεσας δέ με
μόνον· προδοῦναι γάρ σ' ὀκνοῦσα καὶ πόσιν 180
θνήσκω. σὲ δ' ἄλλη τις γυνὴ κεκτήσεται,
σώφρων μὲν οὐκ ἂν μᾶλλον, εὐτυχὴς δ' ἴσως.
κυνεῖ δὲ προσπίτνουσα, πᾶν δὲ δέμνιον
ὀφθαλμοτέγκτῳ δεύεται πλημμυρίδι.
ἐπεὶ δὲ πολλῶν δακρύων εἶχεν κόρον,   185
στείχει προνωπὴς ἐκπεσοῦσα δεμνίων,
καὶ πολλὰ θάλαμον ἐξιοῦσ' ἐπεστράφη
κἄρριψεν αὑτὴν αὖθις ἐς κοίτην πάλιν.
παῖδες δὲ πέπλων μητρὸς ἐξηρτημένοι
ἔκλαιον· ἡ δὲ λαμβάνουσ' ἐς ἀγκάλας   190
ἠσπάζετ' ἄλλοτ' ἄλλον, ὡς θανουμένη.
πάντες δ' ἔκλαιον οἰκέται κατὰ στέγας
δέσποιναν οἰκτίροντες. ἡ δὲ δεξιὰν
προύτειν' ἑκάστῳ, κοὔτις ἦν οὕτω κακὸς
ὃν οὐ προσεῖπε καὶ προσερρήθη πάλιν.   195
τοιαῦτ' ἐν οἴκοις ἐστὶν Ἀδμήτου κακά.
καὶ κατθανών τἂν ὤλετ'· ἐκφυγὼν δ' ἔχει
τοσοῦτον ἄλγος, οὔποθ' οὐ λελήσεται.

ΧΟ. ἦ που στενάζει τοισίδ' Ἄδμητος κακοῖς,
ἐσθλῆς γυναικὸς εἰ στερηθῆναί σφε χρή;   200

ΘΕ. κλαίει γ' ἄκοιτιν ἐν χεροῖν φίλην ἔχων,
    καὶ μὴ προδοῦναι λίσσεται, τἀμήχανα
    ζητῶν· φθίνει γὰρ καὶ μαραίνεται νόσῳ,
    παρειμένη δέ, χειρὸς ἄθλιον βάρος

        *   *   *   *

    ὅμως δὲ καίπερ σμικρὸν ἐμπνέουσ' ἔτι   205
    βλέψαι πρὸς αὐγὰς βούλεται τὰς ἡλίου.   206
    ἀλλ' εἶμι καὶ σὴν ἀγγελῶ παρουσίαν·   209
    οὐ γάρ τι πάντες εὖ φρονοῦσι κοιράνοις,   210
    ὥστ' ἐν κακοῖσιν εὐμενεῖς παρεστάναι.
    σὺ δ' εἶ παλαιὸς δεσπόταις ἐμοῖς φίλος.

ΗΜΙΧ. ἰὼ Ζεῦ, τίς ἂν πῶς πᾷ πόρος κακῶν   στρ.
    γένοιτο καὶ λύσις τύχας ἃ πάρεστιν κοιράνοις;

ΗΜΙΧ. ἔξεισί τις; ἢ τέμω τρίχα,   215
    καὶ μέλανα στολμὸν πέπλων
    ἀμφιβαλώμεθ' ἤδη;

ΧΟ. δῆλα μέν, φίλοι, δῆλά γ', ἀλλ' ὅμως
    θεοῖσιν εὐξόμεσθα· θεῶν γὰρ δύναμις μεγίστη.
    ὦναξ Παιάν,   220
    ἔξευρε μηχανάν τιν' Ἀδμήτῳ κακῶν,
    πόριζε δὴ πόριζε· καὶ πάρος γὰρ
    τοῦτ' ἐφηῦρες τῷδε, καὶ νῦν
    λυτήριος ἐκ θανάτου γενοῦ,
    φόνιον δ' ἀπόπαυσον Ἅιδαν.   225

ΗΜΙΧ. παπαῖ φεῦ παπαῖ φεῦ φεῦ ἰὼ ἰώ.   ἀντ.
    ὦ παῖ Φέρητος, οἷ' ἔπραξας δάμαρτος σᾶς στε-
    ρείς.

ΗΜΙΧ. ἆρ' ἄξια καὶ σφαγᾶς τάδε,
    καὶ πλέον ἢ βρόχῳ δέρην
    οὐρανίῳ πελάσσαι;   230

ΧΟ. τὰν γὰρ οὐ φίλαν ἀλλὰ φιλτάταν

γυναῖκα κατθανοῦσαν εἰν ἄματι τῷδ᾽ ἐπόψει.
ἰδοὺ ἰδού,
ἥδ᾽ ἐκ δόμων δὴ καὶ πόσις πορεύεται.
βόασον ὦ, στέναξον, ὦ Φεραία
χθών, ἰοῦσαν τὰν ἀρίσταν　　　　　　　　　　235
γυναῖκα, μαραινομέναν νόσῳ,
κατὰ γᾶς χθόνιον παρ᾽ Ἅιδαν.
οὔποτε φήσω γάμον εὐφραίνειν
πλέον ἢ λυπεῖν, τοῖς τε πάροιθεν
τεκμαιρόμενος καὶ τάσδε τύχας　　　　　　　　240
λεύσσων βασιλέως, ὅστις ἀρίστης
ἀπλακὼν ἀλόχου τῆσδ᾽ ἀβίωτον
τὸν ἔπειτα χρόνον βιοτεύσει.

ΑΛΚΗΣΤΙΣ.

Ἅλιε καὶ φάος ἀμέρας,　　　　　　　　　στρ.
οὐράνιαί τε δῖναι νεφέλας δρομαίου,　　　　245

ΑΔΜΗΤΟΣ.

ὁρᾷ σὲ κἀμέ, δύο κακῶς πεπραγότας,
οὐδὲν θεοὺς δράσαντας ἀνθ᾽ ὅτου θανεῖ.

ΑΛ.　γαῖά τε καὶ μελάθρων στέγαι　　　　ἀντ.
νυμφίδιοί τε κοῖται πατρίας Ἰωλκοῦ.

ΑΔ.　ἔπαιρε σαυτήν, ὦ τάλαινα, μὴ προδῷς·　250
λίσσου δὲ τοὺς κρατοῦντας οἰκτῖραι θεούς.

ΑΛ.　ὁρῶ δίκωπον ὁρῶ σκάφος ἐν λίμνᾳ,　στρ.
νεκύων δὲ πορθμεὺς
ἔχων χέρ᾽ ἐπὶ κοντῷ Χάρων μ᾽ ἤδη καλεῖ· τί
μέλλεις;
ἐπείγου· σὺ κατείργεις.　　　　　　　　255

τάδε τοί με σπερχόμενος ταχύνει.

ΑΔ. οἴμοι, πικράν γε τήνδε μοι ναυκληρίαν
ἔλεξας. ὦ δύσδαιμον, οἷα πάσχομεν.

ΑΛ. ἄγει μ᾽ ἄγει μέ τις, οὐχ ὁρᾷς; μέθες με· ἀντ.
νεκύων ἐς αὐλὰν   260
ὑπ᾽ ὀφρύσι κυαναυγέσι βλέπων πτερωτὸς ῞Αιδας.
τί ῥέξεις; ἄφες. οἵαν
ὁδὸν ἁ δειλαιοτάτα προβαίνω.

ΑΔ. οἰκτρὰν φίλοισιν, ἐκ δὲ τῶν μάλιστ᾽ ἐμοὶ
καὶ παισίν, οἷς δὴ πένθος ἐν κοινῷ τόδε.   265

ΑΛ. μέθετε μέθετέ μ᾽ ἤδη.
κλίνατ᾽, οὐ σθένω ποσίν·
πλησίον ῞Αιδας·
σκοτία δ᾽ ἐπ᾽ ὄσσοις νὺξ ἐφέρπει.
τέκνα τέκν᾽, οὐκέτι δὴ   270
οὐκέτι μάτηρ σφῷν ἔστιν.
χαίροντες, ὦ τέκνα, τόδε φάος ὁρῷτον.

ΑΔ. οἴμοι· τόδ᾽ ἔπος λυπρὸν ἀκούω
καὶ παντὸς ἐμοὶ θανάτου μεῖζον.
μὴ πρός σε θεῶν τλῇς με προδοῦναι,   275
μὴ πρὸς παίδων οὓς ὀρφανιεῖς,
ἀλλ᾽ ἄνα τόλμα·
σοῦ γὰρ φθιμένης οὐκέτ᾽ ἂν εἴην·
ἐν σοὶ δ᾽ ἐσμὲν καὶ ζῆν καὶ μή·
σὴν γὰρ φιλίαν σεβόμεσθα.

ΑΛ. ῎Αδμηθ᾽, ὁρᾷς γὰρ τἀμὰ πράγμαθ᾽ ὡς ἔχει, 280
λέξαι θέλω σοι πρὶν θανεῖν ἃ βούλομαι.
ἐγώ σε πρεσβεύουσα κἀντὶ τῆς ἐμῆς
ψυχῆς καταστήσασα φῶς τόδ᾽ εἰσορᾶν,
θνήσκω παρόν μοι μὴ θανεῖν ὑπὲρ σέθεν,
ἀλλ᾽ ἄνδρα τε σχεῖν Θεσσαλῶν ὃν ἤθελον,   285

καὶ δῶμα ναίειν ὄλβιον τυραννίδι.
οὐκ ἠθέλησα ζῆν ἀποσπασθεῖσά σου
σὺν παισὶν ὀρφανοῖσιν· οὐδ' ἐφεισάμην,
ἥβης ἔχουσα δῶρ', ἐν οἷς ἐτερπόμην.
καίτοι σ' ὁ φύσας χἠ τεκοῦσα προύδοσαν,   290
καλῶς μὲν αὐτοῖς κατθανεῖν ἧκον βίου,
καλῶς δὲ σῶσαι παῖδα κεὐκλεῶς θανεῖν.
μόνος γὰρ αὐτοῖς ἦσθα, κοὔτις ἐλπὶς ἦν
σοῦ κατθανόντος ἄλλα φιτύσειν τέκνα.
κἀγώ τ' ἂν ἔζων καὶ σὺ τὸν λοιπὸν χρόνον,   295
κοὐκ ἂν μονωθεὶς σῆς δάμαρτος ἔστενες
καὶ παῖδας ὠρφάνευες. ἀλλὰ ταῦτα μὲν
θεῶν τις ἐξέπραξεν ὥσθ' οὕτως ἔχειν.
εἶεν· σὺ νῦν μοι τῶνδ' ἀπόμνησαι χάριν·
αἰτήσομαι γάρ σ' ἀξίαν μὲν οὔποτε·   300
ψυχῆς γὰρ οὐδέν ἐστι τιμιώτερον·
δίκαια δ', ὡς φήσεις σύ· τούσδε γὰρ φιλεῖς
οὐχ ἧσσον ἢ 'γὼ παῖδας, εἴπερ εὖ φρονεῖς·
τούτους ἀνάσχου δεσπότας ἐμῶν δόμων,
καὶ μὴ 'πιγήμῃς τοῖσδε μητρυιὰν τέκνοις,   305
ἥτις κακίων οὖσ' ἐμοῦ γυνὴ φθόνῳ
τοῖς σοῖσι κἀμοῖς παισὶ χεῖρα προσβαλεῖ.
μὴ δῆτα δράσῃς ταῦτά γ', αἰτοῦμαί σ' ἐγώ.
ἐχθρὰ γὰρ ἡ 'πιοῦσα μητρυιὰ τέκνοις
τοῖς πρόσθ', ἐχίδνης οὐδὲν ἠπιωτέρα.   310
καὶ παῖς μὲν ἄρσην πατέρ' ἔχει πύργον μέγαν,   311
σὺ δ' ὦ τέκνον μοι πῶς κορευθήσει καλῶς;   313
ποίας τυχοῦσα συζύγου τῷ σῷ πατρί;
μή σοί τιν' αἰσχρὰν προσβαλοῦσα κληδόνα   315
ἥβης ἐν ἀκμῇ σοὺς διαφθείρῃ γάμους.
οὐ γάρ σε μήτηρ οὔτε νυμφεύσει ποτὲ

οὔτ᾽ ἐν τόκοισι σοῖσι θαρσυνεῖ, τέκνον,
παροῦσ᾽, ἵν᾽ οὐδὲν μητρὸς εὐμενέστερον.
δεῖ γὰρ θανεῖν με καὶ τόδ᾽ οὐκ ἐς αὔριον   320
οὐδ᾽ ἐς τρίτην μοι μηνὸς ἔρχεται κακόν,
ἀλλ᾽ αὐτίκ᾽ ἐν τοῖς μηκέτ᾽ οὖσι λέξομαι.
χαίροντες εὐφραίνοισθε· καὶ σοὶ μέν, πόσι,
γυναῖκ᾽ ἀρίστην ἔστι κομπάσαι λαβεῖν,
ὑμῖν δέ, παῖδες, μητρὸς ἐκπεφυκέναι.   325

ΧΟ. θάρσει· πρὸ τούτου γὰρ λέγειν οὐχ ἅζομαι·
δράσει τάδ᾽, εἴπερ μὴ φρενῶν ἁμαρτάνει.

ΑΔ. ἔσται τάδ᾽ ἔσται, μὴ τρέσῃς· ἐπεί σ᾽ ἐγὼ
καὶ ζῶσαν εἶχον καὶ θανοῦσ᾽ ἐμὴ γυνὴ
μόνη κεκλήσει, κοὔτις ἀντὶ σοῦ ποτε   330
τόνδ᾽ ἄνδρα νύμφη Θεσσαλὶς προσφθέγξεται.
οὐκ ἔστιν οὕτως οὖσα πατρὸς εὐγενοῦς
τό τ᾽ εἶδος ἄλλως ἐκπρεπεστάτη γυνή.
ἅλις δὲ παίδων· τῶνδ᾽ ὄνησιν εὔχομαι
θεοῖς γενέσθαι· σοῦ γὰρ οὐκ ὠνήμεθα.   335
οἴσω δὲ πένθος οὐκ ἐτήσιον τὸ σόν,
ἀλλ᾽ ἔστ᾽ ἂν αἰὼν οὑμὸς ἀντέχῃ, γύναι,
στυγῶν μὲν ἥ μ᾽ ἔτικτεν, ἐχθαίρων δ᾽ ἐμὸν
πατέρα· λόγῳ γὰρ ἦσαν οὐκ ἔργῳ φίλοι.
σὺ δ᾽ ἀντιδοῦσα τῆς ἐμῆς τὰ φίλτατα   340
ψυχῆς ἔσωσας. ἆρά μοι στένειν πάρα
τοιᾶσδ᾽ ἁμαρτάνοντι συζύγου σέθεν;
παύσω δὲ κώμους συμποτῶν θ᾽ ὁμιλίας
στεφάνους τε μοῦσάν θ᾽ ἣ κατεῖχ᾽ ἐμοὺς δόμους.
οὐ γάρ ποτ᾽ οὔτ᾽ ἂν βαρβίτου θίγοιμ᾽ ἔτι   345
οὔτ᾽ ἂν φρέν᾽ ἐξαίροιμι πρὸς Λίβυν λακεῖν
αὐλόν· σὺ γάρ μου τέρψιν ἐξείλου βίου.
σοφῇ δὲ χειρὶ τεκτόνων δέμας τὸ σὸν

εἰκασθὲν ἐν λέκτροισιν ἐκταθήσεται,
ᾧ προσπεσοῦμαι καὶ περιπτύσσων χέρας   350
ὄνομα καλῶν σὸν τὴν φίλην ἐν ἀγκάλαις
δόξω γυναῖκα καίπερ οὐκ ἔχων ἔχειν,
ψυχρὰν μέν, οἶμαι, τέρψιν, ἀλλ᾿ ὅμως βάρος
ψυχῆς ἀπαντλοίην ἄν· ἐν δ᾿ ὀνείρασι
φοιτῶσά μ᾿ εὐφραίνοις ἄν. ἡδὺ γὰρ φίλους   355
κἂν νυκτὶ λεύσσειν, ὅντιν᾿ ἂν παρῇ τρόπον.
εἰ δ᾿ Ὀρφέως μοι γλῶσσα καὶ μέλος παρῆν,
ὥστ᾿ ἢ κόρην Δήμητρος ἢ κείνης πόσιν
ὕμνοισι κηλήσαντά σ᾿ ἐξ Ἅιδου λαβεῖν,
κατῆλθον ἄν, καί μ᾿ οὔθ᾿ ὁ Πλούτωνος κύων   360
οὔθ᾿ οὑπὶ κώπῃ ψυχοπομπὸς ἂν Χάρων
ἔσχον, πρὶν ἐς φῶς σὸν καταστῆσαι βίον.
ἀλλ᾿ οὖν ἐκεῖσε προσδόκα μ᾿, ὅταν θάνω,
καὶ δῶμ᾿ ἑτοίμαζ᾿, ὡς συνοικήσουσά μοι.
ἐν ταῖσιν αὐταῖς γάρ μ᾿ ἐπισκήψω κέδροις   365
σοὶ τούσδε θεῖναι πλευρά τ᾿ ἐκτεῖναι πέλας
πλευροῖσι τοῖς σοῖς· μηδὲ γὰρ θανών ποτε
σοῦ χωρὶς εἴην τῆς μόνης πιστῆς ἐμοί.

ΧΟ. καὶ μὴν ἐγώ σοι πένθος ὡς φίλος φίλῳ
λυπρὸν συνοίσω τῆσδε· καὶ γὰρ ἀξία.   370

ΑΛ. ὦ παῖδες, αὐτοὶ δὴ τάδ᾿ εἰσηκούσατε
πατρὸς λέγοντος μὴ γαμεῖν ἄλλην τινὰ
γυναῖκ᾿ ἐφ᾿ ὑμῖν μηδ᾿ ἀτιμάσειν ἐμέ.

ΑΔ. καὶ νῦν γέ φημι, καὶ τελευτήσω τάδε.

ΑΛ. ἐπὶ τοῖσδε παῖδας χειρὸς ἐξ ἐμῆς δέχου.   375

ΑΔ. δέχομαι φίλον γε δῶρον ἐκ φίλης χερός.

ΑΛ. σὺ νῦν γενοῦ τοῖσδ᾿ ἀντ᾿ ἐμοῦ μήτηρ τέκνοις.

ΑΔ. πολλή μ᾿ ἀνάγκη σοῦ γ᾿ ἀπεστερημένοις.

ΑΛ. ὦ τέκν᾿, ὅτε ζῆν χρῆν μ᾿, ἀπέρχομαι κάτω.

ΑΔ. οἴμοι, τί δράσω δῆτα σοῦ μονούμενος;   380

ΑΛ. χρόνος μαλάξει σ'· οὐδέν ἐσθ' ὁ κατθανών.

ΑΔ. ἄγου με σὺν σοὶ πρὸς θεῶν ἄγου κάτω.

ΑΛ. ἀρκοῦμεν ἡμεῖς οἱ προθνῄσκοντες σέθεν.

ΑΔ. ὦ δαῖμον, οἵας συζύγου μ' ἀποστερεῖς.

ΑΛ. καὶ μὴν σκοτεινὸν ὄμμα μου βαρύνεται.   385

ΑΔ. ἀπωλόμην ἄρ', εἴ με δὴ λείψεις, γύναι.

ΑΛ. ὡς οὐκέτ' οὖσαν οὐδὲν ἂν λέγοις ἐμέ.

ΑΔ. ὄρθου πρόσωπον, μὴ λίπῃς παῖδας σέθεν.

ΑΛ. οὐ δῆθ' ἑκοῦσά γ'. ἀλλὰ χαίρετ', ὦ τέκνα.

ΑΔ. βλέψον πρὸς αὐτούς βλέψον. ΑΛ. οὐδέν εἰμ' ἔτι.

ΑΔ. τί δρᾷς; προλείπεις; ΑΛ. χαῖρ'. ΑΔ. ἀπωλόμην
    τάλας.   391

ΧΟ. βέβηκεν, οὐκέτ' ἔστιν Ἀδμήτου γυνή.

ΕΥΜΗΛΟΣ.

ἰώ μοι τύχας. μαῖα δὴ κάτω   στρ.
βέβακεν, οὐκέτ' ἔστιν, ὦ
πάτερ, ὑφ' ἁλίῳ.   395
προλιποῦσα δ' ἀμὸν βίον
ὠρφάνισεν τλάμων.
ἴδε γὰρ ἴδε βλέφαρον
καὶ παρατόνους χέρας.
ὑπάκουσον ἄκουσον, ὦ μᾶτερ, ἀντιάζω   400
σ' ἐγώ, μᾶτερ, ἐγώ
* * καλοῦμαι ὁ
σὸς ποτὶ σοῖσι πίτνων στόμασιν νεοσσός.

ΑΔ. τὴν οὐ κλύουσαν οὐδ' ὁρῶσαν· ὥστ' ἐγὼ
καὶ σφὼ βαρείᾳ συμφορᾷ πεπλήγμεθα.   405

ΕΥ. νέος ἐγώ, πάτερ, λείπομαι φίλας   ἀντ.
μονόστολός τε ματρός· ὦ

σχέτλια δὴ παθὼν
ἐγὼ ἔργα * * σύ τε,
σύγκασί μοι κούρα,   410
* * * * συνέτλας·
* * * ὦ πάτερ,
ἀνόνατ' ἀνόνατ' ἐνύμφευσας οὐδὲ γήρως
ἔβας τέλος σὺν τᾷδ'·
ἔφθιτο γὰρ πάρος,
οἰχομένας δὲ σοῦ, μᾶτερ, ὄλωλεν οἶκος.   415

ΧΟ. Ἄδμητ', ἀνάγκη τάσδε συμφορὰς φέρειν·
οὐ γάρ τι πρῶτος οὐδὲ λοίσθιος βροτῶν
γυναικὸς ἐσθλῆς ἤμπλακες· γίγνωσκε δὲ
ὡς πᾶσιν ἡμῖν κατθανεῖν ὀφείλεται.

ΑΔ. ἐπίσταμαί γε κοὐκ ἄφνω κακὸν τόδε   420
προσέπτατ'· εἰδὼς δ' αὖτ' ἐτειρόμην πάλαι.
ἀλλ' ἐκφορὰν γὰρ τοῦδε θήσομαι νεκροῦ,
πάρεστε καὶ μένοντες ἀντηχήσατε
παιᾶνα τῷ κάτωθεν ἀσπόνδῳ θεῷ.
πᾶσιν δὲ Θεσσαλοῖσιν ὧν ἐγὼ κρατῶ   425
πένθους γυναικὸς τῆσδε κοινοῦσθαι λέγω
κουρᾷ ξυρήκει καὶ μελαγχίμοις πέπλοις·
τέθριππά θ' οἳ ζεύγνυσθε καὶ μονάμπυκας
πώλους, σιδήρῳ τέμνετ' αὐχένων φόβην.
αὐλῶν δὲ μὴ κατ' ἄστυ, μὴ λύρας κτύπος   430
ἔστω σελήνας δώδεκ' ἐκπληρουμένας·
οὐ γάρ τιν' ἄλλον φίλτερον θάψω νεκρὸν
τοῦδ' οὐδ' ἀμείνον' εἰς ἔμ'· ἀξία δέ μοι
τιμᾶν, ἐπεὶ τέθνηκεν ἀντ' ἐμοῦ μόνη.

ΧΟ. ὦ Πελίου θύγατερ,   στρ. 435
χαίρουσά μοι εἰν Ἀΐδα δόμοισιν
τὸν ἀνάλιον οἶκον οἰκετεύοις.

ἴστω δ' Ἅιδας ὁ μελαγχαίτας θεὸς ὅς τ' ἐπὶ κώπᾳ
πηδαλίῳ τε γέρων   440
νεκροπομπὸς ἵζει,
πολὺ δὴ πολὺ δὴ γυναῖκ' ἀρίσταν
λίμναν Ἀχεροντίαν πορεύ-
σας ἐλάτᾳ δικώπῳ.

πολλά σε μουσοπόλοι   ἀντ. 445
μέλψουσι καθ' ἑπτάτονόν τ' ὀρείαν
χέλυν ἔν τ' ἀλύροις κλέοντες ὕμνοις,
Σπάρτᾳ κύκλον ἁνίκα Καρνείου περινίσσεται ἅρα
μηνὸς ἀειρομένας   450
παννύχου σελάνας,
λιπαραῖσί τ' ἐν ὀλβίαις Ἀθάναις.
τοίαν ἔλιπες θανοῦσα μολ-
πὰν μελέων ἀοιδοῖς.

εἴθ' ἐπ' ἐμοὶ μὲν εἴη,   στρ. 455
δυναίμαν δέ σε πέμψαι
φάος ἐξ Ἀίδα τεράμνων
Κωκυτοῦ τε ῥεέθρων
ποταμίᾳ νερτέρᾳ τε κώπᾳ.
σὺ γάρ, ὦ μόνα ὦ φίλα γυναικῶν,   460
σὺ τὸν αὑτᾶς
ἔτλας πόσιν ἀντὶ σᾶς ἀμεῖψαι
ψυχᾶς ἐξ Ἅιδα. κούφα σοι
χθὼν ἐπάνωθε πέσοι, γύναι. εἰ δέ τι
καινὸν ἕλοιτο λέχος πόσις, ἦ μάλ' ἂν ἔμοιγ' ἂν εἴη
στυγηθεὶς τέκνοις τε τοῖς σοῖς.   465
ματέρος οὐ θελούσας   ἀντ.
πρὸ παιδὸς χθονὶ κρύψαι
δέμας, οὐδὲ πατρὸς γεραιοῦ,
* * * * * * *

ὃν ἔτεκον δ᾽, οὐκ ἔτλαν ῥύεσθαι
σχετλίω, πολιὰν ἔχοντε χαίταν·   470
σὺ δ᾽ ἐν ἥβᾳ
νέᾳ προθανοῦσα φωτὸς οἴχει.
τοιαύτας εἴη μοι κῦρσαι
συνδυάδος φιλίας ἀλόχου· τὸ γὰρ
ἐν βιότῳ σπάνιον μέρος· ἦ γὰρ ἂν ἔμοιγ᾽ ἄλυπος
δι᾽ αἰῶνος ἂν ξυνείη.   475

ΗΡΑΚΛΗΣ.

ξένοι, Φεραίας τῆσδε κωμῆται χθονός,
Ἄδμητον ἐν δόμοισιν ἆρα κιγχάνω;
ΧΟ. ἔστ᾽ ἐν δόμοισι παῖς Φέρητος, Ἡράκλεις.
ἀλλ᾽ εἰπὲ χρεία τίς σε Θεσσαλῶν χθόνα
πέμπει, Φεραῖον ἄστυ προσβῆναι τόδε.   480
ΗΡ. Τιρυνθίῳ πράσσω τιν᾽ Εὐρυσθεῖ πόνον.
ΧΟ. καὶ ποῖ πορεύει; τῷ συνέζευξαι πλάνῳ;
ΗΡ. Θρῃκὸς τέτρωρον ἅρμα Διομήδους μέτα.
ΧΟ. πῶς οὖν δυνήσει; μῶν ἄπειρος εἶ ξένου;
ΗΡ. ἄπειρος· οὔπω Βιστόνων ἦλθον χθόνα.   485
ΧΟ. οὐκ ἔστιν ἵππων δεσπόσαι σ᾽ ἄνευ μάχης.
ΗΡ. ἀλλ᾽ οὐδ᾽ ἀπειπεῖν τοὺς πόνους οἷόν τ᾽ ἐμοί.
ΧΟ. κτανὼν ἄρ᾽ ἥξεις ἢ θανὼν αὐτοῦ μενεῖς.
ΗΡ. οὐ τόνδ᾽ ἀγῶνα πρῶτον ἂν δράμοιμ᾽ ἐγώ.
ΧΟ. τί δ᾽ ἂν κρατήσας δεσπότην πλέον λάβοις; 490
ΗΡ. πώλους ἀπάξω κοιράνῳ Τιρυνθίῳ.
ΧΟ. οὐκ εὐμαρὲς χαλινὸν ἐμβαλεῖν γνάθοις.
ΗΡ. εἰ μή γε πῦρ πνέουσι μυκτήρων ἄπο.
ΧΟ. ἀλλ᾽ ἄνδρας ἀρταμοῦσι λαιψηραῖς γνάθοις.
ΗΡ. θηρῶν ὀρείων χόρτον, οὐχ ἵππων λέγεις.   495
ΧΟ. φάτνας ἴδοις ἂν αἵμασιν πεφυρμένας.

2—2

ΗΡ. τίνος δ' ὁ θρέψας παῖς πατρὸς κομπάζεται;

ΧΟ. Ἄρεος, ζαχρύσου Θρηκίας πέλτης ἄναξ.

ΗΡ. καὶ τόνδε τοὐμοῦ δαίμονος πόνον λέγεις,
σκληρὸς γὰρ αἰεὶ καὶ πρὸς αἶπος ἔρχεται,   500
εἰ χρή με πᾶσιν οὓς Ἄρης ἐγείνατο
μάχην συνάψαι, πρῶτα μὲν Λυκάονι,
αὖθις δὲ Κύκνῳ, τόνδε δ' ἔρχομαι τρίτον
ἀγῶνα πώλοις δεσπότῃ τε συμβαλών.
ἀλλ' οὔτις ἔστιν ὃς τὸν Ἀλκμήνης γόνον   505
τρέσαντα χεῖρα πολεμίων ποτ' ὄψεται.

ΧΟ. καὶ μὴν ὅδ' αὐτὸς τῆσδε κοίρανος χθονὸς
Ἄδμητος ἔξω δωμάτων πορεύεται.

ΑΔ. χαῖρ', ὦ Διὸς παῖ Περσέως τ' ἀφ' αἵματος.

ΗΡ. Ἄδμητε, καὶ σὺ χαῖρε, Θεσσαλῶν ἄναξ.   510

ΑΔ. θέλοιμ' ἄν· εὔνουν δ' ὄντα σ' ἐξεπίσταμαι.

ΗΡ. τί χρῆμα κουρᾷ τῇδε πενθίμῳ πρέπεις;

ΑΔ. θάπτειν τιν' ἐν τῇδ' ἡμέρᾳ μέλλω νεκρόν.

ΗΡ. ἀπ' οὖν τέκνων σῶν πημονὴν εἴργοι θεός.

ΑΔ. ζῶσιν κατ' οἴκους παῖδες οὓς ἔφυσ' ἐγώ.   515

ΗΡ. πατήρ γε μὴν ὡραῖος, εἴπερ οἴχεται.

ΑΔ. κἀκεῖνος ἔστι χἠ τεκοῦσά μ', Ἡράκλεις.

ΗΡ. οὐ μὴν γυνή γ' ὄλωλεν Ἄλκηστις σέθεν;

ΑΔ. διπλοῦς ἐπ' αὐτῇ μῦθος ἔστι μοι λέγειν.

ΗΡ. πότερα θανούσης εἶπας ἢ ζώσης ἔτι;   520

ΑΔ. ἔστιν τε κοὐκέτ' ἔστιν, ἀλγύνει δέ με.

ΗΡ. οὐδέν τι μᾶλλον οἶδ'· ἄσημα γὰρ λέγεις.

ΑΔ. οὐκ οἶσθα μοίρας ἧς τυχεῖν αὐτὴν χρεών;

ΗΡ. οἶδ' ἀντὶ σοῦ γε κατθανεῖν ὑφειμένην.

ΑΔ. πῶς οὖν ἔτ' ἔστιν, εἴπερ ᾔνεσεν τάδε;   525

ΗΡ. ἆ, μὴ πρόκλαι' ἄκοιτιν, ἐς τότ' ἀμβαλοῦ.

ΑΔ. τέθνηχ' ὁ μέλλων, κοὐκέτ' ἔσθ' ὁ κατθανών.

ΗΡ. χωρὶς τό τ᾽ εἶναι καὶ τὸ μὴ νομίζεται.

ΑΔ. σὺ τῇδε κρίνεις, Ἡράκλεις, κείνη δ᾽ ἐγώ.

ΗΡ. τί δῆτα κλαίεις; τίς φίλων ὁ κατθανών;   530

ΑΔ. γυνή· γυναικὸς ἀρτίως μεμνήμεθα.

ΗΡ. ὀθνεῖος ἢ σοὶ συγγενὴς γεγῶσά τις;

ΑΔ. ὀθνεῖος, ἄλλως δ᾽ ἦν ἀναγκαία δόμοις.

ΗΡ. πῶς οὖν ἐν οἴκοις σοῖσιν ὤλεσεν βίον;

ΑΔ. πατρὸς θανόντος ἐνθάδ᾽ ὠρφανεύετο.   535

ΗΡ. φεῦ.
εἴθ᾽ ηὕρομέν σ᾽, Ἄδμητε, μὴ λυπούμενον.

ΑΔ. ὡς δὴ τί δράσων τόνδ᾽ ὑπορράπτεις λόγον;

ΗΡ. ξένων πρὸς ἄλλων ἑστίαν πορεύσομαι.

ΑΔ. οὐκ ἔστιν, ὦναξ· μὴ τοσόνδ᾽ ἔλθοι κακόν.

ΗΡ. λυπουμένοις ὀχληρός, εἰ μόλοι, ξένος.   540

ΑΔ. τεθνᾶσιν οἱ θανόντες· ἀλλ᾽ ἴθ᾽ ἐς δόμους.

ΗΡ. αἰσχρὸν παρὰ κλαίουσι θοινᾶσθαι φίλοις.

ΑΔ. χωρὶς ξενῶνές εἰσιν οἵ σ᾽ ἐσάξομεν.

ΗΡ. μέθες με, καί σοι μυρίαν ἕξω χάριν.

ΑΔ. οὐκ ἔστιν ἄλλου σ᾽ ἀνδρὸς ἑστίαν μολεῖν.   545
ἡγοῦ σὺ τῷδε δωμάτων ἐξωπίους
ξενῶνας οἴξας, τοῖς τ᾽ ἐφεστῶσιν φράσον
σίτων παρεῖναι πλῆθος· ἐν δὲ κλῄσατε
θύρας μεταύλους· οὐ πρέπει θοινωμένους
κλύειν στεναγμῶν οὐδὲ λυπεῖσθαι ξένους.   550

ΧΟ. τί δρᾷς; τοιαύτης συμφορᾶς προσκειμένης,
Ἄδμητε, τολμᾷς ξενοδοκεῖν; τί μῶρος εἶ;

ΑΔ. ἀλλ᾽ εἰ δόμων σφε καὶ πόλεως ἀπήλασα
ξένον μολόντα, μᾶλλον ἄν μ᾽ ἐπῄνεσας;
οὐ δῆτ᾽, ἐπεί μοι συμφορὰ μὲν οὐδὲν ἂν   555
μείων ἐγίγνετ᾽, ἀξενώτερος δ᾽ ἐγώ.
καὶ πρὸς κακοῖσιν ἄλλο τοῦτ᾽ ἂν ἦν κακόν,

δόμους καλεῖσθαι τοὺς ἐμοὺς ἐχθροξένους.
αὐτὸς δ' ἀρίστου τοῦδε τυγχάνω ξένου,
ὅταν ποτ' Ἄργους διψίαν ἔλθω χθόνα.   560

ΧΟ. πῶς οὖν ἔκρυπτες τὸν παρόντα δαίμονα,
φίλου μολόντος ἀνδρός, ὡς αὐτὸς λέγεις;

ΑΔ. οὐκ ἄν ποτ' ἠθέλησεν εἰσελθεῖν δόμους,
εἰ τῶν ἐμῶν τι πημάτων ἐγνώρισε.
καὶ τῷ μὲν οἶμαι δρῶν τάδ' οὐ φρονεῖν δοκῶ,   565
οὐδ' αἰνέσει με· τἀμὰ δ' οὐκ ἐπίσταται
μέλαθρ' ἀπωθεῖν οὐδ' ἀτιμάζειν ξένους.

ΧΟ. ὦ πολύξεινος καὶ ἐλεύθερος ἀνδρὸς ἀεί ποτ'
οἶκος,   στρ.
σέ τοι καὶ ὁ Πύθιος εὐλύρας Ἀπόλλων   570
ἠξίωσε ναίειν,
ἔτλα δὲ σοῖσι μηλονόμας
ἐν δόμοις γενέσθαι,
δοχμιᾶν διὰ κλιτύων   575
βοσκήμασι σοῖσι συρίζων
ποιμνίτας ὑμεναίους.

σὺν δ' ἐποιμαίνοντο χαρᾷ μελέων βαλιαί τε
λύγκες,   ἀντ.
ἔβα δὲ λιποῦσ' Ὄθρυος νάπαν λεόντων   580
ἁ δαφοινὸς ἴλα·
χόρευσε δ' ἀμφὶ σὰν κιθάραν,
Φοῖβε, ποικιλόθριξ
νεβρὸς ὑψικόμων πέραν   585
βαίνουσ' ἐλατᾶν σφυρῷ κούφῳ,
χαίρουσ' εὔφρονι μολπᾷ.

τοιγὰρ πολυμηλοτάταν   στρ.
ἑστίαν οἰκεῖ παρὰ καλλίναον
Βοιβίαν λίμναν· ἀρότοις δὲ γυᾶν   590

καὶ πεδίων δαπέδοις
ὅρον ἀμφὶ μὲν ἀελίου κνεφαίαν
ἱππόστασιν αἰθέρα τὰν Μολοσσῶν * * * τίθεται,
πόντιον δ' Αἰγαίων' ἐπ' ἀκτὰν   595
ἀλίμενον Πηλίου κρατύνει.
καὶ νῦν δόμον ἀμπετάσας   ἀντ.
δέξατο ξεῖνον νοτερῷ βλεφάρῳ,
τᾶς φίλας κλαίων ἀλόχου νέκυν ἐν
δώμασιν ἀρτιθανῆ·   600
τὸ γὰρ εὐγενὲς ἐκφέρεται πρὸς αἰδῶ.
ἐν τοῖς ἀγαθοῖσι δὲ πάντ' ἔνεστιν σοφίας. ἄγαμαι·
πρὸς δ' ἐμᾷ ψυχᾷ θάρσος ἧσται
θεοσεβῆ φῶτα κεδνὰ πράξειν.   605

ΑΔ. ἀνδρῶν Φεραίων εὐμενὴς παρουσία,
νέκυν μὲν ἤδη πάντ' ἔχοντα πρόσπολοι
φέρουσιν ἄρδην ἐς τάφον τε καὶ πυράν·
ὑμεῖς δὲ τὴν θανοῦσαν, ὡς νομίζεται,
προσείπατ' ἐξιοῦσαν ὑστάτην ὁδόν.   610

ΧΟ. καὶ μὴν ὁρῶ σὸν πατέρα γηραιῷ ποδὶ
στείχοντ', ὀπαδούς τ' ἐν χεροῖν δάμαρτι σῇ
κόσμον φέροντας, νερτέρων ἀγάλματα.

ΦΕΡΗΣ.

ἥκω κακοῖσι σοῖσι συγκάμνων, τέκνον·
ἐσθλῆς γάρ, οὐδεὶς ἀντερεῖ, καὶ σώφρονος   615
γυναικὸς ἡμάρτηκας. ἀλλὰ ταῦτα μὲν
φέρειν ἀνάγκη καίπερ ὄντα δύσφορα.
δέχου δὲ κόσμον τόνδε, καὶ κατὰ χθονὸς
ἴτω· τὸ ταύτης σῶμα τιμᾶσθαι χρεών,
ἥτις γε τῆς σῆς προύθανε ψυχῆς, τέκνον,   620
καί μ' οὐκ ἄπαιδ' ἔθηκεν οὐδ' εἴασε σοῦ

στερέντα γήρᾳ πενθίμῳ καταφθίνειν,
πάσαις δ' ἔθηκεν εὐκλεέστερον βίον
γυναιξίν, ἔργον τλᾶσα γενναῖον τόδε.
ὦ τόνδε μὲν σώσασ', ἀναστήσασα δὲ   625
ἡμᾶς πίτνοντας, χαῖρε, κἀν Ἅιδου δόμοις
εὖ σοι γένοιτο.   φημὶ τοιούτους γάμους
λύειν βροτοῖσιν, ἢ γαμεῖν οὐκ ἄξιον.

ΑΔ.   οὔτ' ἦλθες ἐς τόνδ' ἐξ ἐμοῦ κληθεὶς τάφον,
οὔτ' ἐν φίλοισι σὴν παρουσίαν λέγω.   630
κόσμον δὲ τὸν σὸν οὔποθ' ἥδ' ἐνδύσεται·
οὐ γάρ τι τῶν σῶν ἐνδεὴς ταφήσεται.
τότε ξυναλγεῖν χρῆν σ' ὅτ' ὠλλύμην ἐγώ.
σὺ δ' ἐκποδὼν στὰς καὶ παρεὶς ἄλλῳ θανεῖν
νέῳ γέρων ὤν, τόνδ' ἀποιμώζεις νεκρόν;   635
οὐκ ἦσθ' ἄρ' ὀρθῶς τοῦδε σώματος πατήρ·   636
ἔδειξας εἰς ἔλεγχον ἐξελθὼν ὃς εἶ,   640
καί μ' οὐ νομίζω παῖδα σὸν πεφυκέναι.
ἦ τἆρα πάντων διαπρέπεις ἀψυχίᾳ,
ὃς τηλικόσδ' ὢν κἀπὶ τέρμ' ἥκων βίου
οὐκ ἠθέλησας οὐδ' ἐτόλμησας θανεῖν
τοῦ σοῦ πρὸ παιδός, ἀλλὰ τήνδ' εἰάσατε   645
γυναῖκ' ὀθνείαν, ἣν ἐγὼ καὶ μητέρα
πατέρα τ' ἂν ἐνδίκως ἂν ἡγοίμην μόνην.
καίτοι καλόν γ' ἂν τόνδ' ἀγῶν' ἠγωνίσω
τοῦ σοῦ πρὸ παιδὸς κατθανών, βραχὺς δέ σοι
πάντως ὁ λοιπὸς ἦν βιώσιμος χρόνος.   650
καὶ μὴν ὅσ' ἄνδρα χρὴ παθεῖν εὐδαίμονα   653
πέπονθας· ἥβησας μὲν ἐν τυραννίδι,
παῖς δ' ἦν ἐγώ σοι τῶνδε διάδοχος δόμων,   655
ὥστ' οὐκ ἄτεκνος κατθανὼν ἄλλοις δόμον
λείψειν ἔμελλες ὀρφανὸν διαρπάσαι.

οὐ μὴν ἐρεῖς γέ μ' ὡς ἀτιμάζων τὸ σὸν
γῆρας θανεῖν προύδωκά σ', ὅστις αἰδόφρων
πρός σ' ἦν μάλιστα, κἀντὶ τῶνδέ μοι χάριν 660
τοιάνδε καὶ σὺ χἡ τεκοῦσ' ἠλλαξάτην.
τοιγὰρ φυτεύων παῖδας οὐκέτ' ἂν φθάνοις,
οἳ γηροβοσκήσουσι καὶ θανόντα σε
περιστελοῦσι καὶ προθήσονται νεκρόν.
οὐ γάρ σ' ἔγωγε τῇδ' ἐμῇ θάψω χερί· 665
τέθνηκα γὰρ δὴ τοὐπί σ'· εἰ δ' ἄλλου τυχὼν
σωτῆρος αὐγὰς εἰσορῶ, κείνου λέγω
καὶ παῖδά μ' εἶναι καὶ φίλον γηροτρόφον.
μάτην ἄρ' οἱ γέροντες εὔχονται θανεῖν,
γῆρας ψέγοντες καὶ μακρὸν χρόνον βίου· 670
ἢν δ' ἐγγὺς ἔλθῃ θάνατος, οὐδεὶς βούλεται
θνήσκειν, τὸ γῆρας δ' οὐκέτ' ἔστ' αὐτοῖς βαρύ.

ΧΟ. παύσασθ', ἅλις γὰρ ἡ παροῦσα συμφορά,
ὦ παῖ· πατρὸς δὲ μὴ παροξύνῃς φρένας.

ΦΕ. ὦ παῖ, τίν' αὐχεῖς, πότερα Λυδὸν ἢ Φρύγα 675
κακοῖς ἐλαύνειν ἀργυρώνητον σέθεν;
οὐκ οἶσθα Θεσσαλόν με κἀπὸ Θεσσαλοῦ
πατρὸς γεγῶτα γνησίως ἐλεύθερον;
ἄγαν ὑβρίζεις, καὶ νεανίας λόγους
ῥίπτων ἐς ἡμᾶς οὐ βαλὼν οὕτως ἄπει. 680
ἐγὼ δέ σ' οἴκων δεσπότην ἐγεινάμην
κἄθρεψ', ὀφείλω δ' οὐχ ὑπερθνήσκειν σέθεν·
οὐ γὰρ πατρῷον τόνδ' ἐδεξάμην νόμον
παίδων προθνήσκειν πατέρας, οὐδ' Ἑλληνικόν.
σαυτῷ γὰρ εἴτε δυστυχὴς εἴτ' εὐτυχὴς 685
ἔφυς· ἃ δ' ἡμῶν χρῆν σε τυγχάνειν, ἔχεις.
πολλῶν μὲν ἄρχεις, πολυπλέθρους δέ σοι γύας
λείψω· πατρὸς γὰρ ταῦτ' ἐδεξάμην πάρα.

τί δῆτά σ' ἠδίκηκα; τοῦ σ' ἀποστερῶ;
μὴ θνῇσχ' ὑπὲρ τοῦδ' ἀνδρός, οὐδ' ἐγὼ πρὸ σοῦ. 690
χαίρεις ὁρῶν φῶς· πατέρα δ' οὐ χαίρειν δοκεῖς;
ἦ μὴν πολύν γε τὸν κάτω λογίζομαι
χρόνον, τὸ δὲ ζῆν μικρόν, ἀλλ' ὅμως γλυκύ.
σὺ γοῦν ἀναιδῶς διεμάχου τὸ μὴ θανεῖν,
καὶ ζῇς παρελθὼν τὴν πεπρωμένην τύχην,　695
ταύτην κατακτάς· εἶτ' ἐμὴν ἀψυχίαν
λέγεις, γυναικὸς ὦ κάκισθ' ἡσσημένος,
ἣ τοῦ καλοῦ σοῦ προύθανεν νεανίου;
σοφῶς δ' ἐφηῦρες ὥστε μὴ θανεῖν ποτε,
εἰ τὴν παροῦσαν κατθανεῖν πείσεις ἀεὶ　700
γυναῖχ' ὑπὲρ σοῦ· κᾆτ' ὀνειδίζεις φίλοις
τοῖς μὴ θέλουσι δρᾶν τάδ', αὐτὸς ὢν κακός;
σίγα· νόμιζε δ', εἰ σὺ τὴν σαυτοῦ φιλεῖς
ψυχήν, φιλεῖν ἅπαντας· εἰ δ' ἡμᾶς κακῶς
ἐρεῖς, ἀκούσει πολλὰ κοὐ ψευδῆ κακά.　705

ΧΟ.　πλείω λέλεκται νῦν τε καὶ τὸ πρὶν κακά·
παῦσαι δέ, πρέσβυ, παῖδα σὸν κακορροθῶν.

ΑΔ.　λέγ', ὡς ἐμοῦ λέξαντος· εἰ δ' ἀλγεῖς κλύων
τἀληθές, οὐ χρῆν σ' εἰς ἔμ' ἐξαμαρτάνειν.

ΦΕ.　σοῦ δ' ἂν προθνῄσκων μᾶλλον ἐξημάρτανον. 710

ΑΔ.　ταὐτὸν γὰρ ἡβῶντ' ἄνδρα καὶ πρέσβυν θανεῖν;

ΦΕ.　ψυχῇ μιᾷ ζῆν, οὐ δυοῖν ὀφείλομεν.

ΑΔ.　καὶ μὴν Διός γε μείζονα ζώης χρόνον.

ΦΕ.　ἀρᾷ γονεῦσιν οὐδὲν ἔκδικον παθών;

ΑΔ.　μακροῦ βίου γὰρ ᾐσθόμην ἐρῶντά σε.　715

ΦΕ.　ἀλλ' οὐ σὺ νεκρὸν ἀντὶ σοῦ τόνδ' ἐκφέρεις;

ΑΔ.　σημεῖα τῆς σῆς, ὦ κάκιστ', ἀψυχίας.

ΦΕ.　οὔτοι πρὸς ἡμῶν γ' ὤλετ'· οὐκ ἐρεῖς τόδε.

ΑΔ.　φεῦ·

εἴθ' ἀνδρὸς ἔλθοις τοῦδέ γ' ἐς χρείαν ποτέ.

ΦΕ. μνήστευε πολλάς, ὡς θάνωσι πλείονες. 720

ΑΔ. σοὶ τοῦτ' ὄνειδος· οὐ γὰρ ἤθελες θανεῖν.

ΦΕ. φίλον τὸ φέγγος τοῦτο τοῦ θεοῦ, φίλον.

ΑΔ. κακὸν τὸ λῆμα κοὐκ ἐν ἀνδράσιν τὸ σόν.

ΦΕ. οὐκ ἐγγελᾷς γέροντα βαστάζων νεκρόν.

ΑΔ. θανεῖ γε μέντοι δυσκλεής, ὅταν θάνῃς. 725

ΦΕ. κακῶς ἀκούειν οὐ μέλει θανόντι μοι.

ΑΔ. φεῦ φεῦ· τὸ γῆρας ὡς ἀναιδείας πλέων.

ΦΕ. ἥδ' οὐκ ἀναιδής· τήνδ' ἐφηῦρες ἄφρονα.

ΑΔ. ἄπελθε κἀμὲ τόνδ' ἔα θάψαι νεκρόν.

ΦΕ. ἄπειμι· θάψεις δ' αὐτὸς ὢν αὐτῆς φονεύς, 730
δίκας τε δώσεις τοῖσι κηδεσταῖς ἔτι.
ἦ τἄρ' Ἄκαστος οὐκέτ' ἔστ' ἐν ἀνδράσιν,
εἰ μή σ' ἀδελφῆς αἷμα τιμωρήσεται.

ΑΔ. ἔρρων νυν αὐτὸς χἠ ξύνοικος οὖσά σοι
ἄπαιδε παιδὸς ὄντος, ὥσπερ ἄξιοι, 735
γηράσκετ'· οὐ γὰρ τῷδ' ἔτ' ἐς ταὐτὸν στέγος
νεῖσθ'· εἰ δ' ἀπειπεῖν χρῆν με κηρύκων ὕπο
τὴν σὴν πατρῷαν ἑστίαν, ἀπεῖπον ἄν.
ἡμεῖς δέ, τοὐν ποσὶν γὰρ οἰστέον κακόν,
στείχωμεν, ὡς ἂν ἐν πυρᾷ θῶμεν νεκρόν. 740

ΧΟ. ἰὼ ἰώ. σχετλία τόλμης,
ὦ γενναία καὶ μέγ' ἀρίστη,
χαῖρε· πρόφρων σὲ χθόνιός θ' Ἑρμῆς
Ἅιδης τε δέχοιτ'. εἰ δέ τι κἀκεῖ
πλέον ἔστ' ἀγαθοῖς, τούτων μετέχουσ' 745
Ἅιδου νύμφῃ παρεδρεύοις.

ΘΕΡΑΠΩΝ.

πολλοὺς μὲν ἤδη κἀπὸ παντοίας χθονὸς

ξένους μολόντας οἶδ᾽ ἐς Ἀδμήτου δόμους,
οἷς δεῖπνα προύθηκ᾽· ἀλλὰ τοῦδ᾽ οὔπω ξένου
κακίον᾽ ἐς τήνδ᾽ ἑστίαν ἐδεξάμην.   750
ὃς πρῶτα μὲν πενθοῦντα δεσπότην ὁρῶν
ἐσῆλθε κἀτόλμησ᾽ ἀμείψασθαι πύλας.
ἔπειτα δ᾽ οὔτι σωφρόνως ἐδέξατο
τὰ προστυχόντα ξένια, συμφορὰν μαθών,
ἀλλ᾽, εἴ τι μὴ φέροιμεν, ὤτρυνεν φέρειν.   755
ποτῆρα δ᾽ ἐν χείρεσσι κίσσινον λαβὼν
πίνει μελαίνης μητρὸς εὔζωρον μέθυ,
ἕως ἐθέρμην᾽ αὐτὸν ἀμφιβᾶσα φλὸξ
οἴνου· στέφει δὲ κρᾶτα μυρσίνης κλάδοις
ἄμουσ᾽ ὑλακτῶν· δισσὰ δ᾽ ἦν μέλη κλύειν·   760
ὁ μὲν γὰρ ᾖδε, τῶν ἐν Ἀδμήτου κακῶν
οὐδὲν προτιμῶν, οἰκέται δ᾽ ἐκλαίομεν
δέσποιναν· ὄμμα δ᾽ οὐκ ἐδείκνυμεν ξένῳ
τέγγοντες· Ἄδμητος γὰρ ὧδ᾽ ἐφίετο.
καὶ νῦν ἐγὼ μὲν ἐν δόμοισιν ἑστιῶ   765
ξένον, πανοῦργον κλῶπα καὶ λῃστήν τινα,
ἡ δ᾽ ἐκ δόμων βέβηκεν, οὐδ᾽ ἐφεσπόμην
οὐδ᾽ ἐξέτεινα χεῖρ᾽, ἀποιμώζων ἐμὴν
δέσποιναν, ἥ 'μοὶ πᾶσί τ᾽ οἰκέταισιν ἦν
μήτηρ· κακῶν γὰρ μυρίων ἐρρύετο,   770
ὀργὰς μαλάσσουσ᾽ ἀνδρός. ἆρα τὸν ξένον
στυγῶ δικαίως, ἐν κακοῖς ἀφιγμένον;

ΗΡ. οὗτος, τί σεμνὸν καὶ πεφροντικὸς βλέπεις;
οὐ χρὴ σκυθρωπὸν τοῖς ξένοις τὸν πρόσπολον
εἶναι, δέχεσθαι δ᾽ εὐπροσηγόρῳ φρενί.   775
σὺ δ᾽ ἄνδρ᾽ ἑταῖρον δεσπότου παρόνθ᾽ ὁρῶν,
στυγνῷ προσώπῳ καὶ συνωφρυωμένῳ
δέχει, θυραίου πήματος σπουδὴν ἔχων.

δεῦρ' ἔλθ', ὅπως ἂν καὶ σοφώτερος γένῃ.
τὰ θνητὰ πράγματ' οἶδας ἣν ἔχει φύσιν;   780
οἶμαι μὲν οὔ· πόθεν γάρ; ἀλλ' ἄκουέ μου.
βροτοῖς ἅπασι κατθανεῖν ὀφείλεται,
κοὐκ ἔστι θνητῶν ὅστις ἐξεπίσταται
τὴν αὔριον μέλλουσαν εἰ βιώσεται·
τὸ τῆς τύχης γὰρ ἀφανὲς οἷ προβήσεται,   785
κἄστ' οὐ διδακτὸν οὐδ' ἁλίσκεται τέχνῃ.
ταῦτ' οὖν ἀκούσας καὶ μαθὼν ἐμοῦ πάρα,
εὔφραινε σαυτόν, πῖνε, τὸν καθ' ἡμέραν
βίον λογίζου σόν, τὰ δ' ἄλλα τῆς τύχης.
τίμα δὲ καὶ τὴν πλεῖστον ἡδίστην θεῶν   790
Κύπριν βροτοῖσιν· εὐμενὴς γὰρ ἡ θεός.
τὰ δ' ἄλλ' ἔασον ταῦτα καὶ πιθοῦ λόγοις
ἐμοῖσιν, εἴπερ ὀρθά σοι δοκῶ λέγειν·
οἶμαι μέν. οὔκουν τὴν ἄγαν λύπην ἀφεὶς
πίει μεθ' ἡμῶν τάσδ' ὑπερβαλὼν τύχας,   795
στεφάνοις πυκασθείς; καὶ σάφ' οἶδ' ὁθούνεκα
τοῦ νῦν σκυθρωποῦ καὶ ξυνεστῶτος φρενῶν
μεθορμιεῖ σε πίτυλος ἐμπεσὼν σκύφου.
ὄντας δὲ θνητοὺς θνητὰ καὶ φρονεῖν χρεών·
ὡς τοῖς γε σεμνοῖς καὶ συνωφρυωμένοις   800
ἅπασίν ἐστιν, ὥς γ' ἐμοὶ χρῆσθαι κριτῇ,
οὐ βίος ἀληθῶς ὁ βίος, ἀλλὰ συμφορά.

ΘΕ. ἐπιστάμεσθα ταῦτα· νῦν δὲ πράσσομεν
οὐχ οἷα κώμου καὶ γέλωτος ἄξια.

ΗΡ. γυνὴ θυραῖος ἡ θανοῦσα· μὴ λίαν   805
πένθει· δόμων γὰρ ζῶσι τῶνδε δεσπόται.

ΘΕ. τί ζῶσιν; οὐ κάτοισθα τὰν δόμοις κακά;

ΗΡ. εἰ μή τι σός με δεσπότης ἐψεύσατο.

ΘΕ. ἄγαν ἐκεῖνός ἐστ' ἄγαν φιλόξενος.

ΗΡ. οὐ χρῆν μ' ὀθνείου γ' οὕνεκ' εὖ πάσχειν νεκροῦ;

ΘΕ. ἢ κάρτα μέντοι καὶ λίαν οἰκεῖος ἦν.   811

ΗΡ. μῶν ξυμφοράν τιν' οὖσαν οὐκ ἔφραζέ μοι;

ΘΕ. χαίρων ἴθ'· ἡμῖν δεσποτῶν μέλει κακά.

ΗΡ. ὅδ' οὐ θυραίων πημάτων ἄρχει λόγος.

ΘΕ. οὐ γάρ τι κωμάζοντ' ἂν ἠχθόμην σ' ὁρῶν.   815

ΗΡ. ἀλλ' ἢ πέπονθα δείν' ὑπὸ ξένων ἐμῶν;

ΘΕ. οὐκ ἦλθες ἐν δέοντι δέξασθαι δόμοις.   817

ΗΡ. μῶν ἢ τέκνων τι φροῦδον ἢ πατὴρ γέρων;   820

ΘΕ. γυνὴ μὲν οὖν ὄλωλεν Ἀδμήτου, ξένε.

ΗΡ. τί φής; ἔπειτα δῆτά μ' ἐξενίζετε;

ΘΕ. ᾐδεῖτο γάρ σε τῶνδ' ἀπώσασθαι δόμων.

ΗΡ. ὦ σχέτλι', οἵας ἤμπλακες ξυναόρου.

ΘΕ. ἀπωλόμεσθα πάντες, οὐ κείνη μόνη.   825

ΗΡ. ἀλλ' ᾐσθόμην μὲν ὄμμ' ἰδὼν δακρυρροοῦν
κουράν τε καὶ πρόσωπον· ἀλλ' ἔπειθέ με
λέγων θυραῖον κῆδος ἐς τάφον φέρειν.
βίᾳ δὲ θυμοῦ τάσδ' ὑπερβαλὼν πύλας
ἔπινον ἀνδρὸς ἐν φιλοξένου δόμοις,   830
πράσσοντος οὕτω. κᾆτα κωμάζω κάρα
στεφάνοις πυκασθείς; ἀλλὰ σοῦ τὸ μὴ φράσαι,
κακοῦ τοσούτου δώμασιν προσκειμένου.
ποῦ καί σφε θάπτει; ποῦ νιν εὑρήσω μολών;

ΘΕ. ὀρθὴν παρ' οἶμον, ἣ 'πὶ Λάρισσαν φέρει,   835
τύμβον κατόψει ξεστὸν ἐκ προαστίου.

ΗΡ. ὦ πολλὰ τλᾶσα καρδία καὶ χεὶρ ἐμή,
νῦν δεῖξον οἷον παῖδά σ' ἡ Τιρυνθία
Ἠλεκτρυόνος ἐγείνατ' Ἀλκμήνη Διί.
δεῖ γάρ με σῶσαι τὴν θανοῦσαν ἀρτίως   840
γυναῖκα κᾆς τόνδ' αὖθις ἱδρῦσαι δόμον
Ἄλκηστιν, Ἀδμήτῳ θ' ὑπουργῆσαι χάριν.

ἐλθὼν δ' ἄνακτα τὸν μελάμπεπλον νεκρῶν
Θάνατον φυλάξω, καί νιν εὑρήσειν δοκῶ
πίνοντα τύμβου πλησίον προσφαγμάτων. 845
κἄνπερ λοχαίας αὐτὸν ἐξ ἕδρας συθεὶς
μάρψω, κύκλον δὲ περιβαλῶ χεροῖν ἐμαῖν,
οὐκ ἔστιν ὅστις αὐτὸν ἐξαιρήσεται
μογοῦντα πλευρά, πρὶν γυναῖκ' ἐμοὶ μεθῇ.
ἢν δ' οὖν ἁμάρτω τῆσδ' ἄγρας, καὶ μὴ μόλῃ 850
πρὸς αἱματηρὸν πέλανον, εἶμι τῶν κάτω
Κόρης ἄνακτός τ' εἰς ἀνηλίους δόμους
αἰτήσομαί τε· καὶ πέποιθ' ἄξειν ἄνω
Ἄλκηστιν, ὥστε χερσὶν ἐνθεῖναι ξένου,
ὅς μ' ἐς δόμους ἐδέξατ' οὐδ' ἀπήλασε, 855
καίπερ βαρείᾳ συμφορᾷ πεπληγμένος,
ἔκρυπτε δ' ὢν γενναῖος, αἰδεσθεὶς ἐμέ.
τίς τοῦδε μᾶλλον Θεσσαλῶν φιλόξενος,
τίς Ἑλλάδ' οἰκῶν; τοιγὰρ οὐκ ἐρεῖ κακὸν
εὐεργετῆσαι φῶτα γενναῖος γεγώς. 860

ΑΔ. ἰώ. στυγναὶ πρόσοδοι, στυγναὶ δ' ὄψεις
χήρων μελάθρων· ἰώ μοί μοι. αἰαῖ.
ποῖ βῶ; πᾷ στῶ; τί λέγω; τί δὲ μή;
πῶς ἂν ὀλοίμαν;
ἦ βαρυδαίμονα μήτηρ μ' ἔτεκεν. 865
ζηλῶ φθιμένους, κείνων ἔραμαι,
κεῖν' ἐπιθυμῶ δώματα ναίειν.
οὔτε γὰρ αὐγὰς χαίρω προσορῶν
οὔτ' ἐπὶ γαίας πόδα πεζεύων·
τοῖον ὅμηρόν μ' ἀποσυλήσας 870
Ἅιδῃ Θάνατος παρέδωκεν.

ΧΟ. πρόβα πρόβα· βᾶθι κεῦθος οἴκων. στρ.
ΑΔ. αἰαῖ.

ΧΟ. πέπονθας ἄξι' αἰαγμάτων. ΑΔ. ἒ ἔ.

ΧΟ. δι' ὀδύνας ἔβας,
    σάφ' οἶδα. ΑΔ. φεῦ φεῦ. ΧΟ. τὰν νέρθεν
       οὐδὲν ὠφελεῖς.   875

ΑΔ. ἰώ μοί μοι. ΧΟ. τὸ μήποτ' εἰσιδεῖν φιλίας ἀλόχου
    πρόσωπόν σε πάντα λυπρόν.

ΑΔ. ἔμνησας ὅ μου φρένας ἤλκωσεν·
    τί γὰρ ἀνδρὶ κακὸν μεῖζον ἁμαρτεῖν
    πιστῆς ἀλόχου; μή ποτε γήμας   880
    ὤφελον οἰκεῖν μετὰ τῆσδε δόμους.
    ζηλῶ δ' ἀγάμους ἀτέκνους τε βροτῶν·
    μία γὰρ ψυχή, τῆς ὑπεραλγεῖν
    μέτριον ἄχθος·
    παίδων δὲ νόσους καὶ νυμφιδίους   885
    εὐνὰς θανάτοις κεραϊζομένας
    οὐ τλητὸν ὁρᾶν, ἐξὸν ἀτέκνους
    ἀγάμους τ' εἶναι διὰ παντός.

ΧΟ. τύχα τύχα δυσπάλαιστος ἥκει,   ἀντ.

ΑΔ. αἰαῖ.

ΧΟ. πέρας δέ γ' οὐδὲν ἀλγέων τιθεῖς. ΑΔ. ἒ ἔ.   890

ΧΟ. βαρέα μὲν φέρειν,
    ὅμως δὲ ΑΔ. φεῦ φεῦ. ΧΟ. τλᾶθ'· οὐ σὺ
       πρῶτος ὤλεσας

ΑΔ. ἰώ μοί μοι. ΧΟ. γυναῖκα· συμφορὰ δ' ἑτέρους
       ἑτέρα
    πιέζει φανεῖσα θνατῶν.

ΑΔ. ὦ μακρὰ πένθη λῦπαί τε φίλων   895
    τῶν ὑπὸ γαῖαν.
    τί μ' ἐκώλυσας ῥῖψαι τύμβου
    τάφρον ἐς κοίλην καὶ μετ' ἐκείνης
    τῆς μέγ' ἀρίστης κεῖσθαι φθίμενον;

δύο δ' ἀντὶ μιᾶς Ἅιδης ψυχὰς   900
τὰς πιστοτάτας σὺν ἂν ἔσχεν, ὁμοῦ
χθονίαν λίμνην διαβάντε.

ΧΟ.   ἐμοί τις ἦν   στρ.
ἐν γένει ᾧ, κόρος ἀξιόθρηνος
ὤλετ' ἐν δόμοισιν   905
μονόπαις· ἀλλ' ἔμπας
ἔφερε κακὸν ἅλις, ἄτεκνος ὤν,
πολιὰς ἐπὶ χαίτας
ἤδη προπετὴς ὢν
βιότου τε πόρσω.   910

ΑΔ.   ὦ σχῆμα δόμων, πῶς εἰσέλθω;
πῶς δ' οἰκήσω μεταπίπτοντος
δαίμονος; οἴμοι. πολὺ γὰρ τὸ μέσον·
τότε μὲν πεύκαις σὺν Πηλιάσιν   915
σύν θ' ὑμεναίοις ἔστειχον ἔσω,
φιλίας ἀλόχου χέρα βαστάζων·
πολυάχητος δ' εἵπετο κῶμος,
τήν τε θανοῦσαν κἄμ' ὀλβίζων,
ὡς εὐπατρίδαι καὶ ἀπ' ἀμφοτέρων   920
ὄντες ἀριστέων σύζυγες εἶμεν.
νῦν δ' ὑμεναίων γόος ἀντίπαλος
λευκῶν τε πέπλων μέλανες στολμοὶ
πέμπουσί μ' ἔσω
λέκτρων κοίτας ἐς ἐρήμους.   925

ΧΟ.   παρ' εὐτυχῆ   ἀντ.
σοὶ πότμον ἦλθεν ἀπειροκάκῳ τόδ'
ἄλγος· ἀλλ' ἔσωσας
βίοτον καὶ ψυχάν.
ἔθανε δάμαρ, ἔλιπε φιλίαν·   930
τί νέον τόδε; πολλοὺς

Η. Α.

                                                        3

ἤδη παρέλυσεν
θάνατος δάμαρτος.

ΑΔ. φίλοι, γυναικὸς δαίμον' εὐτυχέστερον   935
τοὐμοῦ νομίζω, καίπερ οὐ δοκοῦνθ' ὅμως·
τῆς μὲν γὰρ οὐδὲν ἄλγος ἅψεταί ποτε,
πολλῶν δὲ μόχθων εὐκλεὴς ἐπαύσατο.
ἐγὼ δ', ὃν οὐ χρῆν ζῆν, παρεὶς τὸ μόρσιμον
λυπρὸν διάξω βίοτον· ἄρτι μανθάνω.   940
πῶς γὰρ δόμων τῶνδ' εἰσόδους ἀνέξομαι;
τίν' ἂν προσειπών, τοῦ δὲ προσρηθεὶς ὕπο,
τερπνῆς τύχοιμ' ἂν εἰσόδου; ποῖ τρέψομαι;
ἡ μὲν γὰρ ἔνδον ἐξελᾷ μ' ἐρημία,
γυναικὸς εὐνὰς εὖτ' ἂν εἰσίδω κενὰς   945
θρόνους τ' ἐν οἷσιν ἷζε, καὶ κατὰ στέγας
αὐχμηρὸν οὖδας, τέκνα δ' ἀμφὶ γούνασι
πίπτοντα κλαίῃ μητέρ', οἱ δὲ δεσπότιν
στένωσιν οἵαν ἐκ δόμων ἀπώλεσαν.
τὰ μὲν κατ' οἶκον τοιάδ'· ἔξωθεν δέ με   950
γάμοι τ' ἐλῶσι Θεσσαλῶν καὶ ξύλλογοι
γυναικοπληθεῖς· οὐ γὰρ ἐξανέξομαι
λεύσσων δάμαρτος τῆς ἐμῆς ὁμήλικας.
ἐρεῖ δέ μ' ὅστις ἐχθρὸς ὢν κυρεῖ τάδε·
ἰδοῦ τὸν αἰσχρῶς ζῶνθ', ὃς οὐκ ἔτλη θανεῖν, 955
ἀλλ' ἣν ἔγημεν ἀντιδοὺς ἀψυχίᾳ
πέφευγεν Ἅιδην· εἶτ' ἀνὴρ εἶναι δοκεῖ;
στυγεῖ δὲ τοὺς τεκόντας, αὐτὸς οὐ θέλων
θανεῖν. τοιάνδε πρὸς κακοῖσι κληδόνα
ἕξω. τί μοι ζῆν δῆτα κύδιον, φίλοι,   960
κακῶς κλύοντι καὶ κακῶς πεπραγότι;

ΧΟ. ἐγὼ καὶ διὰ μούσας   στρ.
καὶ μετάρσιος ᾖξα, καὶ

πλείστων ἁψάμενος λόγων
κρεῖσσον οὐδὲν Ἀνάγκας   965
ηὗρον, οὐδέ τι φάρμακον
Θρήσσαις ἐν σανίσιν, τὰς
Ὀρφεία κατέγραψεν
γῆρυς, οὐδ᾽ ὅσα Φοῖβος Ἀ-
σκληπιάδαις ἔδωκε   970
φάρμακα πολυπόνοις
ἀντιτεμὼν βροτοῖσιν.

μόνας δ᾽ οὔτ᾽ ἐπὶ βωμοὺς   ἀντ.
ἔστιν οὔτε βρέτας θεᾶς
ἐλθεῖν, οὐ σφαγίων κλύει.   975
μή μοι, πότνια, μείζων
ἔλθοις ἢ τὸ πρὶν ἐν βίῳ.
καὶ γὰρ Ζεὺς ὅ τι νεύσῃ,
σὺν σοὶ τοῦτο τελευτᾷ.
καὶ τὸν ἐν Χαλύβοις δαμά-   980
ζεις σὺ βίᾳ σίδαρον,
οὐδέ τις ἀποτόμου
λήματός ἐστιν αἰδώς.

καὶ σ᾽ ἐν ἀφύκτοισι χερῶν εἷλε θεὰ δεσμοῖς. στρ.
τόλμα δ᾽· οὐ γὰρ ἀνάξεις ποτ᾽ ἔνερθεν   985
κλαίων τοὺς φθιμένους ἄνω.
καὶ θεῶν σκότιοι φθίνουσι
παῖδες ἐν θανάτῳ.
φίλα μὲν ὅτ᾽ ἦν μεθ᾽ ἡμῶν,   990
φίλα δὲ θανοῦσ᾽ ἔτ᾽ ἔσται·
γενναιοτάταν δὲ πασᾶν
ἐζεύξω κλισίαις ἄκοιτιν.
                                                994
μηδὲ νεκρῶν ὡς φθιμένων χῶμα νομιζέσθω ἀντ.
τύμβος σᾶς ἀλόχου, θεοῖσι δ᾽ ὁμοίως

τιμάσθω, σέβας ἐμπόρων.
καί τις δοχμίαν κέλευθον   1000
ἐμβαίνων τόδ᾽ ἐρεῖ·
αὗτα ποτὲ προύθαν᾽ ἀνδρός,
νῦν δ᾽ ἐστὶ μάκαιρα δαίμων·
χαῖρ᾽, ὦ πότνι᾽, εὖ δὲ δοίης.
τοιαί νιν προσεροῦσι φᾶμαι.   1005
καὶ μὴν ὅδ᾽, ὡς ἔοικεν, Ἀλκμήνης γόνος,
Ἄδμητε, πρὸς σὴν ἑστίαν πορεύεται.

ΗΡ. φίλον πρὸς ἄνδρα χρὴ λέγειν ἐλευθέρως,
Ἄδμητε, μομφὰς δ᾽ οὐχ ὑπὸ σπλάγχνοις ἔχειν
σιγῶντ᾽. ἐγὼ δὲ σοῖς κακοῖσιν ἠξίουν   1010
ἐγγὺς παρεστὼς ἐξετάζεσθαι φίλος·
σὺ δ᾽ οὐκ ἔφραζες σῆς προκείμενον νέκυν
γυναικός, ἀλλά μ᾽ ἐξένιζες ἐν δόμοις,
ὡς δὴ θυραίου πήματος σπουδὴν ἔχων.
κἄστεψα κρᾶτα καὶ θεοῖς ἐλειψάμην   1015
σπονδὰς ἐν οἴκοις δυστυχοῦσι τοῖσι σοῖς.
καὶ μέμφομαι μὲν μέμφομαι παθὼν τάδε,
οὐ μήν σε λυπεῖν ἐν κακοῖσι βούλομαι.
ὧν δ᾽ οὕνεχ᾽ ἥκω δεῦρ᾽ ὑποστρέψας πάλιν
λέξω. γυναῖκα τήνδε μοι σῶσον λαβών,   1020
ἕως ἂν ἵππους δεῦρο Θρῃκίας ἄγων
ἔλθω, τύραννον Βιστόνων κατακτανών.
πράξας δ᾽ ὃ μὴ τύχοιμι, νοστήσαιμι γάρ,
δίδωμι τήνδε σοῖσι προσπολεῖν δόμοις.
πολλῷ δὲ μόχθῳ χεῖρας ἦλθεν εἰς ἐμάς·   1025
ἀγῶνα γὰρ πάνδημον εὑρίσκω τινὰς
τιθέντας, ἀθληταῖσιν ἄξιον πόνον,
ὅθεν κομίζω τήνδε νικητήρια
λαβών· τὰ μὲν γὰρ κοῦφα τοῖς νικῶσιν ἦν

ἵππους ἄγεσθαι, τοῖσι δ' αὖ τὰ μείζονα   1030
νικῶσι, πυγμὴν καὶ πάλην, βουφόρβια·
γυνὴ δ' ἐπ' αὐτοῖς εἵπετ'· ἐντυχόντι δὲ
αἰσχρὸν παρεῖναι κέρδος ἦν τόδ' εὐκλεές.
ἀλλ', ὥσπερ εἶπον, σοὶ μέλειν γυναῖκα χρή·
οὐ γὰρ κλοπαίαν, ἀλλὰ σὺν πόνῳ λαβὼν   1035
ἥκω· χρόνῳ δὲ καὶ σύ μ' αἰνέσεις ἴσως.

ΑΔ. οὔτοι σ' ἀτίζων οὐδ' ἐν ἐχθροῖσιν τιθεὶς
ἔκρυψ' ἐμῆς γυναικὸς ἀθλίου τύχας·
ἀλλ' ἄλγος ἄλγει τοῦτ' ἂν ἦν προσκείμενον,
εἴ του πρὸς ἄλλου δώμαθ' ὡρμήθης ξένου·   1040
ἅλις δὲ κλαίειν τοὐμὸν ἦν ἐμοὶ κακόν.
γυναῖκα δ', εἴ πως ἔστιν, αἰτοῦμαί σ', ἄναξ,
ἄλλον τιν' ὅστις μὴ πέπονθεν οἷ' ἐγὼ
σῴζειν ἄνωχθι Θεσσαλῶν· πολλοὶ δέ σοι
ξένοι Φεραίων· μή μ' ἀναμνήσῃς κακῶν.   1045
οὐκ ἂν δυναίμην τήνδ' ὁρῶν ἐν δώμασιν
ἄδακρυς εἶναι· μὴ νοσοῦντί μοι νόσον
προσθῇς· ἅλις γὰρ συμφορᾷ βαρύνομαι.
ποῦ καὶ τρέφοιτ' ἂν δωμάτων νέα γυνή;
νέα γάρ, ὡς ἐσθῆτι καὶ κόσμῳ πρέπει.   1050
πότερα κατ' ἀνδρῶν δῆτ' ἐνοικήσει στέγην;
καὶ πῶς ἀκραιφνὴς ἐν νέοις στρωφωμένη
ἔσται; τὸν ἡβῶνθ', Ἡράκλεις, οὐ ῥᾴδιον
εἴργειν· ἐγὼ δὲ σοῦ προμηθίαν ἔχω.
ἦ τῆς θανούσης θάλαμον ἐσβήσας τρέφω;   1055
καὶ πῶς ἐπεσφρῶ τήνδε τῷ κείνης λέχει;
διπλῆν φοβοῦμαι μέμψιν, ἔκ τε δημοτῶν,
μή τίς μ' ἐλέγχῃ τὴν ἐμὴν εὐεργέτιν
προδόντ' ἐν ἄλλης δεμνίοις πίτνειν νέας,
καὶ τῆς θανούσης· ἀξία δ' ἐμοὶ σέβειν·   1060

πολλὴν πρόνοιαν δεῖ μ' ἔχειν. σὺ δ' ὦ γύναι,
ἥτις ποτ' εἶ σύ, ταῦτ' ἔχουσ' Ἀλκήστιδι
μορφῆς μέτρ' ἴσθι, καὶ προσήιξαι δέμας.
οἴμοι. κόμιζε πρὸς θεῶν ἐξ ὀμμάτων
γυναῖκα τήνδε· μή μ' ἕλῃς ᾑρημένον.   1065
δοκῶ γὰρ αὐτὴν εἰσορῶν γυναῖχ' ὁρᾶν
ἐμήν· θολοῖ δὲ καρδίαν, ἐκ δ' ὀμμάτων
πηγαὶ κατερρώγασιν· ὦ τλήμων ἐγώ,
ὡς ἄρτι πένθους τοῦδε γεύομαι πικροῦ.

ΧΟ. ἐγὼ μὲν οὐκ ἔχοιμ' ἂν εὖ λέγειν τύχην·   1070
χρὴ δ', ὅστις εἶ σύ, καρτερεῖν θεοῦ δόσιν.

ΗΡ. εἰ γὰρ τοσαύτην δύναμιν εἶχον ὥστε σὴν
εἰς φῶς πορεῦσαι νερτέρων ἐκ δωμάτων
γυναῖκα καί σοι τήνδε πορσῦναι χάριν.

ΑΔ. σάφ' οἶδα βούλεσθαί σ' ἄν. ἀλλὰ ποῦ τόδε; 1075
οὐκ ἔστι τοὺς θανόντας ἐς φάος μολεῖν.

ΗΡ. μή νυν ὑπέρβαλλ', ἀλλ' ἐναισίμως φέρε.

ΑΔ. ῥᾷον παραινεῖν ἢ παθόντα καρτερεῖν.

ΗΡ. τί δ' ἂν προκόπτοις, εἰ θέλοις ἀεὶ στένειν;

ΑΔ. ἔγνωκα καὐτός, ἀλλ' ἔρως τις ἐξάγει.   1080

ΗΡ. τὸ γὰρ φιλῆσαι τὸν θανόντ' ἄγει δάκρυ.

ΑΔ. ἀπώλεσέν με, κἄτι μᾶλλον ἢ λέγω.

ΗΡ. γυναικὸς ἐσθλῆς ἤμπλακες· τίς ἀντερεῖ;

ΑΔ. ὥστ' ἄνδρα τόνδε μηκέθ' ἥδεσθαι βίῳ.

ΗΡ. χρόνος μαλάξει, νῦν δ' ἔθ' ἡβάσκει κακόν.   1085

ΑΔ. χρόνον λέγοις ἄν, εἰ χρόνος τὸ κατθανεῖν.

ΗΡ. γυνή σε παύσει καὶ νέου γάμου πόθος.

ΑΔ. σίγησον· οἶον εἶπας. οὐκ ἂν ᾠόμην—

ΗΡ. τί δ'; οὐ γαμεῖς γάρ, ἀλλὰ χηρεύσει λέχος;

ΑΔ. οὐκ ἔστιν ἥτις τῷδε συγκλιθήσεται.   1090

ΗΡ. μῶν τὴν θανοῦσαν ὠφελεῖν τι προσδοκᾷς;

ΑΔ. κείνην ὅπουπέρ ἐστι τιμᾶσθαι χρεών.

ΗΡ. αἰνῶ μὲν αἰνῶ· μωρίαν δ᾽ ὀφλισκάνεις.

ΑΔ. ὡς μήποτ᾽ ἄνδρα τόνδε νυμφίον καλῶν.

ΗΡ. ἐπήνεσ᾽ ἀλόχῳ πιστὸς οὕνεκ᾽ εἶ φίλος.   1095

ΑΔ. θάνοιμ᾽ ἐκείνην καίπερ οὐκ οὖσαν προδούς.

ΗΡ. δέχου νυν εἴσω τήνδε γενναίως δόμων.

ΑΔ. μή, πρός σε τοῦ σπείραντος ἄντομαι Διός.

ΗΡ. καὶ μὴν ἁμαρτήσει γε μὴ δράσας τάδε.

ΑΔ. καὶ δρῶν γε λύπῃ καρδίαν δηχθήσομαι.   1100

ΗΡ. πίθου· τάχ᾽ ἂν γὰρ ἐς δέον πέσοι χάρις.

ΑΔ. φεῦ·
εἴθ᾽ ἐξ ἀγῶνος τήνδε μὴ ᾽λαβές ποτε.

ΗΡ. νικῶντι μέντοι καὶ σὺ συννικᾷς ἐμοί.

ΑΔ. καλῶς ἔλεξας· ἡ γυνὴ δ᾽ ἀπελθέτω.

ΗΡ. ἄπεισιν, εἰ χρή· πρῶτα δ᾽ εἰ χρεὼν ἄθρει.   1105

ΑΔ. χρή, σοῦ γε μὴ μέλλοντος ὀργαίνειν ἐμοί.

ΗΡ. εἰδώς τι κἀγὼ τήνδ᾽ ἔχω προθυμίαν.

ΑΔ. νίκα νυν. οὐ μὴν ἁνδάνοντά μοι ποιεῖς.

ΗΡ. ἀλλ᾽ ἔσθ᾽ ὅθ᾽ ἡμᾶς αἰνέσεις· πιθοῦ μόνον.

ΑΔ. κομίζετ᾽, εἰ χρὴ τήνδε δέξασθαι δόμοις.   1110

ΗΡ. οὐκ ἂν μεθείην τὴν γυναῖκα προσπόλοις.

ΑΔ. σὺ δ᾽ αὐτὸς αὐτὴν εἴσαγ᾽, εἰ βούλει, δόμους.

ΗΡ. ἐς σὰς μὲν οὖν ἔγωγε θήσομαι χέρας.

ΑΔ. οὐκ ἂν θίγοιμι· δῶμα δ᾽ εἰσελθεῖν πάρα.

ΗΡ. τῇ σῇ πέποιθα χειρὶ δεξιᾷ μόνῃ.   1115

ΑΔ. ἄναξ, βιάζει μ᾽ οὐ θέλοντα δρᾶν τάδε.

ΗΡ. τόλμα προτεῖναι χεῖρα καὶ θιγεῖν ξένης.

ΑΔ. καὶ δὴ προτείνω, Γοργόν᾽ ὡς καρατομῶν.

ΗΡ. ἔχεις; ΑΔ. ἔχω. ΗΡ. ναί, σῶζέ νυν, καὶ τὸν
Διὸς
φήσεις ποτ᾽ εἶναι παῖδα γενναῖον ξένον.   1120

βλέψον πρὸς αὐτήν, εἴ τι σῇ δοκεῖ πρέπειι
γυναικί· λύπης δ' εὐτυχῶν μεθίστασο.

ΑΔ.   ὦ θεοί, τί λέξω; θαῦμ' ἀνέλπιστον τόδε·
γυναῖκα λεύσσω τὴν ἐμὴν ἐτητύμως,
ἢ κέρτομός με θεοῦ τις ἐκπλήσσει χαρά;   1125

ΗΡ.   οὐκ ἔστιν, ἀλλὰ τήνδ' ὁρᾷς δάμαρτα σήν.

ΑΔ.   ὅρα γε μή τι φάσμα νερτέρων τόδ' ᾖ.

ΗΡ.   οὐ ψυχαγωγὸν τόνδ' ἐποιήσω ξένον.

ΑΔ.   ἀλλ' ἣν ἔθαπτον εἰσορῶ δάμαρτ' ἐμήν;

ΗΡ.   σάφ' ἴσθ'. ἀπιστεῖν δ' οὔ σε θαυμάζω τύχῃ.   1130

ΑΔ.   θίγω, προσείπω ζῶσαν ὡς δάμαρτ' ἐμήν;

ΗΡ.   πρόσειπ'. ἔχεις γὰρ πᾶν ὅσονπερ ἤθελες.

ΑΔ.   ὦ φιλτάτης γυναικὸς ὄμμα καὶ δέμας,
ἔχω σ' ἀέλπτως, οὔποτ' ὄψεσθαι δοκῶν.

ΗΡ.   ἔχεις· φθόνος δὲ μὴ γένοιτό τις θεῶν.   1135

ΑΔ.   ὦ τοῦ μεγίστου Ζηνὸς εὐγενὲς τέκνον,
εὐδαιμονοίης, καί σ' ὁ φιτύσας πατὴρ
σῴζοι· σὺ γὰρ δὴ τἄμ' ἀνώρθωσας μόνος.
πῶς τήνδ' ἔπεμψας νέρθεν ἐς φάος τόδε;

ΗΡ.   μάχην συνάψας δαιμόνων τῷ κυρίῳ.   1140

ΑΔ.   ποῦ τόνδε Θανάτῳ φῂς ἀγῶνα συμβαλεῖν;

ΗΡ.   τύμβον παρ' αὐτὸν ἐκ λόχου μάρψας χεροῖν.

ΑΔ.   τί γὰρ ποθ' ἥδ' ἄναυδος ἔστηκεν γυνή;

ΗΡ.   οὔπω θέμις σοι τῆσδε προσφωνημάτων
κλύειν, πρὶν ἂν θεοῖσι τοῖσι νερτέροις   1145
ἀφαγνίσηται καὶ τρίτον μόλῃ φάος.
ἀλλ' εἴσαγ' εἴσω τήνδε· καὶ δίκαιος ὢν
τὸ λοιπόν, Ἄδμητ', εὐσέβει περὶ ξένους.
καὶ χαῖρ'· ἐγὼ δὲ τὸν προκείμενον πόνον
Σθενέλου τυράννῳ παιδὶ πορσυνῶ μολών.   1150

ΑΔ.   μεῖνον παρ' ἡμῖν καὶ συνέστιος γενοῦ.

ΗΡ. αὖθις τόδ᾽ ἔσται, νῦν δ᾽ ἐπείγεσθαί με δεῖ.

ΑΔ. ἀλλ᾽ εὐτυχοίης, νόστιμον δ᾽ ἔλθοις πόδα.
ἀστοῖς δὲ πάσῃ τ᾽ ἐννέπω τετραρχίᾳ,
χοροὺς ἐπ᾽ ἐσθλαῖς συμφοραῖσιν ἱστάναι   1155
βωμούς τε κνισᾶν βουθύτοισι προστροπαῖς.
νῦν γὰρ μεθηρμόσμεσθα βελτίω βίον
τοῦ πρόσθεν· οὐ γὰρ εὐτυχῶν ἀρνήσομαι.

ΧΟ. πολλαὶ μορφαὶ τῶν δαιμονίων,
πολλὰ δ᾽ ἀέλπτως κραίνουσι θεοί·   1160
καὶ τὰ δοκηθέντ᾽ οὐκ ἐτελέσθη,
τῶν δ᾽ ἀδοκήτων πόρον ηὗρε θεός.
τοιόνδ᾽ ἀπέβη τόδε πρᾶγμα.

NOTES ON THE ΥΠΟΘΕΣΕΙΣ.

Δικαιάρχου Flor., where the argument has been added in a later hand. The allusion is probably to the well-known disciple of Aristotle and friend of Theophrastus, admired by Cicero. It is however possible that the Dicaearchus referred to was a Lacedaemonian pupil of the great Aristarchus of Alexandria, ὁ κορυφαῖος τῶν γραμματικῶν. Aristarchus himself in his turn was the pupil of Aristophanes of Byzantium (flor. 200 B.C.), to whom the second hypothesis is attributed: to the latter, who was librarian at Alexandria, the accentuation of Greek is due. These two scholars, with the head of the rival school at Pergamus, Crates (who introduced the study of grammar into Rome, when sent there as ambassador by Attalus), were the greatest critics of antiquity. Aristophanes is supposed to have taken the materials for his introductions to the great Attic dramas from a work of Callimachus of Alexandria, itself based on the lost 'Didascaliae' of Aristotle, which no doubt was founded on a study of the inscribed records of the dramatic contests at Athens itself. (Cf. Haigh, Attic Theatre, pp. 63, 64.)

16. οὐδετέρῳ, neither Aeschylus nor Sophocles.

17. ιζ′, 'seventeenth': Eurip. had now (438 B.C.) been before the public seventeen years: his first play was produced in 455 B.C. Glaucinus was archon for the year 43⅔.

ὀλυμπιάδος πε′ ἔτει δευτέρῳ, Dindorf for MSS. τὸ λ′. 438 B.C.

19. εἰσιδ✳ ἐχορήγει. These words occur in the MSS after Ἀπόλλων in l. 24: Schwartz (after Dindorf) transposed. In εἰσιδ✳ a proper name, e.g. Ἰσίδοτος is supposed to be concealed.

20. τὸ δὲ δρᾶμα κωμικωτέραν κ.τ.λ., cf. infr. 24, 25. These words recur in Aristophanes' argument to the Orestes.

EXPLANATORY NOTES.

1. ἔτλην, 'I took upon me' as a hardship to be borne: cf. infr. 572 ἔτλα δὲ σοῖσι μηλονόμας ἐν δόμοις γενέσθαι. Soph. Ant. 944 ἔτλα καὶ Δανάας οὐράνιον φῶς | ἀλλάξαι δέμας ('to leave the light of day'). Aesch. Ag. 1040 καὶ παῖδα γάρ τοι φασὶν Ἀλκμήνης ποτὲ | πραθέντα τλῆναι καὶ ζυγῶν θιγεῖν βίᾳ.

ἐγώ. Notice the emphatic position of this word at the end of the line, and of θεός περ ὤν in l. 2. 'I, god though I be.'

2. θῆσσαν is a feminine formed from θής, used as an adj. here, and El. 205 θῆσσαν ἑστίαν. Parallel both in formation and use is Κρῆσσα in Soph. Aj. 1295 μητρὸς ἐξέφυς Κρήσσης. In the constitution of Solon (B.C. 594), the fourth and lowest class of Athenian freemen was that of the θῆτες, who had the right to vote in the assembly, and were liable to service as light-armed troops or on ship-board in time of war. As the citizens were classified according to their property, it follows that among the θῆτες were found the poor labourers who worked for hire on the lands of their richer fellow-citizens. Though their position was essentially different to that of slaves (δοῦλοι), it was no doubt a hard one. Cf. Soph. O. T. 1029, where Oedipus cries in contempt ποιμὴν γὰρ ἦσθα κἀπὶ θητείᾳ πλάνης; ('a vagrant hireling,' Jebb). In the society depicted by Homer, the condition of θῆτες seems to have been similar to that which they occupied in later times: cf. Il. XXI. 444 (a passage strongly resembling this), 'Do you forget?' says Poseidon to Apollo, ὅσα δὴ πάθομεν κακὰ Ἴλιον ἀμφὶ | μοῦνοι νῶι θεῶν, ὅτ' ἀγήνορι Λαομέδοντι | πὰρ Διὸς ἐλθόντες θητεύσαμεν εἰς ἐνιαυτὸν | μισθῷ ἔπι ῥητῷ, ὁ δὲ σημαίνων ἐπέτελλεν. To be θὴς to a poor master is selected by Achilles as the most wretched of earthly lots, but still preferable to sovereignty among the dead: Od. XI. 489 βουλοίμην κ' ἐπάρουρος ἐὼν θητευέμεν ἄλλῳ | ἀνδρὶ παρ' ἀκλήρῳ, ᾧ μὴ βίοτος πολὺς εἴη, | ἢ πᾶσιν νεκύεσσι καταφθιμένοισιν ἀνάσσειν. We must be careful to distinguish them from the Helots of

Sparta and the Penestae of Thessaly, who were 'bound to the soil' (*adscripti glebae*), and directly under the power either of the state or of individual nobles.

αἰνέσαι, 'acquiesce in,' 'submit to.' Cf. El. 1247 αἰνεῖν δ᾽ ἀνάγκη ταῦτα (these troubles). Notice that for αἰνεῖν Attic prose uses ἐπαινεῖν, for περ καίπερ. So in the next line, not κατα- but ἀπο-κτείνω, with passive ἀποθνῄσκω (perfect, however, of simple verb τέθνηκα is used), is found in classic Attic prose. The language of tragedy is a literary dialect (just as is the language of the Homeric poems), differing widely from the idiom spoken at the time of the composition of the dramas, and approximating to the older Ionic, of which Attic is a development: cf. Rutherford, New Phrynicus, p. 3, sq.

3. γάρ introduces an explanation of his enforced service.

4. Ἀσκληπιόν. The mention of Asclepios, the great physician, slain by angry Zeus, in punishment for having dared to restore the dead to life (Virgil, Aen. VII. 770, followed the tradition that represented Hippolytus as the object of his skill), is appropriate in this play, where a similar restoration, wrought by the hand of Heracles, is the central fact of interest: nor are we surprised that Apollo is willing to leave the task of rescue to another, after his son's experience and his own.

5. οὗ, masc. 'in wrath for whose fate.' Instances of this genitive after verbs expressing emotion are Hom. Il. I. 429 χωόμενον γυναικός, 'enraged at the loss of the woman,' XXI. 457 μισθοῦ χωόμενοι, 'at the non-payment of the wage.' Soph. Ant. 1177 μηνίσας φόνου, 'for the murder.' The genitive shows the origin or cause of the passion.

6. κτείνω, historic present. Goodw. Gr. Gr. § 200, note.

The Cyclopes, servants of Zeus and forgers of his thunderbolts, described by Hesiod (Theog. 139 sq., 504), seem to be creatures of a different tradition to the lawless shepherds and cannibals of Sicily, encountered by Odysseus (Od. IX.). Homer introduces their chief Polyphemus openly defying the gods (Od. IX. 275): οὐ γὰρ Κύκλωπες Διὸς αἰγιόχου ἀλέγουσιν | οὐδὲ θεῶν μακάρων, ἐπεὶ ἦ πολὺ φέρτεροί εἰμεν, though his companions later on (l. 411) bid him in his troubles betake himself to prayer, νοῦσόν γ᾽ οὔπως ἔστι Διὸς μεγάλου ἀλέασθαι, | ἀλλὰ σύ γ᾽ εὔχεο πατρὶ Ποσειδάωνι ἄνακτι.

The Cyclopes described by Virgil (Aen. VIII. 424 sq.) are of the former type, skilful metal-workers, under the orders of Vulcan, while the Polyphemus of Theocritus (Id. XI.) is the love-lorn shepherd, who with his stores of cheese and skill in piping, tries to win the scornful Galatea to share his peace and plenty.

7. ἄποιν', in apposition to με θητεύειν θνητῷ παρ' ἀνδρί. For similar accus. in apposition to a clause, cf. infr. 352, n., El. 231 εὐδαιμονοίης, μισθὸν ἡδίστων λόγων. H. F. 59, 978 ὁ δ' ἐξελίσσων παῖδα κίονος κύκλῳ, | τόρνευμα δεινὸν ποδός, ἐναντίον σταθεὶς | βάλλει πρὸς ἧπαρ' 992, 1363 πρὸς στέρν' ἐρείσας μητρὶ δούς τ' ἐς ἀγκάλας, | κοινωνίαν δύστηνον. Aesch. Ag. 1419 οὐ τοῦτον ἐκ γῆς τῆσδε χρῆν σ' ἀνδρηλατεῖν, | μιασμάτων ἄποινα ; Goodw. Gr. Gr. § 137, 3.

8. ἐλθὼν δὲ γαῖαν. The accus. without a preposition of the object of *motion towards* is confined to poetry.

ἐβουφόρβουν. In early times far higher value was attached to oxen than to any other stock, as they were not only serviceable for food, but also as beasts of burden. The price of an ox was adopted as a standard of value (cf. Hom. Il. VI. 235 ὃς πρὸς Τυδείδην Διομήδεα τεύχε' ἄμειβεν | χρύσεα χαλκείων, ἑκατόμβοι' ἐννεαβοίων): a beautiful girl was called ἀλφεσιβοία, 'oxen-earning,' because she brought large ἔδνα, 'bride-price,' to her parents. When coinage was invented, says the compiler of the Etymologicum Magnum (320, 50), βοῦν ἐξετύπουν (engraved) ἐν αὐτῷ, τὸ ἀρχαῖον ἔθος ἐπιδεικνύμενοι. Thus βουφορβός, βουκόλος, etc. were used of keepers of stock generally, as βόες were the main object of their care, and the origin of the words was so far forgotten that βουκολεῖν ἵππους, αἶγας etc. did not sound unnatural. (So κυνέη—'dog-skin'—from being the ordinary material of soldiers' helmets came to mean 'helmet' only, and ταυρείη κυνέη (Il. X. 258) a helmet of bull's hide, would provoke no surprise.) So here ἐβουφόρβουν includes sheep, as infr. 572 Apollo is alluded to as μηλονόμας.

9. ἐς τόδ' ἡμέρας, lit. 'to this point of time.' The genit. is partitive, as in such expressions as ποῦ γῆς ; ὡς εἶχε τάχους, δὶς τῆς ἡμέρας. The use of ἡμέρα for 'time' simply is rare : cf. Soph. O. C. 1138 μέλου δικαίως, ὥσπερ ἐς τόδ' ἡμέρας. Hipp. 1003.

10. ὅσιος has relation to the law of the gods or of nature, while δίκαιος refers to the law of man, based on custom and usage (δίκη) : the relation implied by ὅσιος is twofold : first, what is *sanctioned* by the natural law, hallowed : second, what is *permitted* by that law : e.g. ὅσιον χωρίον might be (*a*) a spot dedicated to the gods, or (*b*) a spot permitted, i.e. not forbidden, to mortal feet, and thus 'open to the public,' Lat. *profanus*. When used of persons it means devout or sinless. The ὁσιότης of Admetus, like the *pietas* of Aeneas, is monotonous in its

regularity : both heroes, too, require a considerable share of this virtue to condone behaviour to their fellow men, which if observed in less god-fearing characters would provoke reproof. It would seem that Apollo speaks of himself as ὅσιος mainly for the sake of the rhetorical repetition, as the word is hardly ever used of a god himself, and would be singularly inappropriate of a god under punishment for murder.

11. After verbs of hindering and preventing we find either the simple infin. (as here) or the genit. of the infin. with τοῦ : in both cases μὴ may be also added. ἐρρυσάμην here has the sense 'prevented from' dying : cf. Phoen. 600 κομπὸς εἶ σπονδαῖς πεποιθώς, αἵ σε σώζουσιν θανεῖν. Andr. 44 Θέτιδος εἰς ἀνάκτορον | θάσσω τόδ᾽ ἐλθοῦσ᾽, ἥν με κωλύσῃ θανεῖν. Most usual is the construction μὴ and simple infin.

12. δολώσας, 'having beguiled' with wine, according to the story : cf. Aesch. Eum. 723 sq., where Apollo is in contest with the nether deities, as in this play with Θάνατος (infr. 29) : after reference to his rescue of Admetus, the Furies continue σύ τοι παλαιὰς διανομὰς καταφθί-σας | οἴνῳ παρηπάτησας ἀρχαίας θεάς. In extenuation of the goddesses, it must be urged that, like their kinswomen the Furies, they were not accustomed to libations of wine, their worship being probably older than the wine-culture of Greece : cf. Eum. 107 : Soph. O. C. 100.

ᾔνεσαν for ξυνῄνεσαν, 'promised': cf. Soph. Phil. 1398 ἃ δ᾽ ᾔνεσάς μοι δεξιᾶς ἐμῆς θιγών, | πέμπειν πρὸς οἴκους, ταῦτά μοι πρᾶξον, τέκνον : a passage which also illustrates the non-use of the future infin. here : after verbs of hoping, promising etc., when emphasis is laid on the thing itself hoped or promised, without special reference to the time of accomplishment, the aorist (or more rarely the present) infin. is used : if, however, the time of accomplishment is regarded, the future infin.: for instance here there is a shade of difference in the meanings 'promised escape from death' (aorist) and 'promised that he should escape death' (future). The quotation from Soph. illustrates this, as the infinitival clause πέμπειν πρὸς οἴκους is in apposition to ταῦτα, and practically equivalent to a noun, which is necessarily 'timeless.'

13. ᾄδην, 'death' simply, without reference to the god or his abode : cf. Hipp. 1048 ταχὺς γὰρ Ἅιδης ῥᾷστος ἀνδρὶ δυσσεβεῖ. Aesch. Ag. 667 Ἅιδην πόντιον πεφευγότες.

14. διαλλάξαντα. ἀλλάσσω and its compounds mean both to give and to take in exchange. διαλλάσσω is rare and confined to prose in these senses : its usual meaning is to 'reconcile.' Perhaps here that sense is connoted, 'giving in exchange so as to prevent ill-feeling.'

15. **ἐλέγξας καὶ διεξελθών,** 'having made trial of the friendship of all, one after another.' διεξελθών, of going completely through a list; cf. Thuc. III. 45, διεξεληλύθασι διὰ πασῶν τῶν ζημιῶν, 'have tried every penalty one after another.' ἐλέγχειν is to test, with a view to prove false. Cf. cr. n. on 16.

17. **οὐχ ηὗρε ὅστις ἤθελε.** The indef. relative ὅστις is used when the antecedent also is indefinite : this is necessarily the case in passages like the present, where the existence of a class of persons is denied. The def. relat. ὅς *may* be used when the antecedent is indef., but an indef. relat. must not refer to a definite antecedent.

18. **κείνου.** An indirect reflexive pronoun is one which, occurring in a dependent sentence, refers to the subject of the principal sentence : οὗ, οἷ etc., the personal pronouns of the 3rd person, and αὐτοῦ, αὐτῷ etc. may take the place of ἑαυτοῦ, ἑαυτῷ etc. as indirect reflexives: occasionally we find ἐκείνου, ἐκείνῳ etc. instead of αὐτοῦ, αὐτῷ (cf. Shilleto's n. on Thuc. I. 132 for the use of αὐτὸς and ἐκεῖνος with reference to the same person, and Plat. Prot. 310 D ἂν αὐτῷ διδῷς ἀργύριον καὶ πείθῃς ἐκεῖνον). Here perhaps the use of κεῖνος (in prose always ἐκεῖνος) is natural as from the point of view of the person refusing Admetus' request.

19. 'Is borne up in her husband's arms.' Note the contrast between this picture and that given infr. 917, where Admetus amid the torch-lit throng of crowding well-wishers, which escorts the bride to her new home, is seated in the marriage-car, φιλίας ἀλόχου χέρα βαστάζων.

20. **ψυχορραγοῦσα,** 'gasping out her life': cf. H. F. 324 ὡς μὴ τέκν' εἰσίδωμεν, ἀνόσιον θέαν, | ψυχορραγοῦντα καὶ καλοῦντα μητέρα.

σφε is both sing. and plur. in tragedy.

22. Apollo and Artemis, the divinities of whom brightness and purity are peculiarly characteristic, avoid the ceremonial pollution inseparable from death : cf. Hipp. 1437 where Artemis may not stay to comfort the last moments of her faithful servant Hippolytus. 'Farewell,' she says, ἐμοὶ γὰρ οὐ θέμις φθιτοὺς ὁρᾶν | οὐδ' ὄμμα χραίνειν θανασίμοισιν ἐκπνοαῖς. Aelian too (ap. Suid.) tells us of the comic poet Philemon, how just before his death he saw in a vision the nine Muses leaving his house, θεοῖς γὰρ οὐδαμῇ θεμιτὸν ὁρᾶν ἔτι νεκρούς, καὶ ἐὰν ὦσι πάνυ φίλοι.

24. At this moment Thanatos appears in quest of his victim, a lock of whose hair he is, as sacrificial priest of the dead, to cut off, thus dedicating its owner to the powers below. He is represented with black wings (cf. infr. 843), offering no doubt a strong stage-contrast to the

bright Apollo : a contrast that brings to mind the famous scene in the *Eumenides*, where the rival claims of the upper and the nether powers are urged before the Areopagites. We may imagine that the ʻopened eye' of the dying Alcestis descries the phantom form of the dread priest, when (infr. 261) she cries in terror at the approach of the ʻwinged Death, dark-gleaming under shaggy brows,' who draws her down to the abodes of Hades. This conception of Death is met with in vase-paintings and is strongly contrasted with the brighter presentment of ʻ Death, twin brother of sleep,' often figured as a sleeping youth with inverted torch.

τόνδε is deictic ; ʻhere, close at hand, I see...'

25. ἱερέα, pronounced as a trisyllable : cf. crit. n.

26. μέλλει κατάξειν. After μέλλω Attic usage demands either the present or future infin., though a very few cases of the aorist are allowed : cf. Rutherford, New Phrynichus, p. 420 sq.

σύμμετρος ἀφίκετο, ʻhe arrives to time,' lit. ʻcommensurate with the day' (τῷ ἤματι understood from ἦμαρ) ; cf. Soph. Ant. 387 ποίᾳ σύμμετρος προὔβην τύχῃ ; ἀφίκετο, aorist referring to an occurrence just past.

27. φρουρῶν, ʻwatching for' : so φυλάσσειν, Aesch. Ag. 8 καὶ νῦν φυλάσσω λαμπάδος τὸ σύμβολον. Thuc. II. 3, 3 νύκτα φυλάξαντες : and τηρεῖν, Thuc. III. 22, 1 οἱ Πλαταιῆς, τηρήσαντες νύκτα χειμέριον ὕδατι καὶ ἀνέμῳ καὶ ἅμα ἀσέληνον, ἐξῇεσαν.

29. πολεῖς, ʻhauntest thou,' Lat. *versari* : cf. Or. 1269 τίς ὅδ᾽ ἄρ᾽ ἀμφὶ μέλαθρον πολεῖ σὸν ἀγρότας ἀνήρ ;

30. αὖ, ʻfor the second time.' First in saving Admetus, and now in wishing to rescue Alcestis.

τιμὰς ἐνέρων. τιμαί are the ʻprerogatives' or ʻproper spheres of action' of the subordinate gods : thus El. 993 of the Dioscuri, τιμὰς σωτῆρας ἔχοντες. Aesch. Eum. 419 τιμάς γε μὲν δὴ τὰς ἐμὰς πεύσει τάχα, say the Eumenides to Athene. Madness in H. F. 845 says τιμὰς δ᾽ ἔχω τάσδ᾽, κ.τ.λ.

31. ἀφοριζόμενος καὶ καταπαύων, ʻlimiting at caprice, nay, utterly abolishing.' καταπαύων is a climax. ἀφοριζόμενος is more appropriate to the methods by which Admetus was rescued : ʻif now by force you are to rob me of Alcestis, there is an end to my prerogatives at once.'

32. ʻDid it not suffice thee to arrest the doom of Admetus, which was his due (μόρος = allotted portion), but now thou art, etc.?' Cf. Or. 1589.

34. σφήλαντι, lit. 'having caused to stumble,' a suitable word considering his method; cf. supr. 12, n. ἐπὶ τῇδ' '(art watching) over Alcestis here' (pointing to the palace).

35. χέρα τοξήρη ὁπλίσας, 'having armed thy hand with thy bow.' τοξήρη is proleptic. Cf. El. 376 (πενία) διδάσκει δ' ἄνδρα τῇ χρείᾳ κακόν (teaches to be wicked): Thompson, Gr. Synt. § 346.

36. τόδ', sc. προθανεῖν: cf. I. A. 840 πᾶσιν τόδ' ἐμπέφυκεν, αἰδεῖσθαι φίλους | καινοὺς ὁρῶσι. Hipp. 466 ἐν σοφοῖσι γὰρ | τάδ' ἐστὶ θνητῶν, λανθάνειν τὰ μὴ καλά.

ἐκλύσασα κ.τ.λ., 'to ransom her husband at the cost of her own life.'

For the inclusion of the antecedent, a person expressed by name, in the relative sentence, cf. Hec. 771 πρὸς ἄνδρ' ὃς ἄρχει τῆσδε Πολυμήστωρ χθονός. Hipp. 101 τήνδ' ἣ πύλαισι σαῖς ἐφέστηκεν Κύπρις. Soph. O. T. 1451 ἔνθα κλήζεται | οὑμὸς Κιθαιρών.

38. λόγους κεδνούς, 'weighty arguments': the main idea in κεδνός seems 'wise'; cf. the Homeric κέδν' εἰδυῖα. Pind. P. x. 72 κεδναὶ πολίων κυβερνάσιες.

39. 'What need then,' retorts Thanatos, 'for this equipment of violence, if you rely on the justice of your case?' ἔργον= 'proper sphere of action for': cf. Hipp. 911 σιωπῆς δ' οὐδὲν ἔργον ἐν κακοῖς.

40. Monk quotes Horace (Od. III. 4, 60) *nunquam umeris positurus arcum...Apollo.*

41. 'Aye, and 'tis also thy wont etc.' προσωφελεῖν (like ὠφελεῖν in poet., cf. Jebb's note on Soph. Ant. 559) is followed by a dative in Herod. and Trag.: cf. Heracl. 330 ἀεὶ ποθ' ἥδε γαῖα τοῖς ἀμηχάνοις | σὺν τῷ δικαίῳ βούλεται προσωφελεῖν: so too ἐπωφελεῖν.

42. γὰρ implies assent to the word προσωφελεῖν. 'True, for etc.'

43. νοσφιεῖς. The early usage of this word is as a deponent, with the meaning 'to turn one's back on,' 'forsake': in this sense is frequent in Homer. In Trag. the active voice is usual= 'remove' or 'rob': cf. Supp. 539 τοὺς θανόντας νοσφίσας ὧν χρῆν λαχεῖν.

44. The emphasis is on πρὸς βίαν. 'I am not going to use force, neither did I in the case of Admetus.' With πρὸς βίαν adverbial, cf. πρὸς ὀργήν, 'angrily,' πρὸς καιρόν, 'seasonably,' πρὸς τὸ λιπαρές (Soph. O. C. 1119), 'persistently': slightly different is πρὸς χάριν, 'with a view to gratify,' πρὸς ἡδονήν, πρὸς τὸ τερπνόν (Thuc. II. 53).

45. κάτω χθονός, cf. Soph. O. T. 968 ὁ δὲ θανὼν | κεύθει κάτω δὴ γῆς: infr. 692. When used of the dead κάτω implies *rest* below: in other connections *motion downwards* is often represented.

46. μέτα, 'after,' i.e. 'to fetch,' as in μετέρχομαι, μεταδιώκω, μεταπέμπω (infr. 66).

47. κἀπάξομαί γε, 'aye, and I will carry her off': so supr. 41.

48. The order is οὐ γὰρ οἶδα εἰ πείσαιμι ἄν σε, 'I know not whether I should persuade you,' where πείσαιμι ἄν is potential, implying 'if I tried to do so.' This order of words is not uncommon in sentences of this type with οἶδα, οἴομαι, δοκῶ and the like: cf. Med. 941 where these very words recur: Plat. Tim. 26 B οὐκ ἄν οἶδ' εἰ δυναίμην. Goodwin M. T. § 220.

49. τοῦτο, equivalent to a cognate accus. ταύτην τὴν τάξιν: ἐπὶ τούτῳ would be usual.

50. 'To bring death without more ado (this seems to me the force of the somewhat strange ἐμβαλεῖν) on those who hang back,' i.e. the old, who should be prepared to depart, such as were Admetus' father and mother. To this Thanatos replies, 'I catch your drift: you would have me take Pheres and leave Alcestis.' For the moment Apollo is hopeful. 'Has Alcestis then a chance?' 'No, truly: remember I prize my prerogatives.' 'True,' replies Apollo, 'but I do not see how that affects the question: you get one life, and one only, either way.' 'You forget that when the young die, I get a richer guerdon.' Apollo, taking guerdon to refer to rich funeral offerings, replies that if Alcestis be spared to reach old age, her obsequies will be no whit less costly then than now. Thanatos however had meant guerdon of glory, so he flings a taunt at Apollo—'a low view truly', he says, 'all in favour of the rich.' Apollo, somewhat piqued, with the fine disdain of a young god for the intelligence of the older generation, retorts, 'What, is Thanatos too a wit, and we never knew it? How mean you?' 'Were money the only consideration,' Thanatos explains, 'the rich would purchase long life of me: but money, with me, is not everything.'

52. μόλοι. This is one of the dozen or so instances in Attic Greek, in which it was usual to state that there is an omission of ἄν (μόλοι ἄν would be potential: cf. supr. 48): it is however better to admit the existence to a limited extent in Attic of the usage (allowed in Epic) of a simple optative to express *possibility* regarded entirely in the abstract, not with a view to some immediate practical action. The difference in the meaning introduced by the use of the optative rather than the subjunctive is a shade only, but quite real and very similar, it seems to me, to that remarked upon in the note on supr. l. 12 (aorist or future infin. after μέλλω and similar words). In this passage, for instance, if we read

μόλοι, the meaning is, 'is it then possible for Alcestis to reach old age?' if μόλῃ were in the text, we should render, 'are there any means we may adopt by which Alcestis may reach old age?' For different views on this vexed question one may refer to Goodwin, M. T. § 241, Prof. Jebb's note in Appendix to Soph. O. C. 170, Mr A. Sidgwick's Appendix I. to his edition of Aesch. Agam., and Prof. Hale's Extended and Remote Deliberatives in Greek, in Trans. of Amer. Philol. Assoc. vol. xxiv.

53. κἀμέ, 'I too, as well as you.'

54. Cf. infr. 900. 'Would I too were dead,' cries Admetus, δύο δ' ἀντὶ μιᾶς Ἅιδης ψυχὰς | τὰς πιστοτάτας σὺν ἂν ἔσχεν.

55. γέρας, 'guerdon.' Thanatos means by this 'glory,' but Apollo chooses to assume that he refers to costly funeral observances. Cf. Aesch. fr. 156 μόνος θεῶν γὰρ θάνατος οὐ δώρων ἐρᾷ.

57. πρὸς τῶν ἐχόντων, 'in favour of the rich': cf. fr. 465 (from the Κρῆσσαι, a play produced along with the Alc.) τῶν ἐχόντων πάντες ἄνθρωποι φίλοι. Supp. 240 οἱ δ' οὐκ ἔχοντες καὶ σπανίζοντες βίου | εἰς τοὺς ἔχοντας κέντρ' ἀφιᾶσιν κακά. Soph. Aj. 157 πρὸς γὰρ τὸν ἔχονθ' ὁ φθόνος ἕρπει. For this use of πρός, cf. Soph. O. T. 1434 πρὸς σοῦ γάρ ('in thy interest'), οὐδ' ἐμοῦ, φράσω.

τόν νόμον τιθεῖς: νόμον τιθέναι of a supreme law-giver: νόμον τίθεσθαι of a legislative assembly: or as Cobet puts it (V. L. 613) νόμον ὁ μὲν νομοθέτης τίθησιν, ὁ δὲ δῆμος τίθεται. Cf. Jebb's n. on Soph. Ant. 8. 'You lay down the law.' τὸν νόμον almost = your law.

58. Both πῶς εἶπας; and ἀλλ' ἦ express surprise. Both are common separately, but the combination is rare: it is found Soph. Phil. 414 πῶς εἶπας; ἀλλ' ἦ χοῦτος οἴχεται θανών; Attic Greek prefers to use the 2nd sing. indic. εἶπας (and perhaps 2nd plur. εἴπατε) and 2nd plur. imperat. εἴπατε from the 1st aor. εἶπα (which itself hardly occurs): εἶπον supplies the rest of the aorist forms. Rutherford, N. P. p. 219.

59. οἷς πάρεστι, i.e. 'the rich.'

61. Cf. Ar. Eq. 390 ἐγὼ γὰρ τοὺς τρόπους ἐπίσταμαι.

62. γε = 'yes'; θεοῖς: observe that Apollo only allows Thanatos to rank as a δαίμων at most, declaring that real gods loathe his character and attributes.

63. In relative sentences with an indefinite antecedent the negative is μή. Goodw. Gr. Gr. § 231.

64. ἦ μὴν, familiar form of strong asseveration, regularly employed in oaths, as Soph. Tr. 1185—7.

65. τοῖος κ.τ.λ., gives the reason for the preceding statement; cf. infr. 453: Soph. O. C. 947 τοιοῦτον αὐτοῖς Ἄρεος εὔβουλον πάγον | ἐγὼ ξυνῄδη χθόνιον ὄνθ'. Aj. 562 ('no one will harm thee') τοῖον πυλωρὸν φύλακα Τεῦκρον ἀμφὶ σοι | λείψω.

66. ἵππειον ὄχημα, on the analogy of ἅρματα, refers to the horses that draw the car: cf. H. F. 881 ἅρμασι δ' ἐνδίδωσι κέντρον. The eighth of the twelve labours imposed on Heracles by Eurystheus of Tiryns was to fetch the man-eating mares of Diomedes, king of the Thracian Bistones. Of the rigours of the Thracian climate many an Athenian would have a lively recollection. In 465 B.C. the unlucky attempt to found a colony at Amphipolis had ended in failure and the loss of over 10,000 lives: at the time of the representation of this play preparations were being made for the second attempt under Hagnon, which finally succeeded: the settlement was actually made in the following year, 437 B.C.

69. βίᾳ. 'Heracles will use force: I did not': supr. 44.

ἐξαιρήσεται, 'will deliver from your hand': cf. infr. 848.

71. δράσεις ταῦτα. δρᾶν τοῦτο is a phrase regularly employed when it is wished to repeat an already expressed idea: cf. infr. 702: Thuc. I. 5 δηλοῦσι δὲ τῶν τε ἠπειρωτῶν τινες ἔτι καὶ νῦν, οἷς κόσμος καλῶς τοῦτο δρᾶν (live by piracy): I. 6: II. 49 καὶ πολλοὶ τοῦτο καὶ ἔδρασαν (threw themselves) ἐς φρέατα. Plat. Theaet. 166 c οὐ μόνον αὐτὸς ὑηνεῖς ('act like a pig'), ἀλλὰ καὶ τοὺς ἀκούοντας τοῦτο δρᾶν εἰς τὰ συγγράμματά μου ἀναπείθεις. Soph. Tr. 413 σὺ μέντοι κάρτα τοῦτο δρῶν (speaking in riddles) κυρεῖς. So here δράσεις ταῦτα='you will surrender her.'

οὔτε...τε is not uncommon, often implying a climax ('so far from'), but τε...οὔτε does not occur. Jebb on Soph. O. C. 1397.

72. For the repetition of ἄν cf. Thompson, Gr. Synt. § 182. 'A participle representing a protasis (as λέξας here) is especially apt to have an emphatic ἄν near it. This, by showing that the verb is to form an apodosis, tends to point out the participle as conditional in an early part of the sentence.' Goodw. M. T. § 224.

πλέον λαβεῖν, 'to get an advantage,' πλέον ἔχειν, 'to have an advantage,' and so with πράσσειν, ἐργάζεσθαι, etc.: cf. I. A. 137 μὴ διαβληθῇ στρατῷ | καὶ πλέον πράξωμεν οὐδέν. I. T. 496 τί δ' ἂν μαθοῦσα τόδε πλέον λάβοις, γύναι;

73. A sarcastic echo of line 65. 'No matter how great a man be on his way to the halls of Pheres, this woman at any rate (δ' οὖν) is on

her way to the halls of Hades.' For δ' οὖν cf. Soph. Ant. 769 (a very close parallel), where Creon, in answer to the timid apprehensions of the chorus at Haemon's passionate outburst, replies, δράτω, φρονείτω μεῖζον ἢ κατ' ἄνδρ' ἰών | τὼ δ' οὖν κόρα τώδ' οὐκ ἀπαλλάξει μόρου.

74. **κατάρξωμαι.** The practice of sacrificial consecration by the cutting off from the brow of the victim of a few hairs is familiar to us from Virgil (Aen. VI. 243) *et summas carpens media inter cornua setas | ignibus imponit sacris libamina prima.* So too IV. 698 (the death of Dido) *necdum illi flavum Proserpina vertice crinem | abstulerat, Stygioque caput damnaverat Orco.* Cf. I. T. 40 κατάρχομαι μὲν (says Iphigeneia, priestess now of the Scythian Artemis, to whom shipwrecked mariners are sacrificed), σφάγια δ' (the actual throat-cutting) ἄλλοισιν μέλει. Heracl. 529 the maiden Macaria, offering up her life for her country, cries ἡγεῖσθ' ὅπου δεῖ σῶμα κατθανεῖν τόδε | καὶ στεμματοῦτε καὶ κατάρχεσθ', εἰ δοκεῖ.

75. **ἱερὸς τῶν θεῶν** = the sacred property of the gods: Lat. *sacer*: Cic. Verr. II. 1, 48 *illa insula eorum deorum sacra putatur* (of Delos): cf. Ar. Plut. 937 ἱερὸν γάρ ἐστι τοῦ Πλούτου πάλαι. Herod. II. 41 τὰς δὲ θηλέας οὔ σφι ἔξεστι θύειν, ἀλλ' ἱραί εἰσι τῆς Ἴσιος.

76. The antecedent to ὅτου is really indefinite, as οὗτος = 'that one, whichever it be': cf. n. on supr. 17. For the omission of ἂν with the subj. in a relative conditional sentence, cf. Goodw. Gr. Gr. § 234. It is by no means rare in poetry: cf. Soph. O. C. 395 γέροντα δ' ὀρθοῦν φλαῦρον, ὃς νέος πέσῃ. In Herod. there are several instances, and even in Attic prose (e. g. Thuc. IV. 17 ἐπιχώριον ὂν ἡμῖν οὗ μὲν βραχεῖς ἀρκῶσι μὴ πολλοῖς χρῆσθαι, where it is however suggested that οὗ...πολλοῖς is quoted from an iambic line) it cannot with certainty be entirely denied. Similarly in conditional sentences the use of the subj. with εἰ, though very rare, is well attested.

77. **ἡσυχία πρ. μελ.** All the servants were within, as we learn from infr. 192, taking tearful leave of their dying mistress.

78. **τί σεσίγηται κ.τ.λ.** 'Why has a hush fallen on Admetus' palace?' This is a remarkable use of the passive of σιγάω, which else-where = 'to be kept secret,' 'not spoken of': cf. I. T. 938, τί χρῆμα δράσειν; ῥητὸν ἢ σιγώμενον; Ph. 332 ἀνὰ δὲ Θηβαίαν | πόλιν ἐσιγάθη σᾶς ἔσοδος νύμφας. So too the passive of σιωπάω. When used transitively it was in the sense 'to be quiet concerning' a thing, not 'to make quiet' for which κοιμίζειν was employed: compare Soph. Aj. 675 ἄημα πνευμάτων ἐκοίμισε στένοντα πόντον with Theocr. II. 38 ἠνίδε σιγῇ μὲν

πόντος, σιγῶντι δ' ἀῆται· ἁ δ' ἐμὰ οὐ σιγᾷ στέρνων ἔντοσθεν ἀνία,
where σιγᾶν = κοιμίζεσθαι.

79. ἀλλ' οὐδέ, cf. supr. 44. Not even a friend is to be seen near
Admetus' hospitable door.

80. ἂν εἴποι is potential: 'would tell, if we enquired.'

85. ἀρίστη γεγενῆσθαι, 'to have proved herself a noble helpmeet':
cf. Thuc. III. 54 where the Platæans plead before the Spartans, τὰ δ'
ἐν τῇ εἰρήνῃ καὶ πρὸς τὸν Μῆδον ἀγαθοὶ γεγενήμεθα.

86. Immediately after death an obol was placed in the mouth of the
deceased to pay his ferry-charge over the Styx (ναῦλον): the corpse was
then washed and anointed with perfumes, and dressed in a white robe
was laid out (the πρόθεσις) in a room of the house : around the κλίνη
were gathered the females of the family (within the degree of second
cousin, according to Solon's regulation) loudly bewailing the departed
(cf. infr. 104): at the main entrance was placed a jar of water (ἀρδάνιον),
that those quitting the house might purify themselves from the cere-
monial pollution attendant on the presence of a dead body within the
walls (infr. 98). Cf. Lucian, de luctu 10, 11, 12.

87. κατὰ στέγας, 'within,' as infr. 192, 950. The chorus, after
commenting on the solitude outside the house, are anxious to know if
there are signs of mourning within which may enlighten them as to the
true state of affairs. The χειρῶν κτύπον would be the sound of the
beating of the breasts.

88. ὡς πεπραγμένων, 'as though all were over.' For the partic.
standing alone in genit. absol. cf. Soph. El. 1344 τελουμένων εἴποιμ' ἄν.
I. A. 1022 καλῶς δὲ κρανθέντων, πρὸς ἡδονὴν φίλοις | σοί τ' ἂν γένοιτο.

89. οὐ μὰν οὐδέ, 'nor yet again.' Cf. Thuc. I. 3 (Homer nowhere
gives them collectively the name Ἕλληνες) οὐ μὴν οὐδὲ βαρβάρους εἴρηκε,
where Shilleto points out that a more usual meaning of οὐ μὴν οὐδὲ is
'not that.' Hom. Il. IV. 512 οὐ μὰν οὐδ' Ἀχιλεὺς Θέτιδος πάις ἠυκό-
μοιο | μάρναται (giving an additional reason for the Trojans to attack
the Greeks).

90. Not even is there a door-keeper (πυλωρός) to be seen—πύλης
ἄναξ θυρωρός, as Sophocles calls him in a fragment. στατίζεται : the
word occurs again El. 315 (also of the allotted station of a slave) πρὸς
δ' ἕδραισιν Ἀσίδες | δμωαὶ στατίζουσ'.

Observe the curious jingle ἀμφιπόλων, ἀμφὶ πύλας : instances are
frequent in Eurip., and may be the result of intention: cf. Hec. 538
πρευμενὴς δ' ἡμῖν γενοῦ | λῦσαί τε πρύμνας : infr. 160. ἀμφὶ is the suit-

able preposition here: 'beside the gate': properly ἀμφί refers to the two sides, περί to the circumference.

91. εἰ γὰρ .. φανείης, 'O for thine appearance, God of healing, amid our storms of woe.' For this form of expression of a wish with reference to the future, cf. Goodw. Gr. Gr. § 251. Originally it was a protasis, 'if only, etc.,' the apodosis καλῶς ἂν ἔχοι being suppressed. For a discussion of the view that εἰ was at first an interjection, and that the optative carries the whole idea of 'wish,' cf. Goodw. M. T., p. 376 sq.

μετακύμιος ἄτας. Cf. Leaf's n. on Hom. Il. v. 19. 'For similar cases where an adjective compounded with a preposition and a substantive expresses the same idea as a preposition governing a case (i.e. μετακύμιος = μετὰ τοῖς κύμασι) we may compare μεταδόρπιος, μεταδήμιος, καταθύμιος, μετακόσμιος and others.'

92. The chorus naturally invokes the aid of the god, who had brought relief to similar distress before: cf. infr. 220 sq.: in both passages it is under his attribute of 'healer' that they supplicate him. Paean is not in Homer identical with Apollo, but merely founder of a family or caste of physicians, neither has Apollo any special power of healing.

93. τὰν = τοι ἄν: φθιμένης, genit. absol.: cf. supr. 88 n.: it represents the protasis, οὐκ ἂν ἐσιώπων being the apodosis: 'were she dead, they would not be thus silent': one section of the chorus is more sanguine than the other.

94. 'At any rate she has not been carried from the house for burial': i.e. the ἐκφορὰ has not yet taken place: this usually happened in the early morning (πρὶν ἥλιον ἐξέχειν says a law in Dem. 1071) of the third day after death.

95. πόθεν; = 'on what ground do you base your inference?' This is a somewhat colloquial expression of incredulity or denial: cf. Ar. Ran. 1455 Aeacus asks τὴν πόλιν νῦν μοι φράσον | πρῶτον, τίσι χρῆται· πότερα τοῖς χρηστοῖς; to which the reply is πόθεν; μισεῖ κάκιστα. Cf. Vesp. 1145: Dem. de Cor. 47 ἀλλ' οὐκ ἔστι ταῦτα, οὐκ ἔστι· πόθεν; ('how could it be so?') πολλοῦ γε καὶ δεῖ.

96. τάφον, 'funeral,' the original (and only Homeric) meaning: 'grave' is a later development of the sense. ἄν is repeated, as supr. 72. The Greeks liked to show as early as possible in a sentence, especially in a long one, if it was going to be conditional or negative: hence we often find negatives and ἄν at the opening of a sentence, though the

particular word to which they apply does not occur till the end : commonly ἄν was inserted a second time in its natural position.

Mr Earle points out that ἔρημον τάφον, 'a funeral without mourners,' is like ἐρήμη δίκη, 'a suit without a defendant.' As πράσσειν τάφον is an unusual expression, probably the lost line contained a suitable governing participle, e.g. στείλας : cf. crit. n.

97. κεδνῆς, cf. supr. 38, n.

100. Cf. Ar. Eccl. 1033 ὕδατός τε κατάθου τοὔστρακον (jar) πρὸ τῆς θύρας.

101. The custom of placing locks of hair on the tomb of the dead is frequently alluded to : cf. Aesch. Cho. 167 ὁρῶ τομαῖον τόνδε βόστρυχον τάφῳ. Eur. El. 515 πυρᾶς δ' ἐπ' αὐτῆς...ἐσεῖδον...ξανθῆς τε χαίτης βοστρύχους κεκαρμένους : but this seems to be the only indication of a practice of placing them at the door of a house of mourning.

103. νεολαία. The occurrence of πηγαῖον and τομαῖον within this half-dozen lines is some support of the genuineness of νεολαία : cf. supr. 90, n. Elsewhere it is found only as a feminine substantive : cf. Aesch. Pers. 670, Supp. 686. Similarly formed adjectives in this play are κλοπαῖος 1035, and (probably) λοχαῖος 846.

105. καὶ μὴν is usually employed to introduce and call attention to either a new character or a new thought : here the thought itself can hardly be regarded as new, but it is now for the first time definitely expressed in words κύριον, 'fixed' : cf. infr. 158 : so κυρία ἐκκλησία is one that met on fixed days ; in the fifth century probably the first in each prytany : a special or extraordinary meeting was termed σύγκλητος.

106. The symmetrical construction of the antistrophic arrangement called for a remark from the other half-chorus in this place, but it is little more than interjectional, and does not interrupt the sentence commenced in l. 105.

107. σφε, cf. supr. 20, n.

108. ἔθιγες, cf. Hipp. 310 θιγγάνει σέθεν τόδε ; Supp. 1162 ἔκλαυσα τόδε κλύων ἔπος | στυγνότατον· ἔθιγέ μου φρενῶν.

109. διακναιομένων. This word is used of wasting away from starvation, love, trouble and the like. Aesch. P. V. 541. The original meaning is 'rubbed' or 'worn through,' cf. Cycl. 486 (of boring out the Cyclops' eye). Cf. Ar. Eccl. 955.

111. ἀπ' ἀρχῆς : it should be remembered that the chorus is composed of old men.

112. The order of the words is: ἀλλ' οὐδ' ἔσθ' ὅποι αἴας στείλας τις ναυκληρίαν, ἢ (ἐπὶ) Λυκίαν εἴτ' ἐφ' ἕδρας ἀν. Ἀμμ. (στείλας), δυστ. παρ. ψυχάν. Probably the poet, when beginning with ἀλλ' οὐδὲ, intended subsequently to suggest (only, of course, to reject) other means of rescue besides ναυκληρίαν στείλας, but changed the turn of the sentence at l. 116. In both instances of the use of ἀλλ' οὐδὲ above more than one thing is contemplated, if not expressed : in l. 44 it is, neither Admetus then (nor Alcestis now) : in l. 79 (neither servants) nor friends. For ὅποι αἴας, cf. supr. 9 n.

114. Λυκίαν : the ἐπὶ before ἕδρας Ἀμμωνιάδας does duty also before Λυκίαν. Monk quotes parallels from Phoen. 284 μαντεῖα σεμνὰ Λοξίου τ' ἐπ' ἐσχάρας. Soph. O. T. 734 σχιστὴ δ' ὁδὸς | ἐς ταὐτὸ Δελφῶν κἀπὸ Δαυλίας ἄγει. 761 ἀγρούς σφε πέμψαι κἀπὶ ποιμνίων νομάς, and elsewhere.

The oracle of Apollo at Patara, a flourishing sea-port on the south-west coast of Lycia, was second only to that at Delphi in renown: cf. Virgil, Aen. IV. 143 *qualis ubi hibernam* (the oracle could only be consulted during the six winter months ; cf. Herod. I. 182 and Servius on the passage of Virgil) *Lyciam Xanthique fluenta | deserit, et Delum maternam invisit Apollo.* The ruins attesting its previous importance are extensive : 'a theatre excavated in the northern side of a small hill, a ruined temple on the side of the same hill, and a deep circular pit of singular appearance, which may have been the seat of the oracle.'

116. Ἀμμωνιάδας. The oasis of Ammon lies in the N.E. of the Libyan desert, and was celebrated from the earliest times for the oracle of the ram-headed (Herod. II. 42) Zeus-Amûn, co-eval in foundation with that of Zeus at Dodona (Herod. II. 54). Originally a Libyan divinity, Amûn became known to Greece through the Hellenic colonists of the Cyrenaica, and by their kinsmen of Sparta he was held in high esteem (Paus. III. 18, 2). At Thebes, too, he had a temple and a statue, the gift of the poet Pindar, who composed a hymn in his honour (Paus. IX. 16, 1). In B.C. 332 Alexander the Great, anxious to re-assure himself of his divine origin, made a toilsome visit to his shrine, and had the satisfaction of being addressed by the priest of the temple as none other than the son of the divinity. For a fine rhetorical account of the god and his worship, cf. Lucan IX. 511 sq. The remains of his sanctuary may still be seen, the colouring bright upon the walls. The modern name of the oasis is Siwah. 'Siwah is a little paradise : round the dark blue mirrors of its lakes there are luxurious palm-woods, and orchards full of oranges, figs and olives.' The present population is about 8000, considerably less, no doubt, than in the days when it was the seat of the great '*Jupiter Sortifer*.'

117. **παραλύσει**, cf. crit. n.

118. **ἀπότομος**, 'sheer': Lat. *praeruptus* (cf. Vell. Pat. II. 2, 3 *Tib. Gracchus in praeruptum atque anceps periculum adduxit rempublicam*): infr. 982 and Soph. O. T. 877 ἀπότομον ὤρουσεν εἰς ἀνάγκαν (the reading is doubtful).

119. **πλάθει**. πελάθω and πλάθω are intrans., πελάω and πελάζω both trans. and intrans.: the prose form is πλησιάζω (so πλησίον for πέλας).

ἐσχάραν. These seem to have been properly braziers, which could be carried about, and were used for many purposes, domestic and sacrificial: in the latter connexion, they were employed in the worship of heroes, the βωμὸς or raised altar being appropriated for the service of gods. They seem however to have been sometimes placed on the top of the more formal βωμοί (cf. phrases like βώμιος ἐσχάρα, Phoen. 274), and hence finally the terms became almost interchangeable. So too *altare* was at first the receptacle for the burnt offering placed on the *ara* (cf. Lucan III. 404): it was thus regarded as the 'high' altar and became the more honorable term, supplanting *ara*, while in Greek the more dignified associations still remained with βωμός: cf. Virg. Ecl. v. 66, where the god has *altaria*, Daphnis *aras*.

120. **οὐκ ἔχω**, 'I know not.' **πορευθῶ**, delib. subj.; ἐπορεύθην is the regular aorist.

μηλοθύταν, cf. I. T. 1116 βωμούς τε μηλοθύτας.

122. **μόνος δ' ἂν κ.τ.λ.** For the position of ἂν (which is to be taken with ἦλθεν, l. 125), cf. supr. 96, n.: it does not seem necessary to regard this sentence as anacoluthic (i.e. that Eurip. began the sentence intending to finish with προλιποῦσαν ἕδρ. σκ. ἀνέστησεν, but changed the construction as he wrote, making Ἄλκηστις the subject), though of course it is quite permissible to do so.

ἦν δεδορκώς: the perf. subj. and opt., act., mid. and pass., the 3rd plur. of the perf. indic., and the fut. perf. act. are usually expressed periphrastically by means of a partic. and εἰμί, (sometimes ἔχω), ἔσομαι. Rarer is the use of the periphrastic conjugation for the remaining persons of the perfect, and for the pluperfect indic. (with ἦν, εἶχον). Goodw. Gr. Gr. § 118. Frequently however the participle is treated merely as a predicate adjective, e.g. Soph. Aj. 588 μὴ προδοὺς ἡμᾶς γένῃ. Phil.

772 μὴ σαυτόν θ᾽ ἅμα | κἄμ᾽, ὄντα σαυτοῦ πρόστροπον, κτείνας γένῃ. Eur. Supp. 511 ἐξαρκέσας ἦν Ζεὺς ὁ τιμωρούμενος. H. F. 313 εἰ μὲν σθενόντων τῶν ἐμῶν βραχιόνων | ἦν τίς σ᾽ ὑβρίζων, ῥᾳδίως ἔπαυσά τἄν. Goodw. M. T. 830. As δεδορκὼς (a perf. with pres. sense) commonly means 'alive' (cf. Soph. El. 66 ὡς κἄμ᾽ ἐπαυχῶ τῆσδε τῆς φήμης ἄπο | δεδορκότ᾽ ἐχθροῖς ἄστρον ὡς λάμψειν ἔτι. Aesch. Eum. 322 ἀλαοῖσι καὶ δεδορκόσιν), it is best to regard it here as predicate.

124. **Φοίβου παῖς**, Asclepios, cf. supr. 4.

125. **ἦν (δεδορκὼς)...ἦλθεν**, 'if he *were* alive...she *would have* returned.'

127. **δμαθέντας**, 'the dead'; an echo of Homer: cf. Il. v. 646 ὑπ᾽ ἐμοὶ δμηθέντα πύλας Ἀΐδαο περήσειν. So too Tro. 175 Τροία δύσταν᾽, ἔρρεις, | δύστανοι δ᾽ οἵ σ᾽ ἐκλείποντες | καὶ ζῶντες καὶ δμαθέντες. I. T. 199 τῶν πρόσθεν δμαθέντων.

128. **πρὶν εἷλε**. πρὶν with the indic. is not found in Homer, and rarely in tragedy: in the 10 or 12 instances where it occurs, it is used without distinction after negative and affirmative sentences (though in the latter case some would assert that the *idea* is negative: it would be difficult to apply this argument to the present passage), in the meaning 'until.' In prose, the regular use of πρὶν with indicative is after a sentence of negative meaning only: cf. Goodw. M. T. § 634.

129. **πλῆκτρον**, lit. anything to strike with: cf. Soph. fr. 151 ὡς ναοφύλακες νυκτέρου ναυκληρίας | πλήκτροις ἀπευθύνουσιν οὐρίαν τρόπιν (of a paddle): fr. 164 δορὸς διχόστομον πλᾶκτρον: commonly of the instrument for striking the lyre, which gradually superseded or supplemented the hand.

130. **νῦν δέ**, 'but as it is.'

131. **προσδέχωμαι**, 'can I entertain?' delib. subj.

132. **πάντα** = 'everything possible': nothing was left untried.

βασιλεῦσι: for the dat. of the agent with passive verb, especially with perf. and pluperf., cf. Goodw. Gr. Gr. § 188, 3. 'There seems to be a reference to the agent's interest in the result of the *completed* action expressed by the perf. and pluperf.' The plural is the so-called 'allusive plural.' A single person is meant, but he is 'alluded to' as one of a class rather than specified: cf. Aesch. Cho. 53 δνόφοι καλύπτουσι δόμους | δεσποτῶν (Agamemnon) θανάτοισι (and Paley's n.): Soph. O. T. 1095 ὡς ἐπὶ ἦρα φέροντα τοῖς ἐμοῖς τυράννοις (Oedipus): infr. 138, 210.

134. **πλήρεις**, 'in full number': cf. Herod. VIII. 122 ἐπειρώτων

τὸν θεὸν εἰ λελάβηκε πλήρεα καὶ ἀρεστὰ τὰ ἀκροθίνια ('pick of the spoils'). Eur. fr. 904, 5 θυσίαν ἄπυρον παγκαρπείας | δέξαι πλήρη προχυθεῖσαν.

136. ἥδε, deictic, cf. supr. 24, 34. ὀπαδῶν. A certain number of words are retained in the tragic dialect in their Doric form, e.g. κυναγός, χοραγός, δαρός: by their side, however, we generally find Atticised forms (κυνηγέτης, χορηγέω), but of ὀπαδός we have no such bye-form: this is perhaps due to the influence of ὀπάζω.

138. The leader of the chorus here addresses the maid. τι, by a common euphemism, means something bad.

139. εἰ...εἴτε, for εἴτε...εἴτε: cf. Aesch. Eum. 468 σὺ δ᾽, εἰ δικαίως εἴτε μή, κρῖνον δίκην.

140. οὖν is often inserted in that one of successive or alternative clauses on which it is desired to lay some emphasis: cf. Soph. Phil. 345 λέγοντες εἴτ᾽ ἀληθὲς εἴτ᾽ ἄρ᾽ οὖν μάτην. O. T. 1049 εἴτ᾽ οὖν ἐπ᾽ ἀγρῶν εἴτε κἀνθάδ᾽ εἰσιδών. 90 οὔτε γὰρ θρασὺς | οὔτ᾽ οὖν προδείσας εἰμὶ τῷ γε νῦν λόγῳ.

142. καὶ πῶς. When καί is prefixed to interrogatives it gives an impatient or indignant tone to the question. Soph. Aj. 462 καὶ ποῖον ὄμμα πατρὶ δηλώσω φανείς; Phil. 1247 Odysseus tells Neoptolemus that he is talking nonsense, ἀλλ᾽ εἰ δίκαια (sc. φωνῶ), τῶν σοφῶν κρείσσω τάδε, answers Neoptolemus. καὶ πῶς δίκαιον, retorts Odysseus, ἅ γ᾽ ἔλαβες βουλαῖς ἐμαῖς, πάλιν μεθεῖναι ταῦτα;

αὐτός, generalises, therefore masculine.

βλέποι, cf. supr. 123, n. I. T. 718 ἐπεί σ᾽ ἐγὼ | θανόντα μᾶλλον ἢ βλέπονθ᾽ ἔξω φίλον.

143. προνωπής, lit. 'with the head falling forward' in a swoon: cf. Aesch. Ag. 234 φράσεν πατὴρ...προνωπῆ λαβεῖν ἀέρδην, of the fainting Iphigeneia: very similar is προπετής, Soph. Trach. 975 ξῇ γὰρ προπετής, 'he is alive, but only just.' ψυχορραγεῖ, supr. 20: H. F. 324.

144. οἴας οἵος: of this favourite form of expression Monk quotes many examples: among them Soph. Ant. 942 οἶα πρὸς οἵων ἀνδρῶν πάσχω. Aj. 557 δείξεις ἐν ἐχθροῖς οἶος ἐξ οἵου 'τράφης. 'Miserable Admetus, noble thou, noble too the spouse that thou art losing.'

145. τόδ᾽, sc. οἴας ἁμαρτάνει. οἶδε, 'realises.' πρὶν ἂν πάθῃ, '(nor will he realise it) before he has sad experience of his loss.' Cf. Goodw. M. T. §§ 638, 642.

146. μέν, interrogative. Its use implies that the speaker rather

believes the negative, for the suppressed apodosis is to this effect ἐγὼ
δ' οὐκ ἐλπίζω. Badham on Ion 520: cf. Ar. Av. 1214 ὑγιαίνεις μέν;
It should be added that, though its use may imply a *belief* to the
contrary, in form it often requires an affirmative reply, if the discussion
is to continue: thus in Hipp. 316 the nurse asks Phaedra ἁγνὰς μέν, ὦ
παῖ, χεῖρας αἵματος φέρεις; The question is the result of a misgiving,
but still expects a reply in the affirmative. The English equivalent
seems to be 'I suppose' (=I assume to begin with=μέν), its tone
varying to express the amount of misgiving implied in the context.

147. γὰρ='no, for etc.'

148, 9. These lines no doubt are introduced by the poet to serve
as some sort of palliative and explanation of the extraordinary rapidity
of the funeral. Alcestis dies at l. 392 : at l. 607 Admetus is bearing out
to burial τὸν νέκυν ἤδη πάντ' ἔχοντα.

148. 'The fitting preparations are being made for it, no doubt.'
The use of the word πράσσεται here may be some support of πράσσειν
τάφον, supr. 97. αὐτῇ I take to refer to ἡμέρᾳ. The suggestion of the
scholiast and others that it refers to Alcestis is little short of brutal.

149. κόσμος: funeral offerings of robes, etc.: cf. Hec. 578 ἔστηκας,
ὦ κάκιστε, τῇ νεάνιδι | οὐ πέπλον οὐδὲ κόσμον ἐν χεροῖν ἔχων ; (of the
offerings made by the Greeks at the funeral of Polyxena): Lucian de
luctu 14 πόσοι γὰρ καὶ ἵππους καὶ παλλακίδας, οἱ δὲ καὶ οἰνοχόους, ἐπικατ-
έσφαξαν καὶ ἐσθῆτα καὶ τὸν ἄλλον κόσμον συγκατέφλεξαν ἢ συγκατώρυξαν ;
Herod. v. 92 τῶν γάρ οἱ συγκατέθαψε ἱματίων ὄφελος εἶναι οὐδέν, οὐ
κατακαυθέντων.

150. ἴστω...κατθανουμένη: for the partic. (equivalent to the infin.
in indirect speech) with verb of knowing, cf. Goodw. Gr. Gr. § 280.

151. μακρῷ, with ἀρίστη: cf. Soph. Ant. 895 μακρῷ κάκιστα. Eur.
Bacch. 1232 πάντων ἀρίστας θυγατέρας σπείραι μακρῷ | θνητῶν.

152. πῶς δ' οὐκ ἀρίστη; 'noblest beyond doubt': a common
formula of strong assertion: cf. Thuc. III. 66 πῶς οὐ δεινὰ εἴργασθε;
Soph. O. T. 1015, El. 1307.

τίς δ' ἐναντιώσεται; 'who will gainsay it?' cf. infr. 615 οὐδεὶς ἀν-
τερεῖ, 1083 τίς ἀντερεῖ;

153. Monk translates : 'what must the woman be who has sur-
passed her?' ὑπερβ.: the perfect for argument's sake assumes a case :
cf. Med. 386 καὶ δὴ τεθνᾶσι· 'suppose them dead.' Aesch. Eum. 894
καὶ δὴ δέδεγμαι· 'assume that I have accepted.'

154. ἐνδείξαιτο προτιμῶσ': for the partic., cf. Thuc. I. 21 ὁ πόλεμος

οὗτος δηλώσει μείζων γεγενημένος αὐτῶν. Bacch. 47 ὦν οὕνεκ' αὐτῷ θεὸς γεγὼς ἐνδείξομαι. infr. 764.

156. **μὲν δὴ** dismisses a topic, e.g. Aesch. P. V. 500 τοιαῦτα μὲν δὴ ταῦτα, ' so much then for that.'

157. **θαυμάσομαι** not θαυμάσω is the Attic form of the future.

158. **γάρ** prefatory: cf. Soph. El. 32 (introduces, as here, a recital). **κυρίαν**, cf. supr. 105.

159. **ἤκουσαν**, cf. supr. 150, n. **ποταμίοις**: the belief in the efficacy of ' running' water in purification may be paralleled from the Mosaic books : cf. Levit. xiv. 51 : xv. 13. Cf. too (2 Kings v. 10) the order of Elisha to Naaman. In Plat. Phaedo 116 B Socrates washes before taking the hemlock: so of the passing of Oedipus (Soph. O. C. 1602) λουτροῖς τέ νιν | ἐσθῆτί τ' ἐξήσκησαν ᾗ νομίζεται. **λευκὸν**, fair as her skin was, yet she washed it : to regard λευκὸν as proleptic, as though she washed herself till she became white, is lamentable.

160. **λούειν**, of body : νίπτειν, of hands or feet : πλύνειν, of clothes. **ἐλούσατ', ἐκ δ' ἑλοῦσα**, cf. supr. 90, n. **κεδρίνων δόμων**, 'their dwelling-place of cedar wood': this use of δόμος seems without parallel: it may be that Euripides had in mind a treasure- or store-*chamber* like that to which Priam went to collect costly robes as ransom for Hector's corpse (Il. XXIV. 191), αὐτὸς δ' ἐς θάλαμον κατεβήσετο κηώεντα | κέδρινον, ὑψόροφον, ὃς γλήνεα πολλὰ κεχάνδει. The preservative power of cedar oil (and even of its fragrant scent) was well known in the earliest times (cf. Plin. N. H. XVI. 76) : the cedar known to Homer was probably the sweet-smelling juniper-like species, not the Syrian *cedrelates*, of which Pliny says (N. H. XIII. 11) *materiae ipsi aeternitas*: the oil of both prevented decay.

161. **ἐσθῆτα κόσμον τ'**, cf. supr. 149, n. **ἠσκήσατο**, cf. Soph. O. C. 1602 (quoted on l. 159).

162. **ἑστίας**. The hearth (μεσόμφαλος ἑστία, Aesch. Ag. 1056), the centre and symbol of family life, stood in the dining-hall (ἀνδρών), the apartment which, to one entering a Greek house, faced him on the opposite side of the colonnaded court in which he found himself after passing through the entrance hall : on either side of the ἀνδρών lay the θάλαμος and ἀμφιθάλαμος, bed-chambers of the master and mistress of the house and of the grown-up daughters. These three rooms occupied the whole length of one side of the court. The hearth was in large houses represented by an altar dedicated to Hestia, the actual cooking having been transferred elsewhere. ' A particular occasion for

worshipping Hestia was offered by all important changes in the family, such as a departure, a return from a journey,' and the like.

163. **δέσποινα**, i.e. Hestia. **γάρ**, (' I address you now for the last time), for etc.'

165. **ὀρφανεῦσαι**, 'watch over my orphaned children,' cf. infr. 297, 535: ὀρφανεύεσθαι, be an orphan: so παρθενεύειν, bring up as a maid, παρθενεύεσθαι, be a maid (so κορεύεσθαι): παιδεύω, treat as a child, i.e. educate: πρεσβεύω, treat as an old man, i.e. honour.

166. **σύζευξον**, for the imperat. occurring between infinitives depending on αἰτήσομαι (ὀρφανεῦσαι, θανεῖν), cf. Ar. Ran. 386, σῷζε τὸν σαυτῆς χορόν· | καί μ᾽ ἀσφαλῶς πανήμερον | παῖσαί τε καὶ χορεῦσαι.

167. **αὐτὴν ἡ τεκοῦσα**, cf. El. 335 ὁ ἐκείνου τεκών. Ion 308 ὥς σου τὴν τεκοῦσαν ὤλβισα. **ἀπόλλυμαι**, cf. Andr. 413 ὦ τέκνον, ἡ τεκοῦσά σ᾽, ὡς σὺ μὴ θάνῃς, | στείχω πρὸς Ἅιδην.

169. **ἐκπλῆσαι**, 'live to its natural end,' not be cut off ἄωροι, like their mother.

170. **πάντας δὲ βωμούς**: besides the altar of Hestia, which was found in every house, there was usually in the centre of the first court an altar to Ζεὺς ἑρκεῖος: at the entrance one to Ἀπόλλων ἀγυιεύς, while on either side of the court adjoining the θάλαμοι were probably to be found sanctuaries of the θεοὶ κτήσιοι and the θεοὶ πατρῷοι, the gods who protect property, Zeus in particular, and the gods supposed to interest themselves in the special family : perhaps in this case Hecate, who we know from a line of Lycophron (θύσθλοις Φεραίαν ἐξακεύμενοι θεάν, 'appeasing the goddess of Pherae with sacrifices') was the pre-eminent deity at Pherae.

172. The myrtle was largely used by the Greek on occasions both of joy and sorrow. So great indeed was the demand for wreaths that a quarter of the market was called αἱ μυρρίναι. Cf. Ar. Thesm. 448 (an old woman relates how her husband was killed in Cyprus, leaving her with five children) ἀγὼ μόλις | στεφανηπλοκοῦσ᾽ ἔβοσκον ἐν ταῖς μυρρίναις. Euripides, she adds, by destroying people's faith in the gods has ruined the trade. Cf. too the well-known σκόλιον ('drinking song': each guest, as he sang, held a myrtle-branch, which he passed on at the end of his song to another, who then had to take his turn in entertaining the company, cf. Ar. Nub. 1364) ἐν μύρτου κλαδὶ τὸ ξίφος φορήσω, | ὥσπερ Ἁρμόδιος καὶ Ἀριστογείτων, κ.τ.λ. (in Bergk-Hiller, Anth. Lyr. p. 323), telling how the dagger was concealed in a festal myrtle-branch which slew the tyrant Hipparchus. Wreaths of

myrtle were placed as funeral offerings on the tomb: cf. El. 324 (Aga-
memnon's tomb) οὔπω χοάς ποτ' οὐδὲ κλῶνα μυρσίνης | ἔλαβε, and wreaths
of myrtle were the victor's prize at the Iolaia, as the scholiast on Pind.
Isthm. III. 70 tells us, μυρσίνη γὰρ στεφανοῦνται διὰ τὸ εἶναι τῶν νεκρῶν
στέφος.

173. ἄκλαυστος ἀστένακτος, 'without a tear, without a cry.' These
forms are usually passive in meaning: for the middle sense, cf. Soph. Tr.
1200 ἀλλ' ἀστένακτος κἀδάκρυτος, εἴπερ εἶ | τοῦδ' ἀνδρός, ἔρξον. 1074 ἀλλ'
ἀστένακτος αἰὲν εἰπόμην κακοῖς. Hes. 691 οὐδέποτ' ἀστένακτος ἀδάκρυτος
ἀμέρα ἐπισχήσει.

174. 'nor e'en did near-pressing doom pale the fair fashion of her
cheek.'

175. ἐσπεσοῦσα, 'bursting into her marriage-chamber and casting
herself upon her bed.' A slightly zeugmatic use, cf. Ion 1196 κἄν τῷδε
μόχθῳ πτηνὸς ἐσπίπτει δόμους | κῶμος πελειῶν. εἰσπίπτω = εἰσβάλλομαι
(middle): εἰσβάλλω in the active voice is similarly used: cf. Hipp. 1198
ἐπεὶ δ' ἔρημον χῶρον εἰσεβάλλομεν.

176. ἐνταῦθα δή, *tum demum*, 'then, but not before.' Notice the
force of the tenses: 'she fell a-weeping, and began thus to speak': the
aorist expressing the momentary, the present continued action.

177. παρθένει' ἔλυσ' ἐγὼ κορεύματ', slightly varied from the
Homeric λῦσε δὲ παρθενίην ζώνην : in the Homeric phrase λύειν is said
of the bridegroom. κόρευμα seems to occur here only : as ἔλυσα κορεύ-
ματα = 'I was made wife,' it takes the construction of a passive verb,
and is followed by ἐκ and the genitive, denoting the agent : cf. Soph.
El. 1412 ἀλλ' οὐκ ἐκ σέθεν | ᾠκτίρεθ' οὗτος οὐδ' ὁ γεννήσας πατήρ. This
use is common in Ionic Greek : cf. Her. VII. 175 τὰ λεχθέντα ἐξ
Ἀλεξάνδρου. For ἐκ after a virtual passive (as here) cf. O. T. 854 διεῖπε
χρῆναι παιδὸς ἐξ ἐμοῦ θανεῖν ('be slain').

178. οὗ θνῄσκω πέρι: this is an extension of the Homeric use of
περί with genitive, e.g. μάρνασθαι περί τινος, to fight for (i.e. to get or
to keep) a thing: cf. Thuc. II. 39, 2 τοὺς περὶ τῶν οἰκείων ἀμυνομένους.
Valckenaer (on Phoen. 1336) thinks Attic usage (περὶ concerning, ὑπέρ
on behalf of) so constant, that he would here read οὗ θνῄσκω γ' ὑπέρ :
cf. cr. n.

179. χαῖρ', 'well be it with thee.' γὰρ, '(this I say,) for I bear
thee no ill-will, sole cause though thou art of my undoing.' The γὰρ in
l. 180 introduces the explanation of σὺ μόνον μ' ἀπώλεσας. ὀκνοῦσα,
'loth.'

H. A.   5

181. σὲ δέ, '(with me indeed all is over,) but thee some other wife etc.'

182. 'More loyal wife she could not be, haply more fortunate.' Aristophanes parodies these lines in the Equites (1251) σὲ δ' ἄλλος τις λαβὼν κεκτήσεται, | κλέπτης μὲν οὐκ ἂν μᾶλλον, εὐτυχὴς δ' ἴσως, where Cleon has to retire in favour of the sausage-seller, who usurps his place in the affections of Demos.   The full construction of l. 182 is σώφρων μὲν οὐκ ἂν (γενομένη) κ.τ.λ.

183. δέμνιον is rare in the singular : cf. Or. 229 ἰδοὺ φίλον τοι τῷ νοσοῦντι δέμνιον : infr. 186 we have the plural.

184. Cf. Aesch. Cho. 186 ἐξ ὀμμάτων δὲ δίψιοι πίπτουσί μοι | σταγόνες ἄφρακτοι δυσχίμου πλημμυρίδος.

186. προνωπής, 'reeling': cf. supr. 143.   It is noticeable that Euripides is apt to repeat any strange or rare word very soon after his first employment of it, though perhaps it does not recur in his extant works : it may be that ἐκπεσοῦσα is also an illustration of this tendency : cf. supr. 175 : 'casting herself from the bed': the strength of the word shows the effort required.

187. πολλά, 'ofttimes': with ἐπεστράφη. θάλαμον after ἐπεστράφη, 'turned back to': cf. Hel. 89 τί δῆτα Νείλου τούσδ' ἐπιστρέφει γύας; Ion 352 ἦν δὲ σταλαγμὸς ἐν στίβῳ τις αἵματος; asks Ion : Creusa replies οὔ φησι· καίτοι πόλλ' ἐπεστράφη ('turned back to examine') πέδον.

188. ἔρριψεν αὐτὴν gives the force of ἐσέπεσεν.

190. ἡ δέ : the commonest case of the survival in Attic of the primitive demonstrative force of the article is the contrasted ὁ μὲν…ὁ δὲ (notice the accent) : frequently, as here, we find ὁ δὲ following not ὁ μὲν, in the first clause, but an equivalent : here παῖδες : in l. 193 ἡ δὲ answers οἰκέται :   cf. Hadley Gr. Gr. § 654.

191. ἠσπάζετ' : as χαῖρε was used both in greeting and taking leave, so ἀσπάζομαι could be used on either occasion, though it was more usual in welcoming an arrival.   Cf. for its use in farewells, Tro. 1276 (Hecuba bids farewell to Troy) ἀλλ', ὦ γεραιὲ πούς, ἐπίσπευσον μόλις, | ὡς ἀσπάσωμαι τὴν ταλαίπωρον πόλιν. χαῖρε was somewhat old-fashioned, we learn from Ar. Plut. 322 χαίρειν μὲν ὑμᾶς ἐστιν, ὦνδρες δημόται, | ἀρχαῖον ἤδη προσαγορεύειν καὶ σαπρόν · | ἀσπάζομαι δέ. (So Av. 1378 ἀσπαζόμεσθα φιλύρινον Κινησίαν : Nub. 1145 Στρεψιάδην ἀσπάζομαι.) Fresh modes came into vogue : εὖ πράττειν (introduced by Plato, Lucian says), ὑγιαίνειν (except in early morning, when χαῖρε was

proper : Lucian's tract *pro lapsu in salutando* was an apology for a wrong use of ὑγιαίνειν in the morning). An inferior in saluting a superior would often kiss his hand or knee : so in l. 193 Alcestis extends her hand to each servant to kiss at parting, adding appropriate words and receiving their farewells.

194. **προύτεινε δεξιάν** : cf. note on supr. 191. The giving of the right hand (δεξιὰν προτείνειν or ἐμβάλλειν) was customary, too, as a pledge : cf. Soph. Tr. 1181—1184. Phil. 813 ἔμβαλλε χειρὸς πίστιν, says Philoctetes to Neoptolemus, who replies ἐμβάλλω μενεῖν. χεῖρας προτείνειν was also the mark of a suppliant : ἐκόντας τε ἐλάβετε καὶ χεῖρας προϊσχομένους pleaded the Plataeans, Thuc. III. 58.

κακός, 'humble.' The strength of the aristocratic feeling in early times is evidenced by the adoption of words implying morally or physically ' good ' to denote those of high birth, and the reverse for the lowly born : we have to bear in mind, too, that education in those days and literary training were the privilege only of the well-to-do, whose voices alone accordingly we hear : for such it was natural to speak of themselves as ἐσθλοί, ἀγαθοί and the like, and to brand the many who resented, while they coveted, their privileges, as κακοί and δειλοί : cf. Hom. Od. IV. 63 ἀλλ' ἀνδρῶν γένος ἐστὲ διιτρεφέων βασιλήων | σκηπτούχων· ἐπεὶ οὔ κε κακοὶ τοιούσδε τέκοιεν. So too in Latin *optimi, optimates.*

195. In a sentence of this form it is not necessary to repeat the relative, even though the second clause require it in a different case : if emphasis is required the sentence is carried on with a demonstrative pronoun : here, for instance, we might have had ὃν οὐ προσεῖπε, καὶ ὑπὸ τούτου προσερρήθη πάλιν : cf. Hadley, Gr. Gr. § 1005. For **προσεῖπε**, cf. supr. 191, n.

197, 8. The first hint we receive of the half-contemptuous attitude towards Admetus commonly taken in the play. ' Better have died himself and have done with it,' is the servant's homely criticism. **τἄν**, τοι ἄν : τοι serves to introduce a trite saying, as often. Note the emphasis given to οὔποτε by its unusual position.

199. **ἦ που,** 'I make no doubt,' expresses ' *conjecturam adsignificata persuasione* ' says Ellendt (Lex. Soph.) : frequently its use is ironical.

200. **εἰ** : after many verbs expressing emotion (θαυμάζω ἀγανακτῶ αἰσχύνομαι αἰνῶ etc.), the object of the emotion is stated in a sentence introduced by εἰ. For examples, cf. Goodw. M. T. § 494.

201—3. The contempt expressed in these lines is manifest. ' Aye, he's crying and calling her his dear wife, as he holds her in his arms, and prays her not to desert him—senseless man—when she's at her last gasp,' is a somewhat colloquial equivalent.

202. **μὴ προδοῦναι**, cf. infr. 250, 275. **τἀμήχανα ζητῶν**, 'seeking for the impossible': so Soph. Ant. 90 ἀλλ' ἀμηχάνων ἐρᾷς.

203. **μαραίνεται νόσῳ**: infr. 236.

204. After this verse a line has been lost, containing the sentence of which we have the subject only. **χειρὸς ἄθλιον βάρος**, of Alcestis in her husband's arms: cf. Bacch. 1216 ἔπεσθέ μοι φέροντες ἄθλιον βάρος | Πενθέως.

205. **σμικρὸν ἐμπνέουσ'**, 'barely alive': cf. Hipp. 1246 βραχὺν δὴ βίοτον ἐμπνέων ἔτι.

206. So Phaedra begs to be brought out once more to the light of day, so dear to the Greeks: τόδε σοι φέγγος (says the nurse to her), λαμπρὸς ὅδ' αἰθήρ· | δεῦρο γὰρ ἐλθεῖν πᾶν ἔπος ἦν σοι· ('your one cry was'). Hipp. 178.

209. **σὴν παρουσίαν**, cf. infr. 606 ἀνδρῶν Φεραίων εὐμενὴς παρουσία (vocative).

210. **οὐ γάρ τι**, 'for not by any means': cf. infr. 417 οὐ γάρ τι πρῶτος...γυναικὸς ἤμπλακες. **κοιράνοις**, cf. supr. 132, n., and infr. 212.

211. **παρεστάναι**, 'to stand by them': παραστάτης was one's comrade in the ranks, who stood shoulder-to-shoulder with one in battle.

213. For the fusing of several questions into one, cf. I. A. 356 τίνα δὲ πόρον εὕρω πόθεν, | ὥστε μὴ στερέντας ἀρχῆς ἀπολέσαι καλὸν κλέος; Hel. 873 τί τἀμὰ πῶς ἔχει θεσπίσματα; Soph. Phil. 1090 τοῦ ποτε τεύξομαι | σιτονόμου μέλεος πόθεν ἐλπίδος; Hom. Od. I. 170 τίς πόθεν εἰς ἀνδρῶν; (where Merry quotes Plin. Paneg. 2, 3 *ex ipso genere gratiarum agendarum intellegatur, cui quando sint actae*). Hadley Gr. Gr. § 1013.

πόρος κακῶν. As a rule πόρος means a way of 'getting': here of 'averting.' This use seems based on the analogy of μηχανή: cf. infr. 221: μῆχος in this sense is common, cf. Andr. 536 κακῶν μῆχος.

These lines (213, 214) and the corresponding lines of the antistrophe (226, 227) would be rendered less commonplace than at first sight they appear to be by the use of the rare bacchiac rhythm ('quintuple time') and the music to suit.

215. **ἔξεισί τις**; 'will any one come forth from the palace, to tell us whether the queen be yet actually dead, or no?' This is equivalent to 'shall we wait to hear?' The alternative is conveyed in ἤδη (217): 'or are we to don mourning *at once*?'

τέμω, delib. subj.

218. **δῆλα** for the usual δῆλον (ἐστί): so ἀδύνατα (commonly), ἄπορα, etc. Hadl. Gr. Gr. § 635 a.

ὅμως, 'though too late.'

220. **Παιάν**, cf. supr. 92, n.

222. **καὶ πάρος...καὶ νῦν**, 'as formerly...so now.'

223. **τοῦτ'**, sc. μηχανὴν κακῶν. **τῷδε**, for Admetus.

224. Cf. Aesch. Eum. 298 ἔλθοι (Ἀπόλλων) ὅπως γένοιτο τῶνδ' ἐμοὶ λυτήριος.

227. **οἶ' ἔπραξας**, 'what hap was thine, reft of thy wife.' **στερείς**, poet. for στερηθείς ; the 1st aorist forms only are found in prose : the compound ἀποστερῶ is preferred to the simple form in the present.

228. **ἆρα** by itself merely indicates interrogation (ἆρ' οὐ = *nonne*, ἆρα μή = *num*), without suggesting the reply : sometimes however, where intense feeling calls for an affirmative answer, the seemingly studied moderation of the simple ἆρα, instead of ἆρ' οὐ, heightens the effect of the question : cf. infr. 341 ἆρά μοι στένειν πάρα; asks Admetus : 771 ἆρα τὸν ξένον στυγῶ δικαίως; cries the servant disgusted at Heracles' boisterous mirth. So too Soph. Aj. 277 ἆρ' ἔστι ταῦτα δὶς τόσ' ἐξ ἁπλῶν κακά; cries the distracted Tecmessa. With the passage as a whole we may compare Bacch. 246 ταῦτ' οὐχὶ δεινῆς ἀγχόνης ἔστ' ἄξια ; Her. 246 καὶ τόδ' ἀγχόνης πέλας. Ar. Ach. 125 ταῦτα δῆτ' οὐκ ἀγχόνη ;

σφαγάς, properly of cutting the throat of a victim, then generally.

229. **πλέον ἢ κ.τ.λ.**, quite literally, 'is it not a greater thing than so as to (= such as to) bring the neck near to the suspended halter ?' The expression is a strengthened form of 'great enough to bring etc.', and the infinitival construction is retained in the stronger form : cf. Hec. 1106 κρείσσον' ἢ φέρειν κακά. Soph. O. T. 1293 τὸ γὰρ νόσημα μεῖζον ἢ φέρειν. Prof. Goodwin (M. T. § 764) says that the infinitive depends on the idea of *ability* or *inability* implied in the expression.

230. **οὐρανίῳ**. The word is often employed in exaggerated metaphor : cf. El. 860 οὐράνιον πήδημα κουφίζουσα. Bacch. 1064 λαβὼν γὰρ ἐλάτης οὐράνιον ἄκρον κλάδον | κατῆγεν. Tro. 519 ἵππον οὐράνια βρέμοντα. Aristoph. perhaps parodies Eur.'s use of the word Vesp. 1530, Nub. 357, Ran. 781. Here it = 'high-suspended.'

231. 'Dear, said I? nay, dearest.'

232. **εἶν** = ἐν, but only in lyric passages. **ἐπόψει** : the 'pathetic' compound of ὁρᾶν, often used of living to see evils, e.g. Aesch. Ag. 1246

Ἀγαμέμνονός σέ φημ' ἐπόψεσθαι μόρον prophesies Cassandra. Hom. Od. XIX. 260 Ὀδυσσεὺς | ᾤχετ' ἐποψόμενος Κακοΐλιον οὐκ ὀνομαστήν. Cf. too Med. 1025 and Dr Verrall's note.

236. Cf. supr. 203.

237. "Ἀιδαν: the antistrophic echoes in Euripides' lyrics are note-worthy: to "Ἀιδαν here corresponds "Ἀιδαν in l. 225. Similarly in l. 234 βόασον ὦ στέναξον resembles in form πόριζε δὴ πόριζε in l. 222: and infr. ll. 252, 253 are closely followed by ll. 259, 260. Instances of the way in which sounds lingered in Euripides' ear and reproduced themselves are πλέον ἢ in l. 239 and l. 229, οὐρανίῳ l. 230 and οὐράνιαι l. 245. Cf. Hec. 98, n.

238. 'Ever will I deny that marriage brings greater joy than sorrow': φημί, 'I say yes': οὔ φημι, I say no (φάσκω generally supplies the pres. partic. and infin., and the imperf.).

240. τεκμαιρόμενος τοῖς πάροιθεν, 'judging by the history of past times': cf. Soph. O. T. 916 οὐδ' ὁποῖ' ἀνὴρ | ἔννους τὰ καινὰ τοῖς πάλαι τεκμαίρεται. Eur. fr. 578 τεκμαιρόμεσθα τοῖς παροῦσι τἀφανῆ.

241. ὅστις: the use of the *indefinite* relative with a *definite* antecedent seems at first sight irregular, but the poet is generalizing and the antecedent really indefinite: this is seen if we translate 'when I cast my eyes upon the sorrows of *a* king, who etc.': cf. infr. 620, 1090.

242. ἀπλακὼν ἀλόχου, cf. infr. 418, 1083. For the form of the verb, cf. I. A. 124 καὶ πῶς Ἀχιλεὺς λέκτρων ἀπλακὼν | οὐ μέγα φυσῶν θυμὸν ἐπαρεῖ | σοὶ σῇ τ' ἀλόχῳ;

243. Cf. Hipp. 821 κατακονὰ μὲν οὖν ἀβίοτος βίου. 868 ἐμοὶ μὲν οὖν | ἀβίοτος βίου τύχα. Similar are the phrases γάμος ἄγαμος, μήτηρ ἀμήτωρ and the like.

244. 'O sun and light of day, and you, ye eddying clouds that course on high.' Aristophanes (Nub. 380) parodies these opening words of Alcestis. 'Is it not Zeus,' asks Strepsiades, 'who makes the clouds roll?' ἥκιστ', ἀλλ' αἰθέριος δῖνος, Socrates replies. Whether Eurip. here, as certainly Aristoph. does in the parody, intends any reference to the vortical movement imparted by νοῦς (divine intelli-gence) to inert matter (the theory by which Euripides' friend Anaxagoras accounted for the world as we see it) is extremely doubtful: nor is it probable that allusion is made to the revolution of the οὐρανός, the star-studded vault of heaven, round the earth, as the reference to clouds in such a context would be singularly inappropriate. Except in the

present passage and Or. 984, Euripides always uses δίνη of eddying *water*, nor need we seek here for anything beyond a poetic transference.

246. Admetus makes a sorry figure in this scene. The poet must have intended the contrast between the pathetic beauty of Alcestis' lyric farewell to life and home and the iambic banalities of her husband, who feebly persists in regarding himself as a deserving object of pity. ὁρᾷ, sc. ἥλιος. δύο: such a use of numerals to add distinctness to a picture is a recurring feature of Greek style: e.g. Or. 1536 παρθένον τε καὶ δάμαρτα δύο νεκρὼ κατόψεται. πεπραγότας, a common use of plural for dual: the use of the perf. πέπραγα is restricted to the intransitive meaning 'fare.'

247. Cf. Aesch. Cho. 313 δράσαντι παθεῖν, | τριγέρων μῦθος τάδε φωνεῖ. For the double accus. cf. Soph. Phil. 940 οἵ' ἔργ' ὁ παῖς μ' ἔδρασεν οὐξ Ἀχιλλέως.

248. μελάθρων στέγαι, 'sheltering home.'

249. Pelias was king of Iolcos: the town was about 10 miles east of Pherae.

250. μὴ προδῷς, cf. supr. 202, infr. 275. Line 251 is a repetition of l. 219.

252. A curious parallel to lines 252—256, 259—261 is found below 439—444. Reference is made in both passages to the same persons, Death and Charon: in both the wording is similar: Ἅιδας ὑπ' ὀφρύσι κυαναυγέσι βλέπων is there found as Ἀΐδας ὁ μελαγχαίτας θεός: the words λίμνη, δίκωπος actually recur: λίμνη is again used of the nether lake, infr. 902: Soph. El. 139 Ἀΐδα παγκοίνου λίμνας. Ar. Ran. 181.

254. τί μέλλεις; ἐπείγου· σὺ κατείργεις are the supposed words of Charon. κατείργεις = 'hinder.'

256. σπερχόμενος, 'in haste': equivalent to an adverb, as frequently in Homer, e.g. Il. XXIII. 870 σπερχόμενος δ' ἄρα Μηριόνης ἐξείρυσε χειρὸς | τόξον. The use of the verb is confined to poetry (epic chiefly) and Ionic prose. τάδε is a cognate accus., with ταχύνει: cf. Goodw. Gr. Gr. § 159, 4.

259. μέθες με (as also infr. 262 τί ῥέξεις; ἄφες·) is addressed in horror to the spectre whom she beholds in act to seize her. This is Thanatos of the prologue (cf. n. on supr. 24), who approaches possibly to perform the rite of consecration to the nether powers referred to supr. 73, 74. τις goes with Ἅιδας (261).

262. τί ῥέξεις; The use of the future here and in the similar τί

λέξεις; (Med. 1310, Hipp. 353) denotes that the speaker cannot immediately grasp the horror of the situation.

263. προβαίνω: note the pathos of the compound verb in its reference to the 'forward' journey into the unknown: 'how dread the road on which I am setting forth.'

264. ἐκ δὲ τῶν, cf. supr. 190, n. Soph. O. C. 742 πᾶς σε Καδμείων λεὼς | καλεῖ δικαίως, ἐκ δὲ τῶν μάλιστ' ἐγώ: where Jebb notes that an art. used as demonstr. pron. generally stands first in a clause.

266. These words are addressed to Admetus and her children, who are supporting her. This entry of Alcestis reminds one of Phaedra's appearance in the Hippolytus (198 sq.): she too is supported on to the stage uttering wild words of delirium, and when the fit passes she sinks, exhausted indeed but calm.

269. Cf. Hipp. 1444 αἰαῖ, κατ' ὄσσων κιγχάνει μ' ἤδη σκότος (of the dying Hippolytus): infr. 385.

270. It is worthy of careful note that Alcestis' tenderness is everywhere in the play reserved for her children: it is to them that her last words of loving farewell are addressed: it is with their future that her mind is occupied and for their sake that she begs her husband's promise to remain a widower: Admetus himself she heeds but little: indeed with a galling frankness she makes clear to him how great is her sacrifice, how deep and lasting should be his gratitude: yet her trust in him is slight: χρόνος μαλάξει σε is her answer to his appeals for pity: with many a little touch the poet points the contrast between the heroic woman and the whining man. It will need the brutal plain-speaking of Pheres to stir the king's complacency to shame, and it is only to a repentant Admetus that we do not greatly grudge his final good-fortune.

272. χαίροντες carries the full double force of χαῖρε, 'fare well.' φάος is contrasted with νὺξ supr. 269.

273. τόδ' ἔπος, i.e. χαῖρε, involved in χαίροντες.

274. παντὸς θανάτου, 'every form of death': 'worse than a thousand deaths.' πᾶς is often used (=ἕκαστος) to express 'each one' of a number, e.g. πᾶς ἀνήρ: cf. Soph. Ant. 1000 (Teiresias speaks of his seat of augury) ἵν' ἦν μοι παντὸς οἰωνοῦ λιμήν ('resort of every kind of bird'). Phil. 407 ἔξοιδα γάρ νιν παντὸς ἂν λόγου κακοῦ | γλώσσῃ θιγόντα.

275. The full form of the expression would be μὴ (πρὸς θεῶν σε ἄντομαι) τλῇς κ.τ.λ.: cf. infr. 1098. For this (the usual) order of the

words, cf. I. A. 1233 μὴ πρός σε Πέλοπος κ.τ.λ. Phoen. 1665 ναὶ πρός σε τῆσδε μητρὸς Ἰοκάστης, Κρέον. So in Latin, Liv. XXIII. 9 *per ego te quaecunque jura liberos jungunt parentibus precor, etc.*

μὴ τλῇς, 'have not the cruelty to abandon me.' Monk in a note on this line shows by well-selected examples the use of τολμᾶν, τλῆναι to signify 'to bring oneself to do' a thing in defiance of danger (469), shame, pride (1, 572), grief (552), or pity (as here): and adds that in Latin *posse* is similarly employed. τλῇς, aorist.

277. ἄνα=ἀνάστηθι: cf. Soph. Aj. 194 ἀλλ' ἄνα ἐξ ἑδράνων: an epic use.

278. 'I am in thy hands—to live or die,' a figurative statement of course: for ἐν=*penes*, cf. Thuc. I. 74 ἐν ταῖς ναυσὶ τῶν Ἑλλήνων τὰ πράγματα ἐγένετο. Soph. O. C. 247 ἐν ὕμμι γὰρ ὡς θεῷ κείμεθα τλάμονες. 1443 ταῦτα δ' ἐν τῷ δαίμονι.

279. 'For thy love, as of a god, I reverence.' Admetus recognizes his wife's lofty superiority to himself by the use of the word σέβεσθαι: for the same reason φιλία (often used of friendship between superior and inferior: cf. Cycl. 81), not ἔρως (sexual love), is employed. Cf. infr. 930. φιλία occurs neither in Soph. nor Aesch. γάρ introduces a justification of the strong expression ἐν σοὶ δ' ἐσμέν: 'I am in thy hands: for thou art as a god to me.'

280. γάρ. 'I must speak now, *for* you see how near I am to death.' Alcestis speaks with the almost unnatural quietness and the unsparing directness that tell of great effort and of excitement controlled. Notice the effect of the direct opening ἐγώ σε κ.τ.λ., with no introductory particle.

282. πρεσβεύουσα=προτιμῶσα, 'preferring thee in honour,' sc. to myself: cf. Hipp. 5 τοὺς μὲν σέβοντας τἀμὰ πρεσβεύω κράτη. Aesch. Eum. 1 πρῶτον μὲν εὐχῇ τῇδε πρεσβεύω θεῶν | τὴν πρωτόμαντιν Γαῖαν. ἀντί, 'at the price of': cf. infr. 462.

283. With εἰσορᾶν understand σε: 'having wrought that thou should'st live': cf. the echo infr. 362.

284. παρόν, imperf. partic. in accus. absol.: 'tho' it was open to me not to die for thee, but to get me (aorist, of an act) a husband of the Thessalians whom I would, and dwell (pres. of continued state) in a palace dowered with sovereignty.'

285. ὃν ἤθελον. The tense is past by assimilation to the tense of the principal verb (here represented by παρόν): this is regular in conditional sentences, where the condition is unfulfilled: Goodw. M. T.

§ 559. The expanded form of the sentence is: 'if I had wished (but I did not), I could have etc.,' εἰ ἐβουλήθην, ἔσχον ἄν. (For παρῆν σχεῖν = ἔσχον ἄν, cf. Goodw. M. T. §§ 415, 416.)

286. Mr Earle points out the parallel in Hom. Od. II. 336, where it is assumed that in case of Odysseus' death, his position would devolve on whoever married his widow.

287. οὐκ ἠθέλησα: for the omission of connecting particle, cf. supr. 282 and n. on 280.

288. Dread of the portion of the fatherless for her children (cf. Hom. Il. XXII. 485 sq. the lament of Andromache over the fatherless Astyanax), weighs with Alcestis in determining on her self-sacrifice: cf. n. on supr. 270.

'Nor did I grudge to sacrifice the gladsome gifts of youth, which were mine, in which I joyed.' With ἥβης δῶρα, cf. Hel. 364 δῶρα Κύπριδος. The contrast is between her sacrifice of youth and the parents' tenacity of joyless age.

291. καλῶς μὲν...καλῶς δέ, the antithesis is verbal only, not real: the first καλῶς goes, not with κατθανεῖν, but with ἧκον: a suitable time of life had arrived for natural death, while at the same time they might have died with credit and nobly saved their son. Such is the sense, though somewhat obscurely put in the Greek through the poet's desire for rhetorical balance of clauses. καλῶς ἧκον βίου: ἧκον accus. absol.: ἥκειν with an adverb followed by a (partitive, cf. supr. 9, n.) genitive = 'to have come to a certain point with respect to' a thing: the phrase is particularly common in Herod. (e.g. I. 30 Τέλλῳ τοῦ βίου εὖ ἥκοντι τελευτὴ τοῦ βίου λαμπροτάτη ἐπεγένετο: VIII. 111): cf. El. 751 πῶς ἀγῶνος ἥκομεν; Heracl. 213 γένους μὲν ἥκεις ὧδε τοῖσδε, Δημοφῶν ('in this degree of relationship thou standest').

293. ἦσθα: throughout this passage the speaker is regarding the time when the decision of the parents to live, of Alcestis to die, was made: hence the past tenses.

294. οὔτις ἐλπὶς ἦν φιτύσειν, 'there was no hope that they would get': not 'there was no hope of their getting': cf. supr. 12, n. The thought in Alcestis' mind seems to be: 'they would not die to save the life of their only son, old as they were: while I in the bloom of youth am quitting life to preserve a father to my children.'

295. ἔζων: the correct form of the 1st sing. imperf.: from the 2nd and 3rd persons ἔζης, ἔζη the grammarians inferred and brought into the texts a 1st sing. ἔζην, as though from ζῆμι: in Attic Greek the forms in

use were ζῶ, ἔζων, βιώσομαι (rarely ζήσω), ἐβίων, βεβίωκα. Cf. Cobet N.
L. 494, 525.

297. ὠρφάνευες, cf. supr. 165, n. **ταῦτα μέν.** The place of the δέ
clause is supplied by σὺ νῦν μοι κ.τ.λ.: the contrast is between the sad
past, which she dismisses, and the future with its forebodings, on which
she wishes to speak. **μὲν** almost = μὲν δή: cf. supr. 156, n.

299. **εἶεν** dismisses one point to pass on to the next: cf. Hec. 313,
Med. 386.

ἀπόμνησαι only occurs in the phrase ἀπομνήσασθαι χάριν: this is the
only instance in Tragedy.

300. **ἀξίαν μὲν...δίκαια δέ**: this contrast should be brought out in
translation: 'for I shall ask of thee, not its (τῶνδε, 'my sacrifice') equi-
valent indeed, but a just boon.'

301. Monk quotes Hom. Il. IX. 401 οὐ γὰρ ἐμοὶ ψυχῆς ἀντάξιον οὐδ'
ὅσα φασὶν | Ἴλιον ἐκτῆσθαι.

302. **γάρ**: 'just, as you will yourself admit: for it concerns our
children, and dearly as I love them, you love them dearly too, if your
heart is right.' **εἴπερ εὖ φρονεῖς** are not the words of implicit confi-
dence: cf. n. on supr. 270.

304. **ἀνάσχου**, 'uphold': cf. Hec. 120 ἦν δὲ τὸ μὲν σὸν σπεύδων
ἀγαθὸν | τῆς μαντιπόλου βάκχης ἀνέχων | λέκτρ' Ἀγαμέμνων: Soph. Aj.
212 λέχος δουριάλωτον | στέρξας ἀνέχει θούριος Αἴας.

δεσπότας, 'as rulers': in appos. to τούτους. **ἐμῶν**, cf. cr. n.

305. **ἐπιγήμῃς**: cf. infr. 373. Pflugk quotes Herod. IV. 154 ὃς ἐπὶ
θυγατρὶ ἀμήτορι, τῇ οὔνομα ἦν Φρονίμη, ἐπὶ ταύτῃ ἔγημε ἄλλην γυναῖκα.
ἡ δὲ ἐπεσελθοῦσα ἐδικαίευ εἶναι καὶ τῷ ἔργῳ μητρυιὴ τῇ Φρονίμη.

306. **ἥτις** generalizes: cf. supr. 241, n. **κακίων**: Alcestis knows
her own worth, and also assumes the inferiority of a second wife.

307. 'Will lay a heavy hand upon the children, thy children and
mine.'

308. **δῆτα** strengthens the appeal, as freq.: e.g. Soph. O. T. 1153
μὴ δῆτα πρὸς θεῶν τὸν γέροντά μ' αἰκίσῃ.

309. Cf. Ion 1025 φθονεῖν γάρ φασι μητρυιὰς τέκνοις: Hes. Op. et
D. 825 ἄλλοτε μητρυιὴ πέλει ἡμέρη ἄλλοτε μήτηρ (speaking of auspicious
and inauspicious days). Aesch. P. V. 727 calls the dangerous coast of
Salmydessus μητρυιὰ νεῶν. Eur. fr. 4 πέφυκε γάρ πως παισὶ πολέμιος
γυνὴ | τοῖς πρόσθεν ἡ ζυγεῖσα δευτέρα πατρί.

310. **ἐχίδνης**: cf. Andr. 271 ἐχίδνης καὶ πυρὸς περαιτέρω (of a bad
woman). So Ion 1262.

311. πύργον: for the metaphor, cf. Hom. Od. XI. 556 (of Ajax) τοῖος γάρ σφιν πύργος ἀπώλεο. Soph. O. T. 1201 θανάτων δ' ἐμᾷ | χώρᾳ πύργος ἀνέστα ('tower against death'). Med. 390 ἦν μέν τις ἡμῖν πύργος ἀσφαλὴς φανῇ.

313. σὺ δέ, turning to the daughter. κορευθήσει, cf. supr. 165, n. 'grow to womanhood.'

314. συζύγου τῷ σῷ πατρί: these words together form one idea: for the dative, cf. Goodw. Gr. Gr. § 185.

315. The use of an *independent* subj. with μή, expressing 'apprehension coupled with a desire to avert the object of fear' (Goodw. M.T. § 261) is very common (usually in the third person) in Homer: cf. Il. II. 195 μή τι χολωσάμενος ῥέξῃ κακὸν υἷας Ἀχαιῶν. Od. v. 356 ὤ μοι ἐγώ, μή τίς μοι ὑφαίνῃσιν δόλον αὖτε. The usual constr. with verbs of fearing arose when φοβοῦμαι was paratactically prefixed: 'I fear, may he not do harm' becoming in use 'I fear lest he may etc.' Eurip. and Plato at times recur to the Homeric independent construction: cf. H. F. 1399 ἀλλ' αἷμα μὴ σοῖς ἐξομόρξωμαι πέπλοις. Plat. Legg. 861 E μή τις οἴηται. προσβαλοῦσα κληδόνα: cf. Soph. El. 974 λόγων γε μὴν εὔκλειαν οὐχ ὁρᾷς ὅσην | σαυτῇ τε κἀμοὶ προσβαλεῖς πεισθεῖσ' ἐμοί; κληδών is not used in Attic prose: it occurs again, infr. 959.

316. γάμους: the plural is usual: the singular is generally employed only of a particular marriage of a definite person.

317. νυμφεύσει, 'give in marriage': νυμφεύειν besides means both *nubere* and *ducere*: νυμφεύεσθαι is also used = *nubere*.

318. τόκοισι, 'labour-pains': cf. Med. 1031 στερρὰς ἐνεγκοῦσ' ἐν τόκοις ἀλγηδόνας (a passage somewhat resembling the present). θαρσυνεῖ παροῦσα, 'cheer by her presence.'

320. ἐς αὔριον is frequently found = αὔριον simply.

321. Cf. crit. n. ἐς τρίτην: 'the day after to-morrow': ἡμέραν is nearly always added. The Scholiast's note is οὐκ εἰς τὴν αὔριον τοῦ μηνὸς τούτου οὐδὲ εἰς τὴν μεταύριον. If the κυρία ἡμέρα (supr. 105, 158), on which Alcestis was bound to die, was supposed to be the νουμηνία or first day of the month, the usual date for payment of interest, we may imagine that the words ἐς τρίτην μηνὸς refer to the days of grace allowed to a debtor. While it is not altogether unlikely that the 'new moon' would be regarded as the natural date in an early state of society to be fixed for an obligation to be carried out, the allusion to the Athenian custom of a three-day extension of time reminds us more of an interpolator than a poet.

322. ἐν τοῖς μηκέτ' οὖσι: when a participle 'represents a relative clause with an indefinite antecedent' (Goodw. Gr. Gr. § 283, 4), i.e. refers to a *class*, not to *individuals*, the negative is μή.

λέξομαι, 'shall be numbered': passive in sense, as always: many other verbs also use a fut. mid. form in a passive sense: for a list, cf. Hadl. Gr. Gr. § 496 and Jebb's n. on Soph. O.T. 672, who remarks that the 'middle forms of the aorist were alone peculiar to that voice.'

323. χαίροντες εὐφραίνοισθε, cf. supr. 272, n.

325. μητρός, sc. ἀρίστης.

327. An echo of supr. 303. For οὐχ ἅζομαι in the preceding line, cf. crit. n.

328. ἔσται τάδ' ἔσται: instances of repetition in passages expressing deep feeling are supr. 108, 218, 222, 252, 259, 266, 270, 271. μὴ τρέσῃς, a favourite phrase with Euripides: in the Heracl. alone it occurs five times.

329. 'For in life thou wert mine, and in death thou and thou alone shalt be called my wife.' κεκλήσει: 'the fut. perfect often denotes the continuance of an action, or the permanence of its results in future time.' Goodw. M.T. § 78.

331. τόνδ' ἄνδρα = ἐμέ, as often: cf. infr. 1090. νύμφη, in appos., 'as my bride.'

332. οὕτως qualifies generally the whole sentence πατρὸς εὐγενοῦς—γυνή: 'so nobly-born and beautiful besides beyond compare' ('that I should wed her' we must supply). The superlative ἐκπρεπεστάτη is somewhat irregular, but does not jar upon the ear as it would do if a simple adjective (εὐγενής) preceded.

333. ἄλλως, 'besides': cf. the concluding words of the Phaedo (of Socrates) ἀνδρὸς τῶν τότε ὧν ἐπειράθημεν ἀρίστου καὶ ἄλλως φρονιμωτάτου καὶ δικαιοτάτου. Herod. I. 60.

334. ἅλις means 'enough' (or 'in abundance,' Hom.), *not* 'sufficiently.' Euripides is fond of the construction with the genitive (he uses it 12 times, Sophocles once only).

335. γενέσθαι, cf. n. on supr. 12: supply ἐμοί. σοῦ contrasted with τῶνδε. ὠνήμεθα: ὠνήμην indic., but opt. ὀναίμην, infin. ὄνασθαι. Note the tone of selfishness in these lines. Cf. Med. 1025.

336. οἴσω δὲ πένθος: cf. Soph. O.T. 93 τῶνδε γὰρ πλέον φέρω | τὸ πένθος ἢ καὶ τῆς ἐμῆς ψυχῆς πέρι.

οὐκ ἐτήσιον, 'not for a year only': ceremonial mourning at Athens ended with the observances of the τριακάς on the 30th day: the 3rd and

9th days also after the death were marked by certain rites (τρίτα, ἔνατα), while yearly offerings were made at the tomb. At Sparta eleven days' mourning was considered sufficient. Admetus proposes (infr. 431) to order a twelve months' mourning to be observed by his subjects also. Cf. Soph. El. 103 ἀλλ' οὐ μὲν δὴ | λήξω θρήνων στυγερῶν τε γόων | ἔστ' ἂν παμφεγγεῖς ἄστρων | ῥιπάς, λεύσσω δὲ τόδ' ἦμαρ. **τὸ σόν**=σου objective: cf. Soph. El. 343 τἀμὰ νουθετήματα, 'admonitions to me.' O.C. 332 σῇ προμηθίᾳ, 'through regard for thee.'

337. **αἰών**, 'life': cf. fr. 798 ἀπέπνευσεν αἰῶνα: so in the Hom. hymn to Hermes, the god, having found the tortoise, the shell of which he proposed to use for his lyre, αἰῶν' ἐξετόρησεν ('bored through') ὀρεσκῴοιο χελώνης.

338. **στυγῶν**, cf. his father's retort, infr. 958.

340. **ἀντιδοῦσα**: in words denoting 'barter' the main notion is that of 'exchange,' not 'price': thus we find the same word meaning to 'give' and to 'take' in exchange: cf. ἀλλάσσειν, ἀμείβειν, Lat. *mutare*: here ἀντί is used of giving in exchange, supr. 282 of receiving in exchange. **τὰ φίλτατα**, cf. supr. 301.

341. **ἄρα**, cf. supr. 228, n.

342. **ἁμαρτάνοντι**: ἁμαρτάνειν in this sense of 'lose,' 'fail to keep,' is very rare, though of course frequent with the meaning 'lose,' 'fail to get': it occurs Hom. Od. IX. 512 χειρῶν ἐξ Ὀδυσῆος ἁμαρτήσεσθαι ὀπωπῆς ('be deprived of sight'). Merry there says that no other instance is found in Homer (ἀφαμαρτάνειν however occurring, e.g. Il. VI. 411 ἐμοὶ δέ κε κέρδιον εἴη | σεῦ ἀφαμαρτούσῃ χθόνα δύμεναι), 'though common enough in the Tragedians.' It occurs, indeed, four times in this play, 144, 342, 616, 879 (an instance of Euripides' habit of phrase-echoing), Andr. 373, and fr. 547 (ἴσην γὰρ ἀνδρὶ συμφορὰν εἶναι λέγω | τέκνων θ' ἁμαρτεῖν καὶ πάτρας καὶ χρημάτων, | ἀλόχου τε κεδνῆς), but so far as I know not elsewhere in Eurip., and not at all in Soph. or Aesch. (perhaps Ag. 535). **συζύγου**, echo of supr. 314.

344. **στεφάνους**, cf. supr. 172, n. **κατεῖχε**, 'used to fill': cf. Soph. Phil. 10 ἀλλ' ἀγρίαις | κατεῖχ' ἀεὶ πᾶν στρατόπεδον δυσφημίαις: Aesch. Pers. 427 οἰμωγὴ δ' ὁμοῦ | κωκύμασιν κατεῖχε πελαγίαν ἅλα. The promise is an unfortunate one, considering the impending visit of Heracles.

345. **βαρβίτου**. This was some kind of stringed instrument, of foreign (probably oriental) origin: it was akin to the λύρα. The λύρα of Hermes (cf. n. on supr. 337) differed considerably from the κιθάρα of

Apollo: the sounding-board of the former was a tortoise-shell, while the latter had a more complicated and advanced sound-box of wood or metal. The λύρα was *par excellence* the Athenian instrument, at any rate for gentlemen. Technical skill was no doubt carried to a higher pitch of perfection on the κιθάρα, which for this very reason probably was thought unfit for amateurs, who would be disgraced by 'professional' attainments in such matters. Aristotle (Pol. v. 6) excluded it from education along with the flute. After the Persian wars, he says, with more leisure and money, the Athenians tried all manner of instruments, playing in person: but when experience taught them to discriminate between instruments with a moral tendency and those without, they dropped the latter (and among them the βάρβιτος). Both the λύρα and the κιθάρα had strings of equal length, and it was by the varying *thickness* of the string that different notes were produced: it was in the harp (τρίγωνον) that this effect was produced by the differing *length* of the strings. It is curious that the older word κιθάρα was used for the newer instrument, while the comparatively new word λύρα was adopted for the old-fashioned tortoise-shell 'invention' of Hermes, which was still kept in use for educational purposes and among amateurs. The verb κιθαρίζειν denoted playing on either.

346. ἐξαίροιμι, 'rouse,' differs slightly from ἐπαίρειν, which usually connotes 'unduly': cf. Hipp. 322 τί γὰρ τὸ δεινὸν τοῦθ' ὅ σ' ἐξαίρει θανεῖν;

Λίβυν αὐλόν: the αὐλός, 'clarinet,' (to be distinguished from the σῦριγξ, 'flute') was in its simplest form made of reed, though ivory or metal was afterwards used in its construction. It is here called Λίβυν, because from North Africa came the *lotus*; whether the Nile-lily described by Herod. II. 92, the stalks of which may have been utilized for the purpose, or a tree—*Celtis Australis*—whose ebony-like wood Pliny, Nat. Hist. XIII. 32, tells us *ad tibiarum cantus expetitur*, is uncertain: the clarinet itself is often called λωτός, cf. I. A. 438 κατὰ στέγας λωτὸς βοάσθω: 1036 τίς ἄρ' ὑμέναιος διὰ λωτοῦ Λίβυος κ.τ.λ. Hel. 170 μόλοιτ' ἔχουσαι τὸν Λίβυν λωτὸν ἢ σύριγγας. The αὐλός was the national instrument of Boeotia (cf. Ar. Ach. 862, where the Boeotian, who attends Dicaeopolis' market, is attended by pipers who have been performing all the way from Thebes): and in wide use too, among the Athenians, in spite of their patriotic affectation of contempt for the rival of the lyre.

λακεῖν, a poetical word denoting as a rule confused or noisy utter-

ance: cf. Hipp. 55 πολὺς δ' ἅμ' αὐτῷ προσπόλων ὀπισθόπους | κῶμος
λέλακεν Ἄρτεμιν τιμῶν θεὰν | ὑμνοισιν.

348. **σοφῇ**, as so frequently, referring to skill in the arts (esp.
poetry). **δέμας**, the living body)(σῶμα corpse: the distinction holds
widely. Monk quotes a description of Andromeda, bound to the rock
(fr. 124) παρθένου τ' εἰκώ τινα | ἐξ αὐτομόρφων λαΐνων τυκισμάτων, | σοφῆς
ἄγαλμα χειρός.

349. **εἰκασθέν**, 'counterfeited': cf. Herod. III. 28 (Apis has the
following signs) ἐπὶ μὲν τῷ μετώπῳ λευκὸν τετράγωνον, ἐπὶ δὲ τοῦ νώτου
αἰετὸν εἰκασμένον, ἐν δὲ τῇ οὐρῇ τὰς τρίχας διπλᾶς, ὑπὸ δὲ τῇ γλώσσῃ
κάνθαρον.

350. **ᾧ προσπεσοῦμαι**, 'on which I will cast myself': cf. supr.
175, n.

352. Cf. Hel. 35 (of the Euripidean phantom-Helen) καὶ δοκεῖ μ'
ἔχειν, | κενὴν δόκησιν, οὐκ ἔχων, a quotation which also illustrates ψυχρὰν
τέρψιν in the next line, an accus. in apposition to the sentence, as
supr. 7. **τέρψιν** refers with sad humour to supr. 347: note that τέρψις
is subjective in both cases, 'enjoying,' 'power of enjoyment.' **οἶμαι**,
ironicè, as often, when thus interjected.

354. **ἀπαντλοίην ἄν**, 'I should lighten the heavy load of sorrow at
my heart.' **ψυχῆς** is best taken with ἀπαντλ.: lit. 'should draw off
from my heart.'

356. **κἂν νυκτί** is equivalent to 'if only in dreams.' **παρῇ**, impers.,
'it be permitted.'

357. The connexion seems to be: 'Come thou to visit me in
unsubstantial dreams: would that I could come to thee in bodily form
and rescue thee.'

357. Cf. I. A. 1211 εἰ μὲν τὸν Ὀρφέως εἶχον, ὦ πάτερ, λόγον, | πεί-
θειν ἐπᾴδουσ' ὥσθ' ὁμαρτεῖν μοι πέτρας, | κηλεῖν τε τοῖς λόγοισιν, οὓς
ἐβούλομην (for tense, cf. n. on supr. 285), | ἐνταῦθ' ἂν ἦλθον. Not the
Ὀρφεία γῆρυς but the βίη Ἡρακλείη was to work the deliverance of
which Admetus is vapouring. For **παρῆν** following closely παρῇ in the
preceding line, cf. supr. 90, n.

358. **κόρην Δήμητρος**, Persephone: but this most venerable goddess
was usually spoken of by Athenians as Κόρη simply. **κείνης** referring to
the more distant, i.e. the former of the two persons named.

360. **κατῆλθον ἄν**: all through this sentence Admetus speaks to
his wife as though she were already dead. 'Had I the tongue and
tuneful note of Orpheus, then would I have descended to the nether

world, nor should the dread guardians of Hell have stayed me, etc.':
cf. supr. 293, n.

361. Cf. infr. 439. **ψυχοπομπὸς** and ψυχαγωγὸς are usual attri-
butes of Hermes, whose duty it was to collect and convoy Charon's sad
travellers to their point of embarcation.

362. **ἔσχον, πρὶν καταστῆσαι**: a curious variation from the regular
ἔσχον μὴ καταστῆσαι. Cf. Rhes. 61 εἰ γὰρ φαεννοὶ μὴ ξυνέσχον ἡλίου |
λαμπτῆρες, οὐκ ἂν ἔσχον εὐτυχοῦν δόρυ, | πρὶν ναῦς πυρῶσαι.

ἐς φῶς καταστῆσαι βίον is an echo of supr. 283: cf. Bacch. 1339
μακάρων τ' ἐς αἶαν σὸν καθιδρύσει βίον.

363. **ἐκεῖσε**, pregnant use: 'journey thou thither and await me
there.' For ἐκεῖσε, referring to the world below, cf. infr. 744, 866.
Med. 1073 εὐδαιμονοῖτον, ἀλλ' ἐκεῖ (exclaims Medea to the children whom
she is about to slay).

364. The prevalent conception of the scenery and organization of
the nether world was drawn by the Greeks in the main from the
Homeric poems, and the leading features, deeply embedded in the
popular mind, provided literature with a store of familiar imagery,
indistinct indeed, but the more effective for that very want of definition;
a phenomenon observable among all peoples at all times. Euripides
employs this imagery for purely literary purposes, but never does he
succeed, as did Virgil, Dante or Milton, in giving imaginative reality to
the world of shades: it would be unjust to expect from a dramatist the
same measure of success as from the great epic singers who adapted
from the popular traditions the very frame and setting of their poems;
but Euripides moves with an air of unreality and constraint ἀν' εὐρυπυλὲς
ᵛΑϊδος δῶ, which marks the poet whose theme was living man, life's joys
and sorrows; who could confess the ἀπειροσύνην ἄλλου βιότου κοὐκ ἀπό-
δειξιν τῶν ὑπὸ γαίας (Hipp. 194). The dim hero of the myths he could
invest with reality in fuller measure than another, for he drew him with
his neighbour for a model; but in picturing an unseen world his touch
is always weak. It would seem from γὰρ in l. 365 that their union in
the world below depended in some way on their burial side by side in
the same coffin: probably a mixture of ideas due to the indistinctness
in the poet's mind. The language of l. 364 recalls that of S. John
xiv. 2.

365. **ἐπισκήψω**, 'will lay upon them my dying injunction': ἐπι-
σκήπτειν is specially used in this sense: cf. I. T. 701 (Orestes being
about, as he thinks, to die) πρὸς δεξιᾶς σε τῆσδ' ἐπισκήπτω τάδε (where

H. A.   6 the rare construction of the accus. of the person adjured is on the analogy of words of 'beseeching'). κέδροις, cf. supr. 160, n.; it would appear from Plin. XXIV. 5 (quoted by Monk) that the *Cedrelates* supplied coffin-timber: *defuncta corpora incorrupta aevis servat.*

366.   σοί, for the dat. after words expressing resemblance, etc., cf. Goodw. Gr. Gr. § 186: and Xen. An. II. 6, 22 τὸ δ' ἁπλοῦν καὶ τὸ ἀληθὲς ἐνόμιζε τὸ αὐτὸ τῷ ἠλιθίῳ εἶναι.

τούσδε, the children. For the sentiment, cf. Or. 1051 καὶ μνῆμα δέξαιθ' ἕν, κέδρου τεχνάσματα.

367.   Parodied by Aristophanes (Ach. 893): Dicaeopolis addresses the welcome eel, brought by the Boeotian to his market: μηδὲ γὰρ θανών ποτε | σοῦ χωρὶς εἴην ἐντετευτλανωμένης.

369.   καὶ μὴν introduces here an emphatic statement : when καὶ μὴν is used to emphasize a single word γε is usually added to the word on which stress is to be laid.

371.   This construction, ἀκούειν τί τινος λέγοντος, is used when the actual physical hearing of some important statement is to be emphasized: cf. Soph. Phil. 594 καὶ ταῦτ' Ἀχαιοὶ πάντες ἤκουον σαφῶς | Ὀδυσσέως λέγοντος.

372.   λέγοντος μὴ γαμεῖν: as λέγειν here is used in a sense approximating closely to ' to promise,' ' to swear,' we hardly notice the irregularity of the employment of μὴ instead of οὐ.   After verbs of swearing, consenting and the like, an infinitive is negatived by μή, which, perhaps as an older and more emphatic negative, is found in oaths even with the indicative, not only in Homer (Il. X. 329), but also in Attic: cf. Ar. Av. 194 μὰ γῆν...μὴ 'γὼ νόημα κομψότερον ἤκουσά πω.   Goodwin (M. T. § 685) thinks that 'the use of μὴ with the infin. was so fixed, before the infin. began to be used in indirect discourse, that μὴ always seemed natural, even after οὐ had become the regular form after verbs of *saying, thinking,* etc.'

γαμεῖν is future infinitive.

373.   ἐφ' ὑμῖν, cf. supr. 305, n.   μηδ' ἀτιμάσειν ἐμέ: cf. crit. n. on ἐμῶν, supr. 304 n.

375.   ἐπὶ τοῖσδε, 'on these conditions.'

377.   Cf. Hom. Il. VI. 429 Ἕκτορ, ἀτὰρ σύ μοί ἐσσι πατὴρ καὶ πότνια μήτηρ | ἠδὲ κασίγνητος, σὺ δέ μοι θαλερὸς παρακοίτης.

378.   Cf. Med. 1013 πολλή μ' ἀνάγκη, πρέσβυ (sc. δακρυρροεῖν) : here we must supply μητέρα γενέσθαι.

379.   χρῆν, imperfect = χρὴ ἦν : when the origin of the word was

forgotten, the form ἐχρῆν arose from false analogy. An infin. is frequently used with the imperfect of a verb expressing 'obligation' or the like, implying that what is denoted by the infin. ought to be happening or to have happened, but is not happening or did not happen : so here ζῆν χρῆν με=δικαίως ἂν ἔζων. This use is common with ἔδει, χρῆν, εἰκὸς ἦν, ἄξιον ἦν and similar expressions. Cf. Goodw. M. T. § 415, and n. on supr. 285. The reason that she should live is (not as the Scholiast says, νέα οὖσα δηλονότι,) that her children need her care.

380. τί δράσω δῆτα; 'what then shall I do?' δῆτα here marks consequence only, without any connotation of irony or indignation. μονούμενος, supr. 296.

381. χρόνος μαλάξει σ', 'time will assuage thy grief': cf. infr. 1085.

383. Cf. Soph. Ant. 547 ἀρκέσω θνῆσκουσ' ἐγώ. οἱ προθνῄσκοντες refers to Alcestis alone : when a speaker employs the plural in referring to himself, the masculine plural is always used, even when the speaker is a woman : cf. Soph. El. 399 πεσούμεθ', εἰ χρή, πατρὶ τιμωρούμενοι (Electra is speaking of herself).

384. Mr Earle remarks that 'δαίμων is the individual form of τύχη, as in Homer κήρ is the individual form of θάνατος.' συζύγου, supr. 342. ἀποστερεῖς : the word generally implies wrongful or fraudulent seizure : supr. 378.

385. καὶ μὴν announces a fresh symptom of coming death : cf. supr. 105, n.

σκοτεινόν, semi-proleptic : cf. supr. 35, n. 'A weight of darkness falls upon mine eyes.'

386. ἀπωλόμην ἄρ' κ.τ.λ.: cf. Med. 78 ἀπωλόμεσθ' ἄρ' εἰ κακὸν προσοίσομεν | νέον παλαιῷ. The aorist is vividly used, though with reference to a seeming future. 'If you move, you are a dead man' is a parallel English expression : cf. too Hom. Il. IX. 415 εἰ μέν κ' αὖθι μένων Τρώων πόλιν ἀμφιμάχωμαι, | ὤλετο μέν μοι νόστος, ἀτὰρ κλέος ἄφθιτον ἔσται.

387. ὡς οὐκέτ' οὖσαν κ.τ.λ. The use of ὡς gives the statement with reference to the mind of the person addressed : 'you may speak of me with full assurance that I am no more,' not merely, 'you may speak of me as dead,' which would not require ὡς. See Prof. Jebb's note on Soph. O.T. 848.

390. The rule observed by Aeschylus, that an iambic line should

not be divided between two speakers, holds good for Sophocles' and Euripides' earliest plays also, and when violated the irregularity is intentionally introduced (as here) in order to express great agitation or the like. Cf. Wilamowitz-Moellendorff, Analecta Euripidea, p. 195 sq.

391. προλείπεις; 'dost thou desert us?' or it may be that, as she falls forward, Admetus cries 'art thou swooning?' προλείπειν occurs in this sense Hec. 438.

ἀπωλόμην, supr. 386.

393. Rarely on any stage, certainly not on the sonorous and artificial stage of Athens, is there place for the unaffected simplicity of childhood: censure has very properly been meted out to Euripides for this frigid declamation, which might have been pardoned if inserted among the platitudes of a chorus, put into the mouth of a child presumably of very tender years, heart-broken at a mother's death. The strophe is bearable: the thoughts and language are simple and direct: but the antistrophe, with its far-fetched metaphor (μονόστολος), and sympathetic reflections on the bootlessness of his father's marriage (one almost expects to hear his 'respectful condolence') suggests either that Athenian children were unchildlike, or, a far truer view, that Euripides had little knowledge of and sympathy for children : equally bad is the cry of Medea's child when endeavouring to escape the murderous fury of his mother (Med. 1278) ὡς ἐγγὺς ἤδη γ' ἐσμὲν ἀρκύων ξίφους : the infant Molossus too, when threatened with death (Andr. 526), exclaims τί δ' ἐγὼ μόρου παράτροπον μέλος εὕρω; After all one cannot expect much from an infant in buskins and a mask.

μαῖα, a term of affectionate respect usually addressed to nurses : cf. Hipp. 243, where it is used by Phaedra in speaking to an old family servant. Eur. uses it here as a child's word, presumably in the meritorious endeavour to impart a child-like tone to the passage. Line 394 echoes the words of the chorus-leader, l. 392. The child was afterwards the 'king of men,' Eumelus, ὃς ἱπποσύνῃ ἐκέκαστο (Il. XXIII. 289).

396. ἁμόν : ᾱ̔μός is etymologically equivalent to ἡμέ-τερο-s, without the comparative affix, and though in meaning connected with the plural, is sometimes used for ἐμός both in lyric and iambic passages, for metrical convenience.

398. βλέφαρον, 'her closed eye-lid.'

400. ὑπάκουσον ἄκουσον: it is unusual to repeat in full a compound verb : the preposition is supposed to extend its influence over the repeated simple verb. The best known instance is Bacch. 1065

(Dionysus) λαβὼν γὰρ ἐλάτης οὐράνιον ἄκρον κλάδον | κατῆγεν ἦγεν ἦγεν εἰς μέλαν πέδον. Cf. too Hec. 167 κάκ' ἐνεγκοῦσαι πῆματ' ἀπωλέσατ' ὤλέσατ'. Hipp. 1374 προσαπόλλυτέ μ' ὄλλυτε τὸν δυσδαίμονα.

401. Note the pathetic repetition of ἐγώ: cf. supr. 382, 390, 328 n.

403. πίτνων, 'casting myself': cf. supr. 175, n. στόμασιν, 'lips': cf. Soph. Tr. 938 (Hyllus bewailing his dead mother) ἐλείπετ' οὐδέν, ἀμφί νιν γοώμενος, | οὔτ' ἀμφιπίπτων στόμασιν. νεοσσὸς is frequently used by Eurip. of young children: cf. Androm. 441 ἦ καὶ νεοσσὸν τόνδ', ὑπὸ πτερῶν σπάσας ;

404. τὴν οὐ κλύουσαν κ.τ.λ.: in apposition to σέ, supr. 401. The addition of the article by particularising, emphasizes: cf. Med. 271 σὲ τὴν σκυθρωπὸν καὶ πόσει θυμουμένην, | Μήδειαν, εἶπον. Bacch. 912 σὲ τὸν πρόθυμον ὄνθ' ἃ μὴ χρεὼν ὁρᾶν κ.τ.λ.

406. λείπομαι φίλας ματρὸς νέος μονόστολός τε is the order of the words: 'I am left by my dear mother, young as I am, to tread life's path alone.' For the genit. after λείπεσθαι, cf. Soph. Ant. 548 καὶ τίς βίος μοι σοῦ λελειμμένῃ φίλος ; Ion 680 αὐτὴ δ' ἄπαις ἦ καὶ λελειμμένη τέκνων. El. 1309 σοῦ λειπόμενος. μονόστολος, 'journeying alone': each part of the word is equivalent to a separate epithet: cf. Soph. O. C. 1055 τὰς διστόλους ἀδελφάς, 'two journeying sisters': and Jebb's n. on O. T. 846.

413. ἀνόνατ' ἐνύμφευσας: cf. El. 507 ἀνόνητ' ἔθρεψας σοί τε καὶ τοῖς σοῖς φίλοις; Hipp. 1145 μᾶτερ, ἔτεκες ἀνόνατα: Hec. 766: supr. 335. ἐνύμφευσας, cf. supr. 317, n.

γήρως τέλος, 'full measure of years': cf. Med. 920 ἴδοιμι δ' ὑμᾶς εὐτραφεῖς ἥβης τέλος | μολόντας, 'full measure of youth.'

417. This is the usual line of choric consolation: cf. infr. 892, 931. Hipp. 835 (to Theseus, discovering Phaedra's death) οὐ σοὶ τάδ' ὦναξ ἦλθε δὴ μόνῳ κακά· | πολλῶν μετ' ἄλλων δ' ὤλεσας κεδνὸν λέχος. Soph. El. 154 οὔτοι σοὶ μούνᾳ, τέκνον, ἄχος ἐφάνη βροτῶν. Hel. 464: Andr. 841. Cicero (Tusc. III. 33, 79) refers to the *usitata consolatio*, '*non tibi hoc soli*.'

τι emphasizes the negative: 'for not by any means art thou the first, nor wilt thou be the last to lose a worthy wife': cf. supr. 210.

418. ἤμπλακες, supr. 242.

419. Repeated by Heracles infr. 782. Andr. 1272 πᾶσιν γὰρ ἀνθρώποισιν ἥδε πρὸς θεῶν | ψῆφος κέκρανται κατθανεῖν τ' ὀφείλεται. So Horace, Ars Poet. 63 *debemur morti nos nostraque*.

421. **προσέπτατ'**, 'has swooped down upon me,' used of the sudden falling of unexpected evils: cf. Soph. Aj. 282 τίς γάρ ποτ' ἀρχὴ τοῦ κακοῦ προσέπτατο; Aesch. P. V. 662 θεόσσυτον χειμῶνα...ὅθεν μοι προσέπτατο. ἐπτάμην is un-Attic, and borrowed from Homer by the Tragedians, along with ἔπτην. The Attic forms are πέτομαι, ἐπετόμην, πτήσομαι, ἐπτόμην, πεπότημαι. Cobet, V. L. pp. 305—307.

ἐτειρόμην πάλαι, 'I had long been tortured.' Hadl. Gr. Gr. § 826. So Latin *iamdudum*, e.g. Ovid, Met. III. 656 *iamdudum flebam*, 'I had long been weeping.'

422. **ἀλλὰ...γάρ**: here, as very frequently, there is no ellipse: 'but, since I am about to celebrate the funeral, do ye remain': cf. Hec. 724 ἀλλ' εἰσορῶ γὰρ τοῦδε δεσπότου δέμας | Ἀγαμέμνονος, τοὐνθένδε σιγῶμεν, φίλαι. Sometimes the expression is elliptical, e.g. Soph. El. 595 ἀλλ' οὐ γὰρ οὐδὲ νουθετεῖν ἔξεστί σε· 'but (I will say no more), for I may not even give thee counsel.' The **ἐκφορά** properly took place on the third day after death, the day following the πρόθεσις (cf. supr. 86, n.): cf. Leg. ap. Dem. (adv. Mac.) 1071 ἐκφέρειν δὲ τὸν ἀποθανόντα τῇ ὑστεραίᾳ, ᾗ ἂν προθῶνται, πρὶν ἥλιον ἐξέχειν.

424. **παιᾶνα.** A παιάν was properly a hymn sung, with shouts of ἰώ Παιάν, to the 'Averters' of evil, Apollo and Artemis; but the use was extended to include songs of praise addressed to other gods, notably Ares: its character remained however triumphant and joyful, and it is only by a sort of euphemism or an *oxymoron* that it can be applied to strains of lamentation: cf. Aesch. Cho. 151 ὑμᾶς δὲ κωκυτοῖς ἐπανθίζειν νόμος | παιᾶνα τοῦ θανόντος ἐξανδωμένας. Theb. 869 Ἅιδᾳ τ' ἐχθρὸν παιᾶν' ἐπιμέλπειν (where Paley notes that the epithet is used because the Paean is properly a song of joy). A similar *oxymoron* is found Tro. 1230 νεκρῶν ἴακχον.

κάτωθεν simply = κάτω: so frequently ἄνωθεν, ἔσωθεν = ἄνω, ἔσω: cf. Lat. *stare ab aliquo.* Soph. Ant. 521 τίς οἶδεν εἰ κάτωθεν ('in the nether world') εὐαγῆ τάδε; The termination seems to denote the *quarter whence* a person or thing comes.

ἀσπόνδῳ, 'inexorable,' 'unappeasable by libations.' The word heightens the force of παιᾶνα, as paeans were properly addressed to gods who delighted in and required the accompaniment of drink-offerings.

425. For the reversal of this order, cf. infr. 1154.

426. **γυναικός,** objective genit. **λέγω** = κελεύω, as often: cf. Ion 666 ὑμῖν δὲ σιγᾶν, δμωίδες, λέγω τάδε. H. F. 332 οἴγειν κλῇθρα προσπόλοις λέγω.

427. Cf. Hel. 1087 ἐγὼ δ' ἐς οἴκους βᾶσα βοστρύχους τεμῶ | πέπλων τε λευκῶν μέλανας ἀνταλλάξομαι: I. A. 1437 μήτ' οὖν γε τὸν σὸν πλόκαμον ἐκτέμῃς τριχός, | μήτ' ἀμφὶ σῶμα μέλανας ἀμπίσχῃ πέπλους. Pericles boasted οὐδεὶς δι' ἐμὲ τῶν ὄντων Ἀθηναίων μέλαν ἱμάτιον περιεβάλετο (Plut. Per. 38). An instance of horse-cropping is reported by Herod. (IX. 24): Mardonius and the army in grief for Masistius σφέας τε αὐτοὺς ἔκειρον καὶ τοὺς ἵππους καὶ τὰ ὑποζύγια, οἰμωγῇ χρεώμενοι ἀπλέτῳ. Alexander the Great gave a similar order on the death of Hephaestion.

428. The ἄμπυξ was a frontlet, drawn across a horse's forehead, often richly jewelled: cf. the Homeric χρυσάμπυκας ἵππους: **μονάμπυκας** here is merely a poetic variant for **μόνας** (mares were in higher esteem than horses), the latter part of the compound serving to call up the picture of a richly-caparisoned steed. Many Greek adjectives are similarly suggestive: perhaps we may refer them to the class mentioned supr. 406, n. regarding the compound as equivalent to two separate epithets. Cf. Merry's n. on Od. IV. 458.

429. **φόβην** of a horse's mane, as Soph. fr. 587, 10 (of a clipped mare) πενθοῦσα καὶ κλάουσα τὴν πάρος φόβην.

430. Cf. supr. 345, n. 'Let there be no sound of flute or lyre throughout the city for the waning of twelve moons.' Ovid speaks more precisely (Met. VII. 530) *dumque quater iunctis explevit cornibus orbem | luna, quater plenum tenuata retexuit orbem.*

431. **σελήνας** = 'months': cf. Tro. 1075 Φρυγῶν τε ζάθεοι σελᾶναι συνδώδεκα πλήθει: accus. of duration of time.

432. **νεκρὸν ... φίλτερον ... ἀμείνονα**: as supr. 360 Admetus had spoken of his wife, though still alive, as dead, so here he speaks of her, though now dead, as alive. The adjectives would be grotesque if applied strictly to νεκρόν, which we must regard as = 'she, who here lies dead.'

434. **μόνη** is added as a kind of after-thought. 'For she has died for me, aye, when none other would.'

436. 'Farewell I bid thee (μοι), and may'st thou fare well even as handmaid in thy (τόν) sunless home in Hades' palace.' For **χαίρουσα**, cf. supr. 272, n. **μοι**, ethic dative.

εἰν = ἐν, cf. supr. 232, n. **οἰκετεύοις**, apparently a ἅπαξ λεγόμενον: formed from οἰκέτης, which = a member of the household other than the master. For the wish, cf. Hom. Il. XXIII. 179 **χαῖρέ μοι, ὦ Πάτροκλε, καὶ εἰν Ἀίδαο δόμοισιν.**

439. On this and the following lines, cf. supr. 252, n.: compare also supr. 361 where ἐπὶ κώπῃ ψυχοπομπὸς Χάρων echo ἐπὶ κώπᾳ νεκροπομπὸς γέρων here. The monotony of these pictures bears out the remarks in the note on supr. 364.

442. For the repetition of πολὺ δή, cf. supr. 328, n. γυναῖκα... λίμναν...πορεύσας: the constr. with double accus. recurs Soph. Tr. 559 ὅς τὸν βαθύρρουν ποταμὸν Εὔηνον βροτοὺς | μισθοῦ ’πόρευε χερσίν: λίμναν is accus. of space traversed: though, as Prof. Jebb points out, it would more naturally denote the place *to which*, as in Tro. 1085 ἐμὲ σκάφος...πορεύσει Ἄργος.

443. πορεύσας is strictly applicable to Charon only, to whom also it grammatically refers, but in the task of transference from the upper to the nether world he is assisted by Thanatos, who is I think the 'swart Hades' of line 439 and supr. 261.

444. ἐλάτᾳ, like Lat. *abies*, *pinus*,=a ship: cf. Phoen. 208 Ἰόνιον κατὰ πόντον ἐλάτᾳ πλεύσασα.

445. πολλά, 'oft-times'; cf. supr. 187. μουσοπόλοι, 'servants of the Muses,' poets, that is. It is generally an adjective: for the form, cf. θαλαμηπόλος, πρόσπολος, αἰπόλος, βουκόλος (π = κ by labialism), in all of which the idea of 'service' appears.

446. ἑπτάτονον, 'seven-stringed.' The invention of the seven-stringed lyre was attributed to Hermes (Hom. h. Herm. 51) ἑπτὰ δὲ συμφώνους ὀΐων ἐτανύσσατο χορδάς, though Terpander of Lesbos claimed the honour of having enlarged the range of the instrument by increasing the number of strings from four to seven. The latter, the acknowledged parent of Greek music, settled early in life at Sparta, where he won the prize for music in the first contest of the description introduced into the festival in honour of Apollo Carneius, in the year (so it is stated) B.C. 676. He founded there a school of musicians, members of which were uninterruptedly successful at the Carneia down to B.C. 550, and to him were ascribed all the standard melodies employed on solemn occasions. His hold on the conservative Spartans was so great, that when Euripides' celebrated contemporary, Timotheus of Miletus, appeared as a competitor at the Carneia with his newly-invented eleven-stringed lyre, an outraged Ephor seizing his instrument cut away the offensive surplusage of chords. The florid performances of Timotheus, though at first hissed off the Athenian stage, finally, as Euripides predicted they would, acquired the greatest popularity. Cf. supr. 345, n.

ὀρείαν, cf. h. Herm. 33 χέλυς ὄρεσι ζώουσα: 42 ὀρεσκῴοιο χελώνης. The familiar European tortoise (*testudo Graeca*), common on the eastern shores of the Mediterranean, is referred to.

447. ἐν ἀλύροις κλέοντες ὕμνοις: probably unaccompanied recitation is meant: κλέω (Hom. κλείω, but κλέομαι) is used specially of recitations of bards, e.g. Od. I. 338 ἔργ᾽ ἀνδρῶν τε θεῶν τε, τά τε κλείουσιν ἀοιδοί. Arist. (Rhet. III. 6, 7) gives as an instance of 'description by means of negatives' ἄλυρον μέλος, by which is denoted the music, but music without the usual instrument (the lyre), of the trumpet: somewhat similar is Theognis' φόρμιγξ ἄχορδος for a 'bow.'

449. περινίσσεται κύκλον, 'cometh round on circling course.' κύκλον is cognate accusative. The festival of Apollo Carneius was celebrated in Sparta and other Doric states (Cyrene, Thera etc.) in the month of August (Μεταγειτνιών in the Attic, Καρνεῖος in the Laconian calendar). It seems to have been a warlike festival (μίμημα στρατιωτικῆς ἀγωγῆς, Athen. IV. 141), though musical contests were held: cf. n. on supr. 446. The worship of Apollo Carneius in the Peloponnese was probably of pre-Dorian origin.

450. 'When the moon hangeth aloft the livelong night,' as it would do when at the full: at which time, the scholiast tells us, the festival was held: it began on the 7th and lasted till the 16th, thus including the διχομήνιδες ἑσπέραι (Pind. Isth. VII. 44).

452. λιπαραί was a stock epithet of Athens among poets from Pindar onwards: cf. Pind. fr. 46 ὦ ταὶ λιπαραὶ καὶ ἰοστέφανοι καὶ ἀοίδιμοι, | Ἑλλάδος ἔρεισμα, κλειναὶ Ἀθᾶναι, | δαιμόνιον πτολίεθρον (and the allusion, Ar. Ach. 637 οἱ πρέσβεις ἐξαπατῶντες | πρῶτον μὲν ἰοστεφάνους ἐκάλουν, at which the Athenians could hardly keep their seats for pride: εἰ δέ τις ὑμᾶς ὑποθωπεύσας λιπαρὰς καλέσειεν Ἀθήνας, the speaker could get anything he asked for). Pindar uses λιπαραί of Athens also Nem. IV. 18: Isth. II. 20. So Tro. 803 λιπαραῖσί τε κόσμον Ἀθήναις: I. T. 1130. Pindar uses the same adjective with reference to Naxos and Thebes.

453. τοίαν, cf. supr. 65, n. μελέων ἀοιδοῖς, cf. Her. 403 χρησμῶν ἀοιδούς. H. F. 110 γόων ἀοιδός.

455. εἴθ᾽ ἐπ᾽ ἐμοὶ εἴη: observe that this is the form of a *future* wish, though we might have expected the form implying *non-fulfilment*, namely, a past indicative tense. Prof. Goodwin (M. T. § 740) says: 'it is the *futurity* of the object of a wish, and not its *probability* or *possibility*, that requires the optative. No amount of absurdity or extravagance in a future wish can make anything but the optative

proper in expressing it.' In English an equivalent turn of expression would be 'O for the power, etc.' ἐπ' ἐμοί, 'within my power.'

456. πέμψαι, 'escort': usually of escorting *to* Hades (cf. Ἑρμῆs ὁ πέμπων, Soph. Phil. 133); for a similar use to the present, cf. Hom. Od. XI. 625 τὸν (Cerberus) μὲν ἐγὼν (Heracles) ἀνένεικα καὶ ἤγαγον ἐξ Ἀίδαο· | Ἑρμείας δέ μ' ἔπεμψεν ἰδὲ γλαυκῶπις Ἀθήνη.

457. φάος, acc. of goal, not uncommon after πέμπω in poetry: cf. infr. 479; Soph. O. C. 1770 Θήβας δ' ἡμᾶς πέμψον: cf. supr. 8, n. τεράμνων, a word apparently used only by Euripides.

459. ποτ. νερτ. τε κώπᾳ, 'by the bark that plies upon the nether stream.' κώπᾳ, the part for the whole. Eurip. cannot rid himself of the word: cf. supr. 439, n.

460. μόνα, though vocative, must virtually be taken with ἔτλας. The construction, though slightly irregular, is very natural. φίλα γυναικῶν, as Hipp. 849: cf. δῖα γυναικῶν, Od. IV. 305: φίλ' ἀνδρῶν, Theocr. XV. 74: πότνα θεῶν, Bacch. 370. σύ repeated: cf. supr. 328, n.

461. σύ echoed in the antistrophe 471: more striking is the correspondence of 464, ἦ μάλ' ἂν ἔμοιγ' ἂν εἴη and 474 ἦ γὰρ ἂν ἔμοιγ' ἄλυπος.

462. ἀντί, cf. supr. 282, 340, n. The connexion is, 'O for the power to redeem thee from Hades, even as thou didst redeem thy husband.'

463. Cf. Hel. 851 εἰ γάρ εἰσιν οἱ θεοὶ σοφοί, | εὔψυχον ἄνδρα πολεμίων θανόνθ' ὕπο | κούφῃ καταμπίσχουσιν ἐν τύμβῳ χθονί, | κακοὺς δ' ἐφ' ἕρμα στερεὸν ἐκβάλλουσι γῆς. Martial v. 34, 9 (lines on the death of a favourite little slave-girl) *mollia non rigidus cespes tegat ossa, nec illi,* | *terra, gravis fueris: non fuit illa tibi. Sit tibi terra levis* was the usual *requiescat in pace* of the Roman: s. t. t. l. was often engraved on the *cippus:* cf. Persius I. 37 ('is not the poet now happier in his grave?') *non levior cippus nunc imprimit ossa?* We may contrast Dr Evans' epitaph on Vanbrugh, 'lie heavy on him, earth, for he | laid many a heavy load on thee.'

464. ἔμοιγ': the dative of the agent is rarely found, except with perf. and pluperf. pass.: cf. Hadl. Gr. Gr. § 769. εἴη στυγηθείς, cf. supr. 122, n.

468. δέμας, of the *living* body, is appropriate to the context: cf. supr. 348.

A line has dropped out after πατρὸς γεραιοῦ, corresponding to

supr. 458: it may have been of some such form and meaning as κατ-
θανεῖν σύ γ᾽ ἐτόλμας. If so, Euripides has said the same thing twice
over, slightly varying the expression, 466—468 and 469—472: such
repetition is frequent.

469. ῥύεσθαι, supr. 11.

470. πολ. ἔχοντε χ., 'though their heads were hoar.' The use of
the dual calls attention in a special way to the pair of culprits.

472. φωτός, 'husband': cf. Soph. Tr. 177 εἴ με (Deianira) χρὴ
μένειν | πάντων ἀρίστου φωτὸς (Heracles) ἐστερημένην. Ant. 910.

εἴη μοι κῦρσαι. A slip on the poet's part: the wish is strangely
unsuited to the age of the πρεσβῦται, of whom the chorus is composed.
In these four concluding lines we may imagine that Euripides' thoughts
are prompted by his own sad experiences of married life, which seem to
have begun early and to have lasted long. It is probable enough that
the serious and abstracted poet-philosopher (στρυφνὸς καὶ μισογέλως like
his master Anaxagoras, who φασὶ μὴ γελῶντά ποτε ὀφθῆναι μηδὲ μειδιῶντα
τὴν ἀρχήν. Ael. V. H. VIII. 13) was as a husband difficult.

κῦρσαι: this verb is found only in poetry and late prose: never in
Attic prose or comedy (except, of course, in parody).

473. συνδυάδος: the adjective occurs here only, but the verb is
particularly common in Aristotle.

τὸ: cf. supr. 190, n., 264, n.

474. σπάνιον μέρος: very similar was the view of Simonides of
Amorgus, who gives nine classes of bad, but one only of good wives:
for the latter he reserves all his praise, nor does he stint it: the good
woman is like the bee, he says. τήν τις εὐτυχεῖ λαβών, | κείνῃ γὰρ οἴῃ
μῶμος οὐ προσιζάνει | θάλλει δ᾽ ὑπ᾽ αὐτῆς κἀπαέξεται βίος· | φίλη δὲ σὺν
φιλεῦντι γηράσκει πόσι, | τεκοῦσα καλὸν κοὐνομάκλυτον γένος· | κἀριπρεπὴς
μὲν ἐν γυναιξὶ γίγνεται | πάσῃσι, θείη δ᾽ ἀμφιδέδρομεν χάρις. (Bergk-
Hiller, p. 21). Eurip. seems to have had the older poet in his thoughts
when he wrote (I. A. 1158) συμμαρτυρήσεις (Clytaemnestra addresses
Agamemnon) ὡς ἄμεμπτος ἦν γυνή, | ...καὶ τὸ σὸν | μέλαθρον αὔξουσ᾽,
ὥστε σ᾽ εἰσιόντα τε | χαίρειν θύραζέ τ᾽ ἐξιόντ᾽ εὐδαιμονεῖν. | σπάνιον δὲ
θήρευμ᾽ ἀνδρὶ τοιαύτην λαβεῖν | δάμαρτα· φλαύραν δ᾽ οὐ σπάνις γυναῖκ᾽
ἔχειν. Notice the echo of supr. 464. For ἂν duplicated, cf. supr. 96, n.

476. κωμῆται Φεραίας χθονός: κώμη is an unwalled country town,
so Heracles, when saluting them as κωμῆται, addresses them as inhabit-
ants of the district (χθονός) only, not necessarily denizens of the Φεραῖον
ἄστυ (infr. 480).

477. **ἅρα**, cf. supr. 228, n. **κιγχάνω** is the form used by the Tragedians : κἰχάνω is Epic.

479. **χθόνα**, cf. supr. 457, n.

480. **προσβῆναι** is an infin. of *result* (not *purpose*), rarely found in Attic without ὥστε : cf. Goodw. Gr. Gr. § 265, note.

481. **Τιρυνθίῳ Εὐρυσθεῖ** : Sthenelus, King of Argos, father of Eurystheus, expelled Amphitryon, husband of Alcmena, heiress of Electryon, King of Tiryns, and assumed the sovereignty of Tiryns himself. Hence Eurystheus is both Argive and Tirynthian. Tiryns is but a few miles distant from Argos. **πόνον.** This was the eighth labour : cf. H. F. 380 sq.

482. **συνέζευξαι** : cf. Hipp. 1389 οἵαις συμφοραῖς συνεζύγης : Hel. 262 τίνι πότμῳ συνεζύγην ;

483. **τέτρωρον ἅρμα**, 'the four-horse team' : for ἅρματα = 'the horses' that draw the car, cf. supr. 66, n. ἅρματα means 'chariot and horses,' or 'chariot-horses.'

μέτα, 'after' in the sense of 'to fetch' : cf. supr. 46, n.

484. **μῶν** = *num* : ' Surely you are not unacquainted with him ?'

485. **Βιστόνων.** The Bistones were a Thracian tribe, dwelling near lake Bistonis, in the district where tradition stated that Heracles founded the city of Abdera, in honour of his friend Abderus, who assisted the hero in this enterprise at the cost of his life. As a fact, however, Abdera seems to have been colonized first from Clazomenae, and subsequently, in B.C. 541, from Teos. Roman poets occasionally refer to Thracians generally as Bistones : cf. Hor. Od. II. 19, 20 ; Sen. (?) Herc. 1900.

487. **ἀλλ' οὐδ' κ.τ.λ.** 'You may not,' say the chorus, 'make yourself master of the mares without a struggle.' 'But neither,' retorts Heracles, 'may I decline my toils.' Cf. H.F. 1354 ὧν (πόνων) οὔτ' ἀπεῖπον οὐδέν, οὔτ' ἀπ' ὀμμάτων | ἔσταξα πηγάς (Heracles is speaking). Supp. 343 (Theseus says) οὐκοῦν ἀπαυδᾶν δυνατόν ἐστί μοι πόνους.

488. **ἥξεις**, equivalent to 'return hither': cf. infr. 1153. Hermann compares Ion 1038 οὔποθ' ἵξεται | κλεινὰς Ἀθήνας, κατθανὼν δ' αὐτοῦ μενεῖ.

489. 'I should not then for the first time be competing in a struggle for my life.' This metaphorical use of δραμεῖν ἀγῶνα is frequent : cf. Or. 878 Ὀρέστην κεῖνον οὐχ ὁρᾷς πέλας | στείχοντ', ἀγῶνα θανάσιμον δραμούμενον ; (Orestes on trial for matricide). El. 1264 ἐνταῦθα καὶ σὲ δεῖ δραμεῖν φόνου πέρι (of Orestes' trial before the Areopagus). Herod.

VIII. 102 ἦν γὰρ σύ (Xerxes) τε περιῇς καὶ οἶκος ὁ σός, πολλοὺς πολλάκις ἀγῶνας δραμέονται περὶ σφέων αὐτῶν οἱ Ἕλληνες (Artemisia's advice to Xerxes to leave Mardonius in Greece and himself return to Persia).

490. πλέον λάβοις, cf. supr. 72, n. The mares will still be as difficult to overcome when their owner is laid low.

493. εἰ μή γε κ.τ.λ., 'an easy task, unless indeed from their nostrils they breathe forth flames,' which as a fact they did: a clumsy use of irony.

494. 'But 'tis men's flesh they tear in their ravening jaws.' ἀρταμεῖν properly = 'to cut in pieces' like a cook: cf. El. 816 ταῦρον ἀρταμεῖ καλῶς.

496. ἴδοις ἄν, 'thou wilt see': there is no conscious feeling of any *definite* condition, and thus the sense is but slightly removed from mere futurity.

αἵμασιν: the plural is found nine times in Eurip., eight times in Aesch., but once only (Ant. 121) in Soph. Euripides employs it in the sense of 'bloodshed' in lyric passages only: when used in senarii it means 'blood-gouts': cf. El. 1172 ἀλλ' οἵδε μητρὸς νεοφόνοισιν αἵμασι | πεφυρμένοι βαίνουσιν ἐξ οἴκων πόδα. I. T. 73 (Orestes asks) καὶ βωμός, Ἕλλην οὗ καταστάζει φόνος; (to which Pylades replies) ἐξ αἱμάτων γοῦν ξάνθ' ἔχει θριγκώματα.

497. κομπάζεται, passive. 'As son of what sire is he bruited abroad who reared them?'

498. The principal seats of the worship of Ares were in Thrace and Scythia: it was to Thrace that he betook himself after his disgrace at Hephaestos' hands (Hom. Od. VIII. 361), and Herodotus tells us (IV. 59) that he only of the gods was honoured by the Scythians with temples and statues. In Hellas Ares was not a favourite, nor do we find him frequently figured in works of art: a statue by Alcamenes (circ. B.C. 400) at Athens, and another by the later Scopas, probably brought to Rome B.C. 136 from Pergamum, were the only noteworthy representations of the god, whose worship seems to have been of Thracian origin.

ζαχρύσου refers to the gold-decked arms of the Thracian tribes, who dwelt near the rich gold district, which lay between the Strymon and the Nestus: these mines, though known in early times, were first properly worked by Philip of Macedon, who received nearly a quarter of a million a year from them. ζάχρυσος is (like ζάθεος, ζαπληθής, ζαχρεῖος), an Ionic form.

πέλτης ἄναξ. The πέλτη was a light leather-covered shield without a metallic rim, in common use among the Thracians, from whom it was borrowed for the equipment of the light-armed troops (peltasts), of which we first hear during the Peloponnesian war. Iphicrates trained these troops to great proficiency, and with them performed notable exploits. ἄναξ probably = 'master of,' i.e. proficient in the use of : cf. Cycl. 86 ὁρῶ πρὸς ἀκταῖς ναὸς Ἑλλάδος σκάφος | κώπης τ' ἄνακτας. Aesch. Pers. 378 πᾶς ἀνὴρ κώπης ἄναξ. It is possible that πέλτη here means a body of peltasts (so ἀσπίς, Phoen. 78 πολλὴν ἀθροίσας ἀσπίδ' Ἀργείων ἄγει), and this interpretation is favoured by fr. 700 κώπης ἀνάσσων κἀποβὰς εἰς Μυσίαν (of the piratical Achilles making a descent on the coasts of Mysia).

499. τοὐμοῦ δαίμονος, a sort of genit. of origin : 'arising from my destiny.'

500. σκληρός : cf. Antiph. tetr. γ 4 τῇ δὲ σκληρότητι τοῦ δαίμονος ὀρρωδῶ μὴ κ.τ.λ. The metaphor is from a rough up-hill (πρὸς αἶπος ἔρχεται) road : ὁ δαίμων οὐδέποτέ μοι εὐοδεῖ says the scholiast : cf. Plat. Rep. 364 D τῆς δ' ἀρετῆς ἱδρῶτα θεοὶ προπάροιθεν ἔθηκαν καί τινα ὁδὸν μακράν τε καὶ ἀνάντη.

501. πᾶσιν, a natural exaggeration. Of Lycaon we know nothing, but we learn from Hesiod (Scut. Her. 413 sq.) that Heracles, after slaying Cycnus, drove his angry father back to Olympus with a wounded thigh.

503. ἔρχομαι συμβαλών, 'am on my way to engage.'

506. τρέσαντα : this verb is almost entirely confined to poetry.

507. καὶ μήν, introducing a fresh arrival ; when thus used γε does not follow. ὅδ', cf. supr. 136, n. Cf. Soph. O. T. 531 αὐτὸς δ' ὅδ' ἤδη δωμάτων ἔξω περᾷ.

509. 'Son of Zeus and sprung of Perseus' stock.' Alcmena was grand-daughter of Perseus.

511. θέλοιμ' ἄν, sc. χαίρειν : for the double meaning, cf. supr. 272, n.

512. τί χρῆμα ; 'why ?' a rarer use than the common τί χρῆμα = 'what ?' Cf. El. 831 τί χρῆμ' ἀθυμεῖς ; πρέπεις, 'art thou conspicuous ?' Cf. infr. 1050.

513. θάπτειν : either pres. or fut. infin. (not aor.) should follow μέλλειν : cf. Rutherford N. P. p. 420.

514. ἀπ' οὖν κ.τ.λ. The force of οὖν seems to be, 'if that is so, then I hope, etc.'

516.   γε μήν, 'however': cf. Aesch. Ag. 1378 ἦλθε, σὺν χρόνῳ γε μήν.

ὡραῖος, 'ripe for death.'   εἴπερ, 'if, as I surmise.'

517.   ἔστι, 'lives.'

518.   'Surely, 'tis not thy wife Alcestis who is dead?'

519.   'Twofold is the story I have to tell of her.'   Heracles is intended to take this in the sense that she is both alive, and (since doomed) in a manner dead.   The audience, however, would see that by διπλοῦς μῦθος Admetus means one story for those who know the facts, another for Heracles.

520.   θανούσης ἢ ζώσης: cf. supr. 141 : 'do you speak *about* her as alive or dead': a genit. of reference: cf. Soph. El. 317 τοῦ κασιγνήτου τί φής; Phil. 439 ἀναξίου μὲν φωτὸς ἐξερήσομαι: Hom. Od. XI. 174 εἰπὲ δέ μοι πατρός τε καὶ υἱέος.   For εἶπας, cf. supr. 58, n.

521.   Cf. Hel. 138 τεθνᾶσι κοὐ τεθνᾶσι· δύο δ' ἐστὸν λόγω.

522.   Cf. Hipp. 344 οὐδέν τι μᾶλλον οἶδ' ἃ βούλομαι κλύειν.

523.   μοίρας is attracted to the case of the relative ἧς by *inverted assimilation*.   Goodw. Gr. Gr. § 153, 4.

524.   For the partic. ὑφειμένην after οἶδα (verb of knowing), cf. Goodw. Gr. Gr. § 280.

525.   ἤνεσεν, cf. supr. 2, n.

526.   ἃ expresses impatience, as supr. 28.   ἐς τότ', 'till then,' i.e. her death.   The phrase follows the analogy of εἰσότε, ἐς αὔριον, ἐς ἀεί, etc.   So εἰς πότε, Soph. Aj. 1185 : ἐς οὗ even, Herod. I. 67.

527.   Admetus explains the οὐκέτ' ἔστιν of line 521.   τέθνηχ' means 'is as good as dead': cf. infr. 666.

528.   χωρίς, 'of different nature': cf. Soph. O. C. 808 χωρὶς τό τ' εἰπεῖν πολλὰ καὶ τὰ καίρια.   Aesch. P. V. 927 ὅσον τό τ' ἄρχειν καὶ τὸ δουλεύειν δίχα.   Very similar is Tro. 628 οὐ ταὐτὸν ὦ παῖ τῷ βλέπειν τὸ κατθανεῖν: cf. too the celebrated couplet (fr. 639) τίς δ' οἶδεν εἰ τὸ ζῆν μέν ἐστι κατθανεῖν, | τὸ κατθανεῖν δὲ ζῆν κάτω νομίζεται;

529.   A polite form of agreeing to differ: somewhat rougher is the one quoted by Porson from Suidas, εἰ δὲ ἄλλος νοεῖ ἑτέρως, κρατείτω τῆς ἑαυτοῦ γνώμης, ἐμὲ δὲ μὴ ἐνοχλείτω.

530.   δῆτα implies slight impatience.   Heracles is tired of putting the courteously indirect questions with which he started, and comes straight to the point, τίς ὁ κατθανών;

531.   γυνή corrects the mistake in gender in the use of κατθανών : there is grim humour in the intentional word-play on γυνή, 'wife' or

'woman.' Probably there is a play also on μεμνήμεθα, 'I speak of' and 'I bethink me of.'

ἀρτίως is a word extensively used (some say coined) by Sophocles: it is found first in his plays, where it occurs nearly three times as often as ἄρτι, though Aesch. never uses it, and Eurip. on the whole slightly prefers ἄρτι. When used with a present tense (μέμνημαι has the force of a present in Attic) it refers to a moment *just* passed : cf. Soph. El. 347 ἥτις λέγεις μὲν ἀρτίως κ.τ.λ., 'who hast just said.' Eurip. prefers to use ἄρτι with present tenses, ἀρτίως with past.

532. ὀθνεῖος, 'strange to thy blood,' seems to occur only here and infr. 646 in tragedy.

533. ἄλλως, by other ties than blood. ἀναγκαία, 'connected,' Lat. *necessarius.*

535. ὠρφανεύετο, cf. supr. 165, n.

536. εἴθ᾽ ηὕρομεν, of an unattained wish : cf. Goodw. Gr. Gr. § 251, 2. Homeric Greek expresses unattained wishes by ὤφελον with infin.: the idiom in this passage is of later development. μὴ must from its position be taken with λυπούμενον, where οὐ would be regular, as expressing mere reversal of meaning : μὴ is due to the general feeling that the sentence as a whole presents a wish : cf. Hadl. Gr. Gr. § 1027.

537. ὑπορράπτεις : ὑπο- probably refers to the *concealed* intention: ῥάπτειν is always used of 'devices' disagreeable to the speaker.

540. λυπουμένοις ὀχληρός, sc. ἔστι : this line, then, is an instance of a *mixed* conditional sentence, where 'the present indicative in the apodosis *precedes*, containing a general statement, and the optative adds a remote future condition, where we should expect a general present supposition'; in other words εἰ πάρεστι would be usual here : had the εἰ-clause *preceded* we should have had the apodosis ἂν εἴη expressed : cf. Goodw. M. T. § 501.

541. ἀλλ᾽, the so-called *precative* use : cf. Soph. O. C. 1405 ὦ τοῦδ᾽ ὅμαιμοι παῖδες, ἀλλ᾽ ὑμεῖς...μή μ᾽ ἀτιμάσητε.

542. The lengthening of a naturally short syllable (παρὰ) before κλ- may be paralleled from El. 1058 ἆρα κλύουσα, but both lines are suspected : cf. crit. n.

543. ξενῶνες, 'guest-chambers': similarly formed are ἀνδρών, γυναικών, παρθενών, ἱστών (weaver's room), κοιτών, πυλών (door-keeper's room), μυλών (mill-house). There is no authority for ἀνώγεων: cf. Rutherford N. P. p. 358.

546. σύ, addressing a servant. τῷδε, Heracles. δωμάτων ἐξω-πίους, a favourite periphrasis of Euripides, the precise meaning of which ('out of sight of') must not be pressed: it merely=ἔξω with some further idea of detachment: it is also found in Med. 624, Supp. 1038. Aristophanes laughs at it, Thesm. 881 αὐτὸς δὲ Πρωτεὺς ἔνδον ἐστ᾽ ἢ 'ξώπιος; δωμάτων refers to the main block of the palace.

547. 'Give orders to those set over them (sc. the guest-chambers) that abundance of food be set before him': παρεῖναι is from πάρειμι in the sense of the Latin *praesto esse:* the scholiast explains by παρα-κεῖσθαι.

548. ἐν δέ, 'and withal': ἐν is adverbial: cf. Soph. O. T. 27 ἐν δ᾽ ὁ πυρφόρος θεὸς | σκήψας ἐλαύνει, λοιμὸς ἔχθιστος, πόλιν.

549. μεταύλους θύρας. In an ordinary large Athenian house the μέταυλος (or μέσαυλος) θύρα gave access from the first to the second court, from the peristyle, that is, of the andronitis to that of the gynaeconitis: here the expression is more vaguely used for the folding doors (θύραι) separating the range of guest-rooms from the palace. Heracles leaves the stage at l. 550.

552. τολμᾷς, cf. supr. 275, n.

τί μῶρος εἶ; 'what is this folly?' like *Galle, quid insanis?* Verg. Ecl. x. 22 (Monk).

553. εἰ ἀπήλασα ξένον μολόντα σφε, 'if I had chased him from my home and kingdom, though he had come as my guest.' Admetus and Heracles were bound by ties of mutual hospitality, like Glaucus and Diomede: Hom. Il. vi. 224 τῶ νῦν σοὶ μὲν ἐγὼ ξεῖνος φίλος Ἄργεϊ μέσσῳ | εἰμί, σὺ δ᾽ ἐν Λυκίῃ, ὅτε κεν τῶν δῆμον ἵκωμαι. It is just possible that Eurip. in his choice of words had in mind the Spartan ξενη-λασίαι.

555. 'My trouble would be no whit the less, my churlishness the more.'

557. Cf. infr. 1039.

560. Ἄργους διψίαν χθόνα. It is the eastern side of the Argive plain (called by Sophocles O. C. 378 τὸ κοῖλον Ἄργος, as except where it touches the sea it is mountain-girt) which justifies the epithet πολυ-δίψιον applied to it by Homer (Il. iv. 171): the west side is well-watered and fertile, in some places even marshy. One is tempted to add that Heracles found Thessaly διψία in his turn.

561. πῶς, 'how came you to,' i.e. 'why?' τὸν παρόντα δαίμονα, 'thy present fortune': cf. Soph. El. 76 ἐπείπερ εἶ | γενναῖος, ὡς ἰδόντι,

πλὴν τοῦ δαίμονος: fr. 58 μὴ σπεῖρε ('tell not abroad') πολλοῖς τὸν παρόντα δαίμονα.

565. 'I am aware' says Admetus 'that different people may hold different views of my conduct: to one person (τῷ μὲν) I appear foolish' (with οὐ φρονεῖν cf. τί μῶρος εἶ; supr. 552): strictly he should have added 'but to another (τῷ δέ), not so,' but the sentence runs into another form after the amplifying clause οὐδ' αἰνέσει με.

566. οὐκ ἐπίσταται, 'is incapable of': cf. Soph. Ant. 686 οὔτ' ἂν δυναίμην μήτ' ἐπισταίμην λέγειν.

568. πολύξεινος καὶ ἐλεύθερος ἀνδρὸς οἶκος = (by a not uncommon idiom) πολυξείνου καὶ ἐλευθέρου ἀνδρὸς οἶκος: cf. Hipp. 395 θυραῖα φρονή-ματ' ἀνδρῶν for φρ. θυραίων ἀνδρῶν. The master and his house are identified both in Admetus' speech (supr. 566), and by the chorus: note particularly infr. 570, 572, where σε refers to the house, σοῖσι to its master.

570. σέ τοι: for this use of τοι in earnest address, cf. Soph. Phil. 1095 σύ τοι, σύ τοι κατηξίωσας. Aj. 359 σέ τοι, σέ τοι μόνον δέδορκα πημονῶν ἐπ' ἄρκος ὄντ'.

571. ἠξίωσε, 'deigned': cf. Soph. O. T. 1413 ἀξιώσατ' ἀνδρὸς ἀθλίου θιγεῖν: ἀξιοῦν, like τολμᾶν and τλῆναι (cf. supr. 275 n.), expresses a variety of meanings according to the context, all however derived from the root idea 'think fit.'

572. μηλονόμας, like infr. 577 ποιμνίτας, is found here only in classical Greek. These forms in -as are very characteristic of Attic lyrics.

575. 'Through the winding slopes': δόχμιος occurs also infr. 1000, Or. 1261.

576. On the σῦριγξ, cf. supr. 346, n. 'Piping the shepherds' loves,' the ordinary theme of pastoral poetry.

579. σὺν δ', adverbial: the point of ἐποιμαίνοντο is that properly it can be applied to *tame* animals only: 'there came herded for joy of thy strains.'

580. After βαλιαί τε λύγκες we should expect ἅ τε δαφοινὸς ἴλα λεόντων, joint subjects to ἐποιμαίνοντο: but, as often, Eurip. changes the turn of the sentence. Some would read ἔβα τε quite unnecessarily: the form of sentence changes to one where contrast is more appropriate than enumeration: cf. Soph. Tr. 143 (and Jebb's n.).

Ὄθρυος: the lions came a long way, as Othrys is between 30 and 40 miles south of Pherae. Herodotus (VII. 125) tells the story of the attack made by lions on the camels of Xerxes' army in the march through Macedonia: he adds that lions and long-horned wild oxen are common there, but that lions are never found in Europe east of the Nestus or west of the Achelous. This statement is repeated by Aristotle and Pliny. Pausanias (VI. 5), after telling the story of the camels, recounts the achievement of Polydamas of Scotussa (near Pherae), who emulating Heracles slew a huge lion on the slopes of Olympus: οὕτω πολλάκις, he adds, οἱ λέοντες καὶ ἐς τὴν περὶ τὸν Ὄλυμπον πλανῶνται χώραν. Vergil introduces lions and lynxes into his pastorals, Ecl. V. 27; VIII. 3.

581. **ἵλα**: the force is much the same as in σὺν δ' ἐποιμαίνοντο. The usually solitary lions formed a 'tawny herd.' **δαφοινὸς** is a Homeric word, found also in Aesch. P. V. 1022, of an eagle.

582. **χόρευσε**: the augment is frequently dropped in lyrical passages: cf. infr. 598 δέξατο: rarely in senarii (occasionally in the course of a long ῥῆσις). **ἀμφί**, 'about' in a local sense. **κιθάραν**, the natural instrument of εὐλύρας Ἀπόλλων, though above (576) he piped to the flocks.

585. **πέραν ἐλατᾶν**: though timorous, they ventured out of cover. πέρα = ultra, at a point beyond, on the other side; hence of exceeding due limit, where the line is already passed: πέραν = trans, to a point on the other side, emphasizing the intervening space: most frequently used with reference to the sea: here 'to a point on the other (seen from within cover) side of the tall firs.' **σφυρῷ κούφῳ**, 'on nimble pastern.'

587. **μολπᾷ**, not necessarily of the voice: cf. Soph. Phil. 214 οὐ μολπὰν σύριγγος ἔχων.

588. **τοιγάρ**, by reason of Apollo's protection. **πολυμηλοτάταν**, an old-world epithet, recalling the times when wealth was flocks and herds. According to Leake this district still keeps up its ancient reputation.

590. **Βοιβίαν λίμναν**, usually Βοιβηΐς, a narrow lake about 20 miles long, near whose southern shores lay Pherae, while Ossa towered high to the northwards (Ossaea Boebeis, Lucan VII. 176): modern Karla. It is mentioned in the Iliad in connexion with Eumelus (II. 711) οἳ δὲ Φερὰς ἐνέμοντο παραὶ Βοιβηΐδα λίμνην, | ...τῶν ἦρχ' Ἀδμήτοιο φίλος πάις ἕνδεκα νηῶν, | Εὔμηλος, τὸν ὑπ' Ἀδμήτῳ τέκε δῖα γυναικῶν | Ἄλκηστις. **ἀρότοις γυᾶν**, arable land: **πεδίων δαπέδοις**, pasture: γύης is a measure of arable land. δάπεδον is a flat surface: Attic ἔδαφος.

592. 'As the limit in the region of the Sun's dark stabling (the west) he sets the Molossian clime.' **ὅρον** = 'landmark,' generally a stone.

594. **αἰθέρα** (fem., as always in Homer and often in Eurip.), 'clime': so only in this passage. The Molossians lived 50 or 60 miles westward in Epirus: they were one of the three most powerful Epirot tribes, a rough pastoral people famous for their dogs and horses.

595. 'While towards the wave-swept rock-bound coast of the Aegean (i.e. eastwards) he is lord of Pelion.' The reference is to the rocky coast of Magnesia; on it the east wind drove the fleet of Xerxes: cf. Herod. VII. 188.

596. **κρατύνει**='is lord,' c. genit.: cf. Soph. O. T. 14 ὦ κρατύνων Οἰδίπους χώρας ἐμῆς: its usual meaning is to 'strengthen.' Pelion is his ὅρος eastwards.

597. **καὶ νῦν**, 'now too,' for Heracles, as once for Apollo.

598. **νοτερῷ βλεφάρῳ**, 'though with tear-stained eyes.'

601. Specially characteristic of the innate nobility of mind of the well-born is an almost exaggerated (ἐκφέρεται) regard for the feelings of others (αἰδῶ). In ἐκφέρεται there is some idea of excess: here it may be represented by our colloquial 'go out of one's way' to do a thing, do more than is necessary. The meaning is derived from the use of ἐκφέρεσθαι to denote being turned or driven from a direct course, of a chariot or ship: cf. Soph. El. 628 πρὸς ὀργὴν ἐκφέρει says Electra to her mother.

602. The connexion is 'but after all it may be the truest wisdom.' The chorus remember their hasty τί μῶρος εἶ; (supr. 552). **πάντα σοφίας**=the whole of wisdom; we may compare Cic. Fin. III. 7, 24 omnes numeros virtutis continet. **ἄγαμαι**, 'I marvel.'

604. 'But I have a sure trust abiding at my heart.'

605. **κεδνὰ πράξειν**=καλῶς πράξειν: cf. Tro. 683 οὐδὲ κλέπτομαι φρένας ('am cheated into believing') | πράξειν τι κεδνόν.

606. 'Ye men of Pherae who are kindly present.' **εὐμενὴς παρουσία**=εὐμενῶς παρόντες: cf. Soph. El. 418 λόγος τις αὐτήν ἐστιν εἰσιδεῖν πατρὸς | ...δευτέραν ὁμιλίαν, where πατ. ὁμ.=πατέρα ὁμιλοῦντα. Heracl. 581 ὑμεῖς δ', ἀδελφῶν ἡ παροῦσ' ὁμιλία, | εὐδαιμονοῖτε. Similar are φυγή =φυγάδες, Thuc. VIII. 64: δουλεία=δοῦλοι v. 23: πόλει μείζονι τῆς ὑμετέρας παρουσίας, VI. 86.

607. **ἤδη πάντ' ἔχοντα**, 'already (i.e. soon though it may appear) provided with all things needful.' Two or three days usually elapsed between death and burial: cf. supr. 94, n. : the poet both here and supr. 148 apologizes for the abridgment of the period caused by dramatic necessity.

608. **ἄρδην**, carried shoulder-high on a κλίνη: cf. supr. 86, n.

ἐς τάφον τε καὶ πυράν: τάφον does not necessarily imply inhumation, cf. supr. 96, n.: in Dionys. Halic. Ant. Rom. v. 48 (quoted in Becker's Charicles, p. 391 Engl. tr.) ἐμέλλησαν αὐτὸν καίειν τε καὶ θάπτειν, the reference contained in θάπτειν is to the disposal of the ashes after burning.

610. The farewell of the chorus is given infr. 741—746. Pheres also delivers his farewell infr. 625—627. Cf. Suppl. 804 προσαυδῶ σε τὸν θανόντα. The custom was general in Greece and Rome. ὑστάτην ὁδόν, cf. Soph. Tr. 874 βέβηκε Δηάνειρα τὴν πανυστάτην | ὁδῶν ἁπασῶν ἐξ ἀκινήτου ποδός.

611. καὶ μήν, cf. supr. 507 n.

612. ὀπαδούς. Like χοραγός κυναγός δαρός τιμάορος ξυνάορος etc., this word occurs in Tragic dialect in its Doric form. Cf. Rutherford, N. P. p. 496, and supr. 136, n.

613. κόσμον φέροντας: cf. supr. 149, n. The addition of ἐν χεροῖν implies care or ceremony.

614. συγκάμνων, cf. Aesch. P. V. 412 σοῖς πήμασι συγκάμνουσι θνητοί: 1059 αἱ πημοσύναις συγκάμνουσαι ταῖς τοῦδε.

615. Cf. for the form of the sentence supr. 152, infr. 1083. Note the contrast between the σώφρονος of the formal commiseration and the ἄφρονα (infr. 728) of his real sentiments.

616. γυναικὸς ἡμάρτηκας, cf. supr. 342, n.

618. κατὰ χθονὸς ἴτω: cf. supr. 149 κόσμος γ' ἕτοιμος, ᾧ σφε συνθάψει πόσις.

619. σῶμα, 'corse': cf. supr. 348, n.

620. (ταύτης) ἥτις γε, 'of one like thy wife here, who has etc.' Cf. supr. 241, n. ψυχῆς, 'life,' cf. supr. 341.

621. Notice the point of the proximity to the vocative τέκνον of the words καί μ' οὐκ ἄπαιδ' ἔθηκεν. For ἔθηκεν (=made so-and-so) here and infr. 623, Attic would use ἐποίησε. So Plato (Phaedr. 227 B) quoting Pind. Isth. I. 2 πρᾶγμα καὶ ἀσχολίας ὑπέρτερον θήσομαι Atticizes it οὐκ ἂν οἴει με κατὰ Πίνδαρον καὶ ἀσχολίας ὑπέρτερον πρᾶγμα ποιήσεσθαι κ.τ.λ. Cobet V. L. p. 303.

622. στερέντα, the use of the 2nd aor. of this verb is confined to poetry : Attic prose employs the 1st aorist.

623. It will have been observed that the Greeks had no objection to repetitions of the same (ἔθηκεν here and supr. 621) or similar sounds: cf. supr. 90, 160 nn.

625 sq. Cf. supr. 610, n.

626. κἀν "Αιδου δόμοις εὖ σοι γένοιτο, cf. supr. 436, infr. 745.
So Achilles, at Patroclus' burial (Hom. Il. xxiii. 179) χαῖρέ μοι, ὦ
Πάτροκλε, καὶ εἰν ᾽Αίδαο δόμοισιν. The words φημὶ τοιούτους γάμους
λύειν βροτοῖσι acquire a cynical sense when read in the light of lines
699 sq., where Pheres exhorts his son to go on marrying devoted wives,
and thereby attain immortality. The chorus were more sincere in their
wishes, supr. 473.

628. λύειν=λυσιτελεῖν : cf. Med. 566 ἐμοί τε λύει τοῖσι μέλλουσιν
τέκνοις | τὰ ζῶντ᾽ ὀνῆσαι.

ἤ, 'otherwise,' i.e. if one cannot secure such a wife.

629. ἐξ ἐμοῦ κληθείς, 'bidden of me,' as were the chorus, supr.
423. ἐξ ἐμοῦ=ὑπ᾽ ἐμοῦ, the agent being regarded as the source of the
action : an Ionic rather than an Attic usage.

τάφον, cf. supr. 96, n.

630. σὴν παρουσίαν=σε παρόντα, cf. supr. 606 : 'nor, for all thy
appearance here, do I reckon thee among my friends.'

631. Observe the contemptuous recurrence of τὸν σὸν, τῶν σῶν
(l. 632).

632. 'She will not need aught of thy giving at her burial.' Mr
Earle compares Verg. Aen. ii. 521 *non tali auxilio nec defensoribus*
istis | *tempus eget.*

633. χρῆν=χρὴ ἦν : the form ἐχρῆν is probably due to a false
analogy with other imperfects.

ὅτ᾽ ὠλλύμην, 'when I was like to die': cf. H. F. 538 τἄμ᾽ ἔθνῃσκε
τέκν᾽, ἀπωλλύμην δ᾽ ἐγώ.

634. ἄλλῳ, 'another'; generalises, and therefore masc.: cf. infr.
666.

636. οὐκ ἦσθ᾽ ἄρ᾽ κ.τ.λ. 'Now I know thou art not truly, etc.'
'The imperf. ἦν (generally with ἄρα) may express a *fact* which is just
recognized by the speaker, having previously been overlooked or not
understood.' Goodw. M. T. § 39: cf. Hipp. 359 Κύπρις οὐκ ἄρ᾽ ἦν θεός
('is not, as I now see').

640. 'When put to the proof thou shewedst what in truth thou
art,' sc. a stranger: ὅς=οἷος. Cf. Soph. Aj. 1259 οὐ μαθὼν ὃς εἶ (sc.
δοῦλος) φύσιν | ἄλλον τιν᾽ ἄξεις ἄνδρα κ.τ.λ.

ἐξελθὼν εἰς ἔλεγχον, cf. Hec. 226 μήτ᾽ ἐς χερῶν ἄμιλλαν ἐξέλθῃς
ἐμοί.

642. διαπρέπεις: cf. Supp. 841 πόθεν ποθ᾽ οἵδε διαπρεπεῖς εὐψυχίᾳ |
θνητῶν ἔφυσαν ; cf. cr. n.

645. **εἰάσατε**, sc. you and my mother. The 2nd pl. can never be used for 2nd sing.

646. **ὀθνείαν**, cf. supr. 532, n. **ἣν ἐγὼ καὶ μητέρα κ.τ.λ.**: cf. Homer quoted to supr. 377.

647. **ἄν** may be repeated to emphasise particular words: Goodw. M. T. § 223. Cf. supr. 72, 96.

648. Cf. supr. 291.

650. **πάντως**, 'in any case.' Pericles is made to urge this reflection as a consolation to bereaved parents (Thuc. II. 44, 4) ὅσοι δ' αὖ παρηβήκατε, τόν τε πλείονα κέρδος ὃν ηὐτυχεῖτε βίον ἡγεῖσθε, καὶ τόνδε ('what remains') βραχὺν ἔσεσθαι, καὶ τῇ τῶνδε εὐκλείᾳ κουφίζεσθε.

653. **καὶ μὴν** introduces a new thought: cf. supr. 105, n. 'All the experiences a man should have to be called happy were thine.'

654. 'Thou wert in the prime of youth a sovereign' seems to be the force of the aorist ἥβησας: the general sense is 'you had power at an age when power is most prized, in youth: and when old you had a son to succeed you.'

657. **ὀρφανὸν διαρπάσαι (ἄλλοις)**, 'defenceless for others to plunder.'

658. **οὐ μὴν ἐρεῖς γέ μ'**, cf. infr. 704, 954: Andr. 645 τί δῆτ' ἂν εἴποις τοὺς γέροντας, ὡς σοφοί; Soph. El. 520 καίτοι πολλὰ πρὸς πολλούς με δὴ | ἐξεῖπας ὡς θρασεῖα. A similar construction is found with οἶδα, e.g. Soph. Phil. 444 τοῦτον οἶσθ' εἰ ζῶν κυρεῖ; and other verbs, cf. Soph. Phil. 544 ἐκέλευσ' ἐμοί σε ποῦ κυρῶν εἴης φράσαι.

659. **ὅστις**, referring to the apparently *definite* relative με, looks irregular, but an indefinite idea is present, 'me, who am of such a character, that etc.': cf. Hadl. Gr. Gr. § 699, a.

αἰδόφρων. Admetus claims that towards no one has he showed his well-known αἰδώς (supr. 601) more than to his father.

661. **τοιάνδε χάριν**, observe the fine indignation of the outraged son.

662. **οὐκέτ' ἂν φθάνοις**, 'you have no time to lose in begetting children' (Monk): lit. 'you could not now be too soon.' The expression is a very common one: cf. Her. 721 φθάνοις δ' ἂν οὐκ ἂν τοῖσδε συγκρύπτων δέμας: (other examples in Monk's n., and Goodw. M. T. § 894).

664. **περιστελοῦσι καὶ προθήσονται**: cf. supr. 86, n. Cf. Med. 1032 ἦ μήν ποθ' ἡ δύστηνος εἶχον ἐλπίδας | πολλὰς ἐν ὑμῖν, γηροβοσκήσειν τ' ἐμὲ | καὶ κατθανοῦσαν χερσὶν εὖ περιστελεῖν.

665. **οὐ γάρ σ' ἔγωγε κ.τ.λ.** The most striking repudiation of a father possible to a Greek. So great was the importance attached to burial that even a stranger's corpse was not passed unregarded by, but received the ceremonial tribute of a handful of earth: how deep the obligation incumbent on a son we may gather from a law of Solon, referred to by Aeschines (Timarch. 40), that when a father had so behaved towards a son as to forfeit every claim to respect, μὴ ἐπάναγκες εἶναι τῷ παιδὶ ἡβήσαντι τρέφειν τὸν πατέρα μηδὲ οἴκησιν παρέχειν· ἀποθανόντα δὲ αὐτὸν θαπτέτω καὶ τἆλλα ποιείτω τὰ νομιζόμενα.

666. **τοὐπί σε,** *quod ad te attinet* or *quantum in te fuit:* 'so far as concerns you,' or 'so far as depended on you.' In the latter sense, cf. Hec. 514 ἡμεῖς δ' ἄτεκνοι τοὐπί σε (Hecuba bewails Polyxena's death); Or. 1345 σώθηθ' ὅσον γε τοὐπ' ἔμ' (='I will do what I can to save you'). In the former, Soph. Ant. 889 ἡμεῖς γὰρ ἁγνοὶ τοὐπὶ τήνδε τὴν κόρην. The latter sense seems most suitable here.

ἄλλου, cf. supr. 634, n.

668. This line is spoken with bitter allusion to supr. 663: the meaning is 'all the love and care that naturally would go to a father are diverted to the person who has taken a father's responsibilities': both παῖδα and γηροτρόφον, considered with sole reference to Alcestis, would be grotesque.

For **λέγω παῖδά μ' εἶναι** (a variation for emphasis' sake of παῖς εἶναι), cf. Plat. Hipp. maj. 282 E οἶμαι ἐμὲ πλείω χρήματα εἰργάσθαι ἢ ἄλλους σύνδυο: cf. Hadl. Gr. Gr. § 940, b.

669. **ἄρα,** 'as now I see': cf. supr. 636, n. Lines 669, 670 are found among the fragments of the writings of Euripides' enthusiastic admirer and disciple, Menander.

671. This line violates the rule that when a verse ends with a cretic, the fifth foot must be an iambus: the pause after θάνατος may account in some measure for the irregularity, but probably desire for emphatic expression (which often produces intentional breaches of rule) is responsible.

673. **ἅλις γὰρ ἡ παροῦσα συμφορά,** cf. Soph. Tr. 332 ἅλις γὰρ ἡ παροῦσα (λύπη) : cf. supr. 334, n.

675. **τίν' αὐχεῖς κ.τ.λ.** ; 'whom think you in your insolence that you are assailing with your taunts? Some base slave, Lydian or Phrygian, bought with your money?'

αὐχεῖν=*confidenter dicere,* in usage equivalent to 'think' with some connotation of assurance: cf. Aesch. Ag. 506 οὐ γάρ ποτ' ηὔχουν τῇδ' ἐν

Ἀργείᾳ χθονὶ | θανὼν μεθέξειν φιλτάτου τάφου μέρος. The allusion to Lydian and Phrygian slaves is somewhat anachronistic, as it was not till after their conquest by Persia that the dreamy, peaceful and luxurious traders and farmers of Asia Minor, descendants of a family which once had spread far into Europe (even perhaps into Attica, cf. Thuc. II. 22), became a byword for their cowardice and vice: cf. Cic. pro Flac. 65 *utrum igitur nostrum est an vestrum hoc proverbium, Phrygem plagis fieri solere meliorem? quid de tota Caria? nonne hoc vestra voce vulgatum est, si quid cum periculo experiri velis, in Care id potissimum esse faciendum?* (ἐν τῷ Καρὶ κινδυνεύειν, i.e. *corpore vili,* Cycl. 647) *quid porro in Graeco sermone tam tritum atque celebratum est quam si quis despicatui ducitur, ut Mysorum ultimus esse dicatur? nam quid ego dicam de Lydia? quis unquam comœdiam Graecus scripsit in qua servus primarum partium non Lydus esset?* Aristoph. parodies this passsage, Av. 1244 φέρ' ἴδω, πότερα Λυδὸν ἢ Φρύγα | ταυτὶ λέγουσα μορμολύττεσθαι δοκεῖς;

676. **κακοῖς,** 'taunts': cf. Andr. 31 κακοῖς πρὸς αὐτῆς σχετλίοις ἐλαύνομαι (of Andromache now a slave).

677. **Θεσσαλόν**: we must remember that in early times Thessaly was the home of heroes (of Achilles, for instance), and that from it the Hellenes issued to conquer and occupy Greece : cf. Thuc. I. 3.

678. **γνησίως,** 'in wedlock.'

679. **νεανίας,** 'boastful': adjective: so frequently: cf. γέρων λόγος (Aesch. Ag. 750), γραῦς γυνή (Tro. 490), *anus charta* (Cat. 68, 46).

680. **ῥίπτων,** cf. Tro. 734 ῥίπτειν ἄρας: Herod. VII. 13 ἡ νεότης ἐπέξεσε, ὥστε ἀεικέστερα ἀπορρῖψαι ἔπεα ἐς ἄνδρα πρεσβύτερον ἢ χρεόν.

βαλών, cf. Plat. Symp. 189 B βαλών γε, φάναι, ὦ Ἀριστόφανες, οἴει ἐκφεύξεσθαι.

οὕτως, 'unanswered': lit. 'just as you are.' So the Latin, *sic abire*: cf. Ter. Andr. 175 *mirabar hoc si sic abiret,* 'whether this would blow over without any trouble.' Cat. 14, 16 *non, non hoc tibi, salse, sic abibit.* Here οὕτως=ὥσπερ ἔχεις : in Soph. Ant. 315 εἰπεῖν τι δώσεις, ἢ στραφεὶς οὕτως ἴω; it=ὥσπερ ἔχω.

682. Notice the emphatic effect produced by the unusual position of the negative : 'but I am under no sort of obligation.'

683. **πατρῷον** contrasted with Ἑλληνικόν in the next line : 'neither in narrow Pherae, nor wide Greece.' (This seems to contradict Cobet's *dictum,* πατρῷα=τὰ τοῦ πατρός, πάτρια=τὰ τῶν προγόνων. We could, of course, construe πατρῷον ἐδεξάμην, 'received from my father.' Cf.

infr. 688 πατρὸς ταῦτ' ἐδεξάμην πάρα.) Compare infr. 858, where we find the same antithesis.

687. 'Much you have already, more you will receive at my death.'

689. δῆτα, *indignantis*. ἀποστερῶ, 'do I defraud you?'

690. Cf. I. A. 1420 σὺ δ' ὦ ξένε | μὴ θνῆσκε δι' ἐμὲ μηδ' ἀποκτείνῃς τινά. οὐδ' ἐγώ, sc. θανοῦμαι.

691. This passage is parodied in the scene between Pheidippides and his father (Nub. 1411 sq.), where, however, it is the younger man who is the aggressor: κλάουσι ('smart') παῖδες, πατέρα δ' οὐ κλάειν δοκεῖς ('think right'). The father replies ἀλλ' οὐδαμοῦ νομίζεται τὸν πατέρα τοῦτο πάσχειν : cf. too Thesm. 194.

692. Cf. I. A. 1250 τὸ φῶς τόδ' ἀνθρώποισιν ἥδιστον βλέπειν. | τὰ νέρθε δ' οὐδέν· μαίνεται δ' ὃς εὔχεται | θανεῖν· κακῶς ζῆν κρεῖσσον ἢ καλῶς θανεῖν. Cat. v. 5 *nobis, cum semel occidit brevis lux, nox est perpetua una dormienda.*

694. 'You, at any rate (γοῦν), share my opinion that life is sweet, for you held on to it with disgraceful pertinacity.' τὸ μὴ θανεῖν is accus. of the inner object depending on διεμάχου : cf. Soph. Phil. 1253 οὐδέ τοι τῇ χειρὶ πείθομαι τὸ δρᾶν : cf. Goodw. M. T. § 791.

696. ταύτην κατακτάς, this extremely blunt statement of Admetus' own meanness adds point to the following words, εἶτ' ἐμὴν ἀψυχίαν κ.τ.λ. εἶτα introduces an indignant question in the course of an argument : cf. infr. 701 ; Andr. 666 ; Phoen. 548. κατακτάς = prose ἀποκτείνας : cf. supr. 2, n.

697. γυναικὸς ἡσσημένος, the genit. is due to the comparative idea in ἡσσημένος : cf. Ion 1117 τὸ μὴ δίκαιον τῆς δίκης ἡσσώμενον : so κρεισσόνων νικώμενοι, Med. 315 : ξύνεσιν οὐδενὸς λειπόμενος, Thuc. VI. 72.

698. τοῦ καλοῦ, the article by particularizing heightens the contemptuous irony of καλοῦ : for καλὸς in this sense, cf. Soph. El. 393 καλὸς γὰρ οὑμὸς βίοτος, cries the wretched Electra, ὥστε θαυμάσαι.

700. τὴν παροῦσαν ἀεί, 'whoever happens from time to time to be your wife.' This common use of ἀεί is imitated by Cicero, Verr. v. 12 *omnes Siciliae semper praetores.*

702. δρᾶν τάδ', cf. supr. 71, n. μή, in a generic statement.

704. ἡμᾶς, cf. supr. 658, n.

705. Cf. Hec. 576 ὁ δ' οὐ φέρων | πρὸς τοῦ φέροντος τοιάδ' ἤκουεν κακά (and my note). ἀκούσει serves as passive of ἐρεῖς : as a rule, not neut. accus. plur., but masc. nomin. sing. or an adverb is used with

ἀκούω in this sense: cf. infr. 726. κοὺ ψευδῆ, 'not false,' implying 'as yours are.' For the sense, cf. Hom. Il. xx. 250 ὁπποῖόν κ' εἴπησθα ἔπος, τοῖόν κ' ἐπακούσαις: Hes. Opp. 721 εἰ δὲ κακὸν εἴποις, τάχα κ' αὐτὸς μεῖζον ἀκούσαις. **κακά**= 'abuse,' cf. supr. 676.

706. **πλείω**, 'too many.'

707. **παῦσαι κ.τ.λ.**, 'cease from reviling': cf. Hipp. 340 συγγόνους κακορροθεῖς; Note that in the present tense not παύου, but παῦε is used.

708. 'Speak on, as I have had my say: but if it stings thee to hear the truth, then should'st thou not have acted so wrongly towards me.'

710. 'Much more wrongly should I be acting in dying for such as thou.' The play on the two senses of ἐξαμαρτάνειν (to err in *judgment* or in *morality*) can be reproduced in English by the use of the word 'wrong.' The emphatic position of σοῦ must be brought out in translation.

προθνήσκων= εἰ προύθνησκον.

713. **καὶ μὴν** calls attention to a deliberate statement: **γε** emphasizes Διός, 'than Zeus himself': cf. supr. 369, n.

714. Swift's savage playfulness has sketched the horrors of immortality without youth: to the Greek pre-eminently the Struldbrug's lot would have been appalling.

γονεῦσιν, the allusive plural: cf. supr. 132, n. For the sense, cf. Hes. Opp. 331 ὅς τε γονῆα γέροντα κακῷ ἐπὶ γήραος οὐδῷ | νεικείῃ χαλεποῖσι καθαπτόμενος ἐπέεσσιν, | τῷ δ' ἤτοι Ζεὺς αὐτὸς ἀγαίεται, ἐς δὲ τελευτὴν | ἔργων ἀντ' ἀδίκων χαλεπὴν ἐπέθηκεν ἀμοιβήν.

715. **γάρ**, 'aye, for I saw etc.'

716. 'You speak of my love of life: is not yours as great? otherwise, why this funeral?' For **ἐκφορά**, cf. supr. 422.

717. **σημεῖα**, accus. in apposition to νεκρὸν τόνδε: 'No,' answers Admetus, ''tis rather of *thy* cowardice that she is a victim.'

718. 'However that may be,' retorts Pheres, 'you cannot say that her death is directly attributable to *me*: it is to *you*.' This last thrust tells: Admetus can but say φεῦ.

719. **ἀνδρὸς τοῦδε**, i.e. ἐμοῦ: cf. supr. 331. **χρείαν**, cf. Hec. 976 ἀλλὰ τίς χρεία σ' ἐμοῦ;

721. 'That taunt recoils upon yourself: women have the courage and the will, but you showed that you have not': this is I believe the force of the line, which is further brought out in l. 723, 'for your heart is a coward's (κακὸν), not worthy to be called a man's.'

722. **τοῦ θεοῦ**, 'the sun': cf. Or. 1025 φέγγος εἰσορᾶν θεοῦ: Soph. Tr. 145 οὐ θάλπος θεοῦ | οὐδ' ὄμβρος οὐδὲ πνευμάτων οὐδὲν κλονεῖ.

723. **κακὸν τὸ λῆμα**: notice how bitterly Admetus takes up the form and order of his father's words: 'dear is the light,' Pheres had said: 'nay, cowardly is thy heart,' the son retorts. **οὐκ ἐν ἀνδράσιν**, 'fit to be classed among men': cf. Or. 1528 (Orestes addresses a Phrygian in contempt) οὔτε γὰρ γυνὴ πέφυκας οὔτ' ἐν ἀνδράσιν σύ γ' εἶ: Andr. 591 σοὶ ποῦ μέτεστιν ὡς ἐν ἀνδράσιν λόγου;

724. **ἐγγελᾷς** = *irrides*, 'chuckle.' **βαστάζων**, 'carrying out for burial.'

726. **κακῶς ἀκούειν**, cf. supr. 705, n. The sentiment is ignoble and un-Greek.

728. **ἀναιδής**: the word denotes a cynical disregard for what men usually respect.

ἐφηῦρες ἄφρονα, sc. οὖσαν: for similar omission of the participle, cf. Soph. Ant. 281 μὴ 'φευρεθῇς ἄνους τε καὶ γέρων ἅμα.

731. **κηδεσταῖς**, *affinibus*: a wide term including all relations by marriage.

ἔτι, minatory: it is frequently used in threats, e.g. Soph. Tr. ἦ μὴν τὸν ἀγχιστῆρα τοῦδε τοῦ πάθους | ξὺν παιδὶ καὶ γυναικὶ δουλώσειν ἔτι.

732. **ἦ τᾱρ'**, a mocking echo perhaps of Admetus' words, supr. 642: as is οὐκέτ' ἔστ' ἐν ἀνδράσιν of l. 723. Acastus, son of Pelias, king of Iolcos, brother to Alcestis.

733. **σ' αἷμα τιμωρήσεται**, for the double accus. (a rare constr.), cf. Cycl. 695 εἰ μή σ' ἑταίρων φόνον ἐτιμωρησάμην: εἰ with fut. is specially used in threats and warnings.

735. 'A childless couple, though your child still lives': the combination of dual and plural is common.

737. **νεῖσθ'**, future: 'ye shall not come under the same roof with me' (τῷδε). Except once in Soph. (νεῖσθαι, Ant. 33) and twice in Eur. (here and El. 723 νεόμενος), the word does not occur in tragedy.

ἀπειπεῖν, 'disown': cf. Plat. Legg. 928 D οἵ τε πατέρες ἡγοῦντ' ἂν δεῖν τὸν νομοθέτην νομοθετεῖν ἐξεῖναί σφισιν ἐὰν βούλωνται τὸν υἱὸν ὑπὸ κήρυκος ἐναντίον ἁπάντων ἀπειπεῖν υἱὸν κατὰ νόμον μηκέτ' εἶναι κ.τ.λ. A son so disowned was said to be ἀποκεκηρυγμένος. Herod. I. 59 (Hippocrates advised in consequence of a portent) τὴν γυναῖκα ἐκπέμπειν, καὶ εἴ τίς οἱ τυγχάνει ἐὼν παῖς, τοῦτον (Peisistratus) ἀπείπασθαι.

739. **ἡμεῖς**, the funeral cortége. **τοὐν ποσὶν κακόν**, 'the sorrow

that confronts us': cf. Soph. Ant. 1326 βράχιστα γὰρ κράτιστα τὰν ποσὶν κακά: Andr. 397 τὰ ἐν ποσὶν κακά.

740. **ὡς ἄν**, final: very common in Homer, fairly common in Attic poets, once only (Thuc. VI. 91) in Attic prose: ὡς final itself almost disappears from Attic prose, but comes into favour again with Xenophon. Eurip. greatly prefers ὡς to ἵνα and ὅπως (the tables give ὡς and ὡς ἄν 209, ἵνα 71, ὅπως and ὅπως ἄν 26). See the interesting Appendix III. to Goodw. M.T.

741 sq. Cf. supr. 610, n. **σχετλία τόλμης**, 'hapless by reason of thy brave heart.' Goodw. Gr. Gr. § 173, 3.

742. **μέγ' ἀρίστη**, 'greatly best': μέγα as an adverb qualifying an adj. is epic: cf. Aesch. P. V. 647 ὦ μέγ' εὔδαιμον: Hes. 493 μέγ' ὄλβιον: Hom. Il. II. 82 μέγ' ἄριστος. It is one of Xenophon's many un-Attic usages: Rutherford, N. P. p. 28.

744. **ἐκεῖ** = ἐν Ἅιδου: cf. Med. 1073 εὐδαιμονοῖτον ἀλλ' ἐκεῖ. Soph. El. 356 λυπῶ δὲ τούτους, ὥστε τῷ τεθνηκότι | τιμὰς προσάπτειν, εἴ τις ἔστ' ἐκεῖ χάρις.

745. Very similar had been Pheres' wish, supr. 625. **πλέον** = 'advantage'; cf. supr. 72, n.

τούτων refers to εἴ τι above, which is a virtual plural.

746. 'May'st thou have an honoured seat beside Hades' queen.' Possibly Persephone may have had πάρεδροι, as her husband had. Compare Odysseus' vision of noble women in the Odyssey (XI. 225 sq.) νῶι μὲν ὣς ἐπέεσσιν ἀμειβόμεθ', αἱ δὲ γυναῖκες | ἤλυθον, ὄτρυνεν γὰρ ἀγαυὴ Περσεφόνεια, | ὅσσαι ἀριστήων ἄλοχοι ἔσαν ἠδὲ θύγατρες.

The chorus now leave the stage, returning at line 861: such a departure was extremely rare. Aeschylus in the Eumenides, Sophocles in the Ajax, and Euripides in this play and the Helena allow themselves to commit this breach of stage tradition: in the first two cases the structure of the play made it unavoidable; in the two latter the development of the plot is greatly benefited by the absence of the chorus: the working out of the surprise at the end of this play would have been very difficult, had the chorus been aware of Heracles' intention to attempt the rescue of Alcestis.

747. The servant who now appears on the stage is the one addressed as σύ in line 546.

752. **ἀμείψασθαι πύλας**, 'to pass our gates': both in the active and middle ἀμείβειν is used in this sense: the context must decide whether passing in or out is meant.

755. εἴ τι μὴ φέροιμεν, ὤτρυνεν φέρειν: both this sentence and
supr. 671 ἢν δ᾽ ἐγγὺς ἔλθῃ θάνατος, οὐδεὶς βούλεται θνῄσκειν, are instances
of *general* suppositions, the one in past, the other in present time: had
the suppositions been *particular*, the regular construction would have
required the indicative, both in apodosis and protasis. In general
suppositions of this form εἰ and ἐὰν are almost the same as ὅτε and
ὅταν: cf. Goodw. M. T. § 462.

756 sq. As it is in this scene that the Alcestis most nearly ap-
proaches the Satyric drama, it will not surprise us to find many verbal
resemblances between it and the similar scene in the one Satyric play we
possess, the Cyclops, which describes the drinking bout of its immode-
rate hero. ποτήρ occurs only here and Cycl. 151: the cup of ivy wood
(κίσσινον 756) is found Cycl. 390 (it is taken from Hom. Od. IX. 106:
ivy was sacred to Bacchus: cf. too Theocr. I. 27): Heracles ἄμουσ᾽
ὑλακτεῖ (760) παρ᾽ οἰκέταις κλαίουσι (762), Cyclops ἄμουσ᾽ ᾄδει παρὰ
κλαίουσι συνναύταις (425): σκύφος (798), a very rare word in trag.,
occurs four times in the Cycl.: ἐθέρμηνε, of the effects of wine, Alc. 758,
Cycl. 424. Cf. too Alc. 766 πανοῦργον κλῶπα καὶ λῃστήν τινα with
Cycl. 223 λῃσταί τινες κατέσχον ἢ κλῶπες χθόνα; also Alc. 773 σεμνὸν
βλέπεις with Cycl. 553 καλὸν βλέπω.

756. χείρεσσι: the non-tragic character of this part of the play may
be some excuse for the intrusion of this epic form: Soph. uses it once
(Ant. 1297) in an iambic line inserted in a lyric system.

757. μελαίνης μητρὸς refers to the οἰνομήτωρ ἄμπελος: conversely
Pindar calls wine ἀμπέλου παῖδα (Nem. IX. 52): cf. Aesch. Pers. 614
ἀκήρατόν τε μητρὸς ἀγρίας ἄπο | πότον, παλαιᾶς ἀμπέλου γάνος τόδε.
εὔζωρον (Attic for ζωρός, Phryn. 120) means wine with little or no
admixture of water: such potations were considered barbarous by the
Greeks (cf. Herod. VI. 84 ἐπεὰν ζωρότερον βούλωνται πιεῖν, ᾽Επισκύθισον
λέγουσι, of Cleomenes of Sparta, who had been debauched by association
with Scythians), who usually drank in the proportion of two or three
measures of water to one of wine. Odysseus indeed had the good
fortune to receive a present of wine which required twenty times its
own bulk of water (Od. IX. 209): this the man of many wiles offered
neat to the Cyclops, who fell an easy victim: but the making of such
wine was a lost art in historic times.

758. φλὸξ οἴνου, we speak rather of the 'fumes' of wine: however,
flamma fumo proxima est.

759. μυρσίνης, cf. supr. 172, n.

760. ὑλακτῶν, 'howling': cf. Soph. El. 299 (of the enraged Clytaemnestra) τοιαῦθ' ὑλακτεῖ: Aesch. Ag. 1631 σὺ δ' ἐξορίνας νηπίοις ὑλάγμασιν | ἄξει.

761. ὃ μὲν, cf. supr. 190, n.; followed by οἰκέται δέ.

762. οὐδὲν προτιμῶν τῶν κακῶν, 'recking naught of the woe': cf. Ar. Plut. 883 οὐδὲν προτιμῶ σου: the accus. is usual, but with the meaning of 'care for' προτιμῶ follows the analogy of μέλει, φροντίζω etc.

763. ἐδείκνυμεν τέγγοντες: δείκνυμι c. partic. generally means 'to *make* a person see that one is, or is doing, something,' i.e. to prove: e.g. Or. 802 ποῦ γὰρ ὢν δείξω φίλος; Here it = 'to *let* a person see.' It is possible that ὄμμα should be regarded as direct accus. after ἐδείκνυμεν, τέγγοντες being added as explanatory.

766. κλῶπα καὶ λῃστήν τινα: the λῃστὴς was the more dignified evildoer. Thucydides (I. 5) has an interesting chapter on the prevalence of λῃστεία in early Greece, οὐκ ἔχοντός πω αἰσχύνην τούτου τοῦ ἔργου, φέροντος δέ τι καὶ δόξης μᾶλλον. The term was more frequently applied to sea-robbers of the buccaneer type; but, says Thuc., ἐλῃΐζοντο δὲ καὶ κατ' ἤπειρον ἀλλήλους, adding that so late as his time the Acarnanians and Aetolians (cf. the joke in Ar. Eq. 79 τὼ χεῖρ' ἐν Αἰτωλοῖς, ὁ νοῦς δ' ἐν Κλωπιδῶν) were addicted to these predatory habits. The κλὼψ (Attic κλέπτης) on the other hand was half bandit, half footpad; he would pilfer a camp (Rhes. 645), or break into a treasury (Herod. II. 150): a band of them would waylay travellers (Herod. I. 41) or even venture to raid a town and carry off the women (Herod. VI. 16).

767. ἐκ δόμων βέβηκεν, i.e. the ἐκφορὰ has already taken place. Cf. Aesch. Cho. 8 οὐ γὰρ παρὼν ᾤμωξα σόν, πάτερ, μόρον, | οὐδ' ἐξέτεινα χεῖρ' ἐπ' ἐκφορᾷ νεκροῦ.

ἐφεσπόμην: both an aspirated and an unaspirated 2nd aor. of ἕπομαι are found: the former is probably derived from a reduplicated form σεσεπόμην (ἕπομαι = σέπομαι, Lat. *sequor*), which became σεσπόμην (the ε being lost through accentual influence), ἑσπόμην: cf. Veitch Gr. V. s. v., Leaf on Il. v. 423.

768. ἀποιμώζων: ἀπ. here is intensive: with other verbs signifying grief, ἀπ- has the force of 'cease,' e.g. ἀπαλγεῖν (Thuc. II. 61), ἀπολοφύρεσθαι (II. 46), ἀποτύπτεσθαι (Herod. II. 40). It is tempting to translate here 'making my farewell moan,' but the usage of the word elsewhere is against this meaning.

770. μήτηρ, 'a very mother': notice the emphasis of position.

771. **ὀργάς,** 'fits of passion.' The plural has also the meaning of 'disposition': cf. Tro. 53 ὀργὰς ἠπίους ἐπῄνεσα: H. F. 276 ὀργὰς δικαίας τοὺς φίλους ἔχειν χρεών. For ὀργὰς μαλάσσουσ' ἀνδρός, cf. fr. 819 γυνὴ γὰρ ἐν κακοῖσι καὶ νόσοις πόσει | ἥδιστόν ἐστι δώματ' ἢν οἰκῇ καλῶς, | ὀργήν τε πραΰνουσα καὶ δυσθυμίας | ψυχὴν μεθιστᾶσ'.

ἆρα, cf. supr. 228, n.

773. **οὗτος,** 'you there,' 'sirrah': cf. Hec. 1127 οὗτος, τί πάσχεις; Soph. Aj. 71 οὗτος, σὲ τὸν τὰς αἰχμαλωτίδας χέρας | δεσμοῖς ἀπευθύνοντα προσμολεῖν καλῶ. **τί σεμνὸν κ.τ.λ.,** 'wherefore that solemn and thought-laden look?' The expression, like others in this scene, is non-tragic: Cycl. 553 καλὸν βλέπω occurs. Similar is the usage with a noun, e.g. Ἄρη δεδορκότων (Aesch. Sept. 53), ὁρῶντ' ἀλκάν, 'with valour in his look' (Pind. Ol. IX. 119): and frequently in comedy νᾶπυ (Ar. Eq. 631), κάρδαμα (Vesp. 455), πυρρίχην (Av. 1169). By σεμνὸν καὶ πεφρ. βλ. Heracles means the supercilious looks cast upon his efforts at enjoyment by a philosopher (φροντίζειν was the popular word to express the higher thought, cf. Ar. Nub. 94 and *passim*), into whose scheme of life jollity did not enter: he expounds his own 'laughing philosophy' infr. 782—786. There is a hint of impertinence in the use of σεμνόν: cf. Ar. Plut. 275 ὡς σεμνὸς οὑπίτριπτος: Ran. 178 ὡς σεμνὸς ὁ κατάρατος.

774. **τοῖς ξένοις,** generalising plural: notice the emphasis of ξένοις and πρόσπολον juxtaposed.

775. **εὐπροσηγόρῳ,** Lat. *affabilis*: cf. Hipp. 95, where σεμνὸς and εὐπροσήγορος are again contrasted.

777. **συνωφρυωμένῳ,** cf. infr. 800; Hipp. 172 στυγνὸν δ' ὀφρύων νέφος αὐξάνεται: Soph. Tr. 869. Monk compares Hor. Sat. II. 2, 125 *explicuit vino contractae seria frontis.*

778. **πήματος,** objective genitive: so Thuc. VI. 31, 4 ὅπλων σπουδή, 'care in selecting arms.'

779. **ὅπως ἄν,** cf. supr. 740, n.

780. **οἶδας:** this Ionic form, which may have existed in old Attic, was in mature Attic entirely supplanted by οἶσθα: there is no authority for the form οἶσθας. Rutherford, N. P. pp. 227, 8.

781. **οἶμαι μὲν οὔ,** 'nay, I trow not': cf. infr. 794. **πόθεν γάρ;** cf. supr. 95, n.; 'how should you?' sc. being a slave.

782. The line is found also supr. 419: cf. Andr. 1272 πᾶσιν γὰρ ἀνθρώποισιν ἥδε πρὸς θεῶν | ψῆφος κέκρανται κατθανεῖν τ' ὀφείλεται: Simon. in Anth. Pal. X. 105 θανάτῳ πάντες ὀφειλόμεθα. On the gradual growth of the *articular* infinitive from Pindar onwards, cf. Goodw. M. T.

§ 788. The non-articular infin. (as here), as subject nomin. of a finite verb, is found in the earliest Greek.

784. τὴν αὔριον, sc. ἡμέραν: cf. supr. 321, n.

785. Mr Earle points out the appropriately humorous effect of the similarity of the endings of ll. 782—785.

786. οὐ is to be taken closely with διδακτόν. 'The goal whither Fortune will direct her steps is hidden from us: no craft thereof is there that may be taught, nor is the knowledge of it attained unto by skill': cf. Soph. Phil. 863 τὸ δ' ἁλώσιμον ἐμᾷ φροντίδι, 'as far as my thoughts can seize the truth' (Jebb).

788, 9. The creed is a common one: cf. Bacch. 910 τὸ δὲ κατ' ἦμαρ ὅτῳ βίοτος | εὐδαίμων, μακαρίζω. fr. 196 τί δῆτ' ἐν ὄλβῳ μὴ σαφεῖ βεβηκότες | οὐ ζῶμεν ὡς ἥδιστα μὴ λυπούμενοι; Horace is its happiest professor: cf. Od. I. 9, 13 *quid sit futurum cras, fuge quaerere et,* | *quem fors dierum cunque dabit, lucro* | *appone, nec dulces amores* | *sperne puer neque tu choreas.*

790. πλεῖστον ἡδίστην, cf. Soph. Phil. 631 πλεῖστον ἐχθίστης: Med. 1323 μέγιστον ἐχθίστη: Hipp. 1421 μάλιστα φίλτατος. This reference to the Cyprian goddess in the house of Alcestis would doubtless seem outrageous to the already scandalised retainer: but Heracles' conduct does not appear in so shameful a light, if we deem it probable that the hero's views of the position held by the ὀθνεῖος γυνή of supr. 533 were such as would suggest themselves to his own heroic morality. This theory would explain his abrupt dropping of the subject (l. 535), his acceptance of hospitality, his enjoyment of it, and his shock on learning the truth.

793. εἴπερ, 'if, as I think I must do, I seem to you to reason aright.'

795. ὑπερβαλών, 'rising superior to' seems to be the force of the word, if it is genuine. For the sentiment, cf. fr. 471 (from the Κρῆσσαι, a play produced at the same time as the Alcestis) τὰ δ' ἄλλα χαῖρε κύλικος ἑρπούσης κύκλῳ.

796. στεφ. πυκ., repeated repentantly infr. 832. ὀθούνεκα=ἕνεκα τούτου ὅτι, i.e. 'because': but sometimes it='that,' as here and Soph. El. 47 ὅρκον προστιθεὶς ὀθούνεκα | τέθνηκ' Ὀρέστης: ib. 617 μανθάνω δ' ὀθούνεκα | ἔξωρα πράσσω.

797. ξυνεστῶτος: the metaphor seems to be taken from 'congealed' liquids, though the word does not occur in that sense till late: it may be only another way of saying συνωφρυωμένῳ (supr. 777): for the use of

the neut. of the partic. as an abstract noun, cf. Goodw. M. T. § 829 : the appearance of the neut. adj. in the same expression shows the identity of origin of the adjectival and participial uses.

798. **μεθορμιεῖ**, 'will move you to better anchorage.' **πίτυλος**, 'the plash' not of oars in the sea, but of wine in the cup. On **σκύφου**, cf. supr. 756, n. A similar metaphor is found Med. 442 σοὶ δ' οὔτε πατρὸς δόμοι, | δύστανε, μεθορμίσασθαι | μόχθων.

799. For the sentiment cf. fr. 796 ὥσπερ δὲ θνητὸν καὶ τὸ σῶμ' ἡμῶν ἔφυ, | οὕτω προσήκει μηδὲ τὴν ὀργὴν ἔχειν | ἀθάνατον ὅστις σωφρονεῖν ἐπίσταται: Pind. Isth. IV. 16 θνατὰ θνατοῖσι πρέπει.

801. **ὥς γ' ἐμοὶ χρῆσθαι κριτῇ**, 'in my opinion': lit. 'to take me as judge': for the absolute use of the infin. (ὡς εἰπεῖν, ὡς ἐμοὶ δοκεῖν and the like), cf. Goodw. M. T. §§ 777, 778; Gr. Gr. § 268.

802. 'Their life is not life truly, but mischance.' **συμφορά** generally connotes 'evil' fortune: very rarely (as in Ar. Eq. 406—a quotation from Simonides—πῖνε πῖν' ἐπὶ συμφοραῖς) good luck.

806. **δεσπόται**, i.e. Admetus and Alcestis.

807. **τί ζῶσιν**; 'how say you "live"?' The actual word of Heracles is quoted: cf. I. A. 460 τὴν δ' αὖ τάλαιναν παρθένον (τί παρθένον; | Ἅιδης νιν ὡς ἔοικε νυμφεύσει τάχα,) | ὡς ᾤκτισ'. The servant summoned in l. 546 had not been present at the earlier part of the interview, and has been assuming full knowledge of Alcestis' death on the part of Heracles.

808. **εἰ μή τι**: τι is adverbial='perchance.' 'I know your sorrow, unless perchance etc.'

809. The servant's reply is suggested by ἐψεύσατο. 'Aye, his hospitable nature prompted that deceit.'

810. 'Was I to be debarred of enjoyment because a stranger-maid was dead?' Cf. Hec. 135 τὸν ἄριστον Δαναῶν πάντων | δούλων σφαγίων εἵνεκ' ἀπωθεῖν, 'slight the hero to save a slave-girl's life' (lit. on account of a slave's sacrifice).

811. **κάρτα** is un-Attic: Rutherford N. P. p. 8.

812. **ἔφραζε**, sc. Admetus. The suspicion deepening to conviction in Heracles' mind is skilfully depicted.

813. **χαίρων ἴθ'**, a polite form of dismissal: cf. Phoen. 921 χαίρων ἴθ'· οὐ γὰρ σῶν με δεῖ μαντευμάτων.

814. 'Such words prelude no story of sorrow for a stranger's death.'

815. This line is suggested by θυραίων, supr. 814. 'Had it been for a stranger, I should not be distressed etc.'

816. **ἀλλ' ἦ** = *an vero?* 'In this formula ἦ asks the question; ἀλλά marks surprise, as it so often marks remonstrance.' Jebb on Soph. Phil. 414. **πέπονθα δεινά**, 'has sore wrong been done me by my host?' i.e. in concealing some real affliction, of which I should have been informed. **ξένων**, allusive plural: cf. supr. 132, n.

817. **ἐν δέοντι δέξ. δόμ.**: the passive infin. would seem more natural, as the sense is 'at a fitting time to be received in the palace': but this common use of an active infin., when its implied subject is distinct from that of the word on which it depends ('*you* were not well-timed for *us* to receive you') may be traced to its datival origin, as here 'you came not at a fitting time *for the receiving* you': cf. Goodw. M. T. § 763.

820. Cf. crit. n. Heracles is now sure that it is for some one near and dear that the palace is mourning.

821. **μὲν οὖν** corrects a previous statement as incorrect or inadequate: 'nay, sir, not child, not father: 'tis Admetus' wife, none other, who has passed.'

822. **ἔπειτα δῆτα** introduces an astonished and sometimes indignant question: cf. Ar. Av. 911 ἔπειτα δῆτα δοῦλος ὢν κόμην ἔχεις; ib. 1217, and freq. in Aristophanes.

823. **ᾐδεῖτο ἀπώσασθαι**: αἰδ. with partic. = 'I am ashamed' of doing or having done something: with infin. = 'I am ashamed' to do (something which I have not yet done). Goodw. M. T. § 903.

824. **οἵας ἥμπλ. ξυν.**, cf. supr. 242, n.

825. Cf. Hipp. 839 (Theseus to his dead wife) ἀπώλεσας γὰρ μᾶλλον ἢ κατέφθισο.

826. **ἀλλά** here prefaces assent: cf. Soph. Tr. 1179, Phil. 48 and Jebb's nn. ad loc. **ᾐσθόμην μέν, ἀλλ' ἔπειθε**, 'I had a feeling that it was so, but Admetus over-persuaded me.'

829. **βίᾳ θυμοῦ**, 'in spite of my strong wish': Monk compares Aesch. Theb. 612 βίᾳ φρενῶν, 'against his better judgment.' **ὑπερβαλὼν πύλας**, 'intruding on the palace': this gives the force of ὑπερβαλών, which is often used of crossing barriers, or what should be barriers.

832. **στεφ. πυκ.**, cf. supr. 796. **ἀλλὰ σοῦ τὸ μὴ φράσαι**: the infin. with τὸ is used in exclamations of surprise or indignation: cf. Ar. Ran. 741 τὸ δὲ μὴ πατάξαι σ' ἐξελεγχθέντ' ἄντικρυς | ὅτι δοῦλος ὢν ἔφασκες εἶναι δεσπότης: Med. 1051 ἀλλὰ τῆς ἐμῆς κάκης, τὸ καὶ προσέσθαι μαλθακοὺς λόγους φρενί ('out on my weakness, that I should even admit it etc.' Verrall). The infin. without the article is also thus used: cf.

Goodw. M. T. §§ 787, 805. The genitive σοῦ is possessive: 'to think of your not telling.'

834. **ποῦ καί σφε θάπτει;** 'where, tell me (καί), is he laying her?' For καί *interrogativis postpositum*, cf. infr. 1049: Hec. 515 πῶς καί νιν ἐξε-πράξατ'; 'how, tell me, did ye take her life?' Hipp. 1171 πῶς καὶ διώλετ';

835. **ὀρθὴν παρ' οἶμον,** 'close beside the direct road, which takes you to Larissa.' οἶμος and οἴμη both occur, but the latter has usually a metaphorical sense. Larissa probably in Pelasgic meant 'city,' as many Pelasgic towns bore this name. Pausanias speaking of the citadel of Argos (II. 23) says τὴν δὲ ἀκρόπολιν Λάρισσαν μὲν καλοῦσιν ἀπὸ τῆς Πελασγοῦ θυγατρός. ἀπὸ ταύτης δὲ καὶ δύο τῶν ἐν Θεσσαλίᾳ πόλεων, ἥ τε ἐπὶ θαλάσσῃ (ἡ κρεμαστὴ Λάρισσα on a spur of Mt. Othrys) καὶ ἡ παρὰ τὸν Πηνειὸν ὠνομάσθησαν.

836. Intramural burial was customary in early times (frequently a man was interred in his own dwelling), and in historic times was at some places (Sparta, for instance) not forbidden. Most commonly however the burial places were situated just outside the city gates; at Athens, those who fell in war were interred in the outer Ceramicus, by the Dipylon gate, τὸ κάλλιστον προαστεῖον τῆς πόλεως, καὶ ἀεὶ ἐν αὐτῷ θάπτουσι τοὺς ἐκ τῶν πολέμων, Thuc. II. 34: the ordinary place of sepulture was outside the Itonian gate. At Rome too similarly intra-mural burial was forbidden in the Twelve Tables, and tombs were commonly built by those who could afford them by the side of the great roads that led from Rome; cf. Juv. I. 170 ('I will not attack the living, but') *experiar, quid concedatur in illos | quorum Flaminia tegitur cinis atque Latina.* Practical Bishop Latimer recommended to the citizens of London 'the laudable custom of the citizens of Nain, who buried their corses without the city,' and doubtless the ravages of plague in the xvth, xvith, and xviith centuries were largely due to neglect of this sanitary precaution. **ἐκ προαστίου:** this may mean 'looking from the προάστιον, you will see below you beside the road that stretches over the plain to Larissa etc.,' or ἐκ may = ἔξω, an early use, here supported by the scholiast who notes ἐκτὸς τοῦ προαστείου.

837. Cf. Soph. Tr. 1046 (Heracles speaks) ὦ πολλὰ δὴ καὶ θερμὰ κοὐ λόγῳ κακὰ | καὶ χερσὶ καὶ νώτοισι μοχθήσας ἐγώ.

839. **Ἠλεκτρυόνος,** cf. supr. 481, n.

841. **ἱδρῦσαι** gives the idea of stability, 'establish firmly.'

842. **ὑπουργῆσαι χάριν,** cf. Aesch. Prom. 635 σὸν ἔργον, Ἰοῖ, ταῖσδ' ὑπουργῆσαι χάριν.

843. μελάμπεπλον, cf. supr. 24, n.

844. φυλάξω, 'will watch for,' 'lie in wait for': cf. Hom. Od. IV. 670 δότε νῆα θοὴν...ὄφρα μιν αὐτὸν ἰόντα λοχήσομαι ἠδὲ φυλάξω | ἐν πορθμῷ Ἰθάκης τε Σάμοιό τε παιπαλοέσσης: cf. supr. 27, n.

845. πλησίον τύμβου: πλησίον, like πέλας and ἐγγύς, is found both with genit. and dat.: cf. Latin *prope ad* and *prope ab*.

πίνοντα προσφαγμάτων, partitive genitive: cf. Goodw. Gr. Gr. § 170: Hom. Od. XI. 96 (the ghost of Teiresias speaks to Odysseus) ἀλλ' ἀποχάζεο βόθρου...αἵματος ὄφρα πίω καί τοι νημερτέα εἴπω, a passage which (with Merry's note) well illustrates the practice of blood-offering to the dead (cf. infr. 851 αἱματηρὸν πέλανον): Herod. III. 11 ἐμπιόντες τοῦ αἵματος πάντες οἱ ἐπίκουροι οὕτω δὴ συνέβαλον.

846. λοχαίας, cf. supr. 103, n.: it is formed from λόχος, 'ambush.' ἕδρα is similarly used Rhes. 512.

847, 8. Cf. Ar. Pax 316 (a parody of this passage) οὔτι καὶ νῦν ἔστιν αὐτὴν ὅστις ἐξαιρήσεται, | ἢν ἅπαξ ἐς χεῖρας ἔλθῃ τὰς ἐμάς. ἐξαιρήσεται, cf. supr. 69.

849. πρὶν μεθῇ, for ἂν omitted, cf. Goodw. M. T. § 648, Gr. Gr. § 239, 1.

851. The character and attributes here assigned to Thanatos are apparently similar to those which Aeschylus gives to his Chthonian kinswomen, the Eumenides: cf. Eum. 265 ἀπὸ δὲ σοῦ | βοσκὰν φεροίμαν πώματος δυσπότου (say they to Orestes). The πέλανος is identical with the προσφάγματα explained supr. 845.

852. Κόρης, cf. supr. 357, n.

854. Mr Earle compares Hom. Il. I. 446 (Odysseus restores Chryseis to her father) ὣς εἰπὼν ἐν χερσὶ τίθει ὁ δὲ δέξατο χαίρων | παῖδα φίλην. Both θεῖναι ἐς and θεῖναι ἐν are regular in this sense, cf. Meisterhans, Gramm. d. Att. Inschr., p. 176.

857. ἔκρυπτε, sc. τὴν συμφοράν. αἰδεσθείς: the passive aorist form is regularly employed in an active sense: the middle form, ᾐδεσάμην, is rare, even in poetry.

858. τίς Θεσσαλῶν...τίς Ἑλλάδ' οἰκῶν, cf. supr. 683, n.

860. Cf. infr. 1120. Heracles now quits the stage, which is at once occupied by Admetus and the chorus on their return from the obsequies of Alcestis.

861. ὄψεις, the plural is extremely rare, except in the senses 'eyes' and 'visions': in Supp. 945 πικραὶ γὰρ ὄψεις αἷμα κώτειλαὶ νεκρῶν is the manuscript reading, though editors correct to πικρὰ γὰρ ὄψις.

862. **χήρων**: the adj. χῆρος is a comparatively late formation from the subst. χήρα, 'widow': the present is the only instance quoted by L. and S. from classical Greek.

863. Cf. Hec. 1056 πᾷ βῶ; πᾷ στῶ; πᾷ κέλσω; The subj. are of course deliberative.

864. **πῶς ἀν ὀλοίμαν;** the phrase recurs Med. 97. For this form of wish, cf. Hadl. Gr. Gr. § 870 e.

866. **ζηλῶ**, echoed infr. 882. **κείνων**, i.e. τῶν ἐν ᾿Αιδου: cf. supr. 744, n.

ἔραμαι and imperf. ἠράμην only in lyrics: ἐράω, ἤρων in senarii and prose, but other tenses from ἔραμαι. Aristoph. parodies these lines (Vesp. 751) κείνων ἔραμαι, κεῖθι γενοίμαν, | ἵν᾽ ὁ κῆρύξ φησι 'τίς ἀψήφι- | στος; ἀνιστάσθω.'

869. **πόδα πεζεύων**: 'to verbs denoting motion of the body may be added a dative or an accusative of the part of the body in motion.' Lobeck, quoted by Jebb on Aj. 40: the dative expresses the instrument, the accus. is one of specification or limitation: cf. Goodw. Gr. Gr. § 160: similar expressions are Her. 805 ἐκβὰς πόδα: El. 94 βαίνω πόδα: Phoen. 1412 προβὰς δὲ κῶλον δεξιόν; infr. 1153 νόστιμον δ᾽ ἔλθοις πόδα (so some MSS). Prof. Jebb regards βαίνειν as transitive in these passages. **πεζεύων**: the verb occurs elsewhere only in somewhat late prose.

870. Admetus seems to mean that Alcestis' life was held as a hostage for his own, and that Thanatos has fraudulently seized (ἀπο-συλήσας) it and handed it over to Hades (the loss thus becoming irremediable): implying that really he would have preferred to die himself.

τοῖον, cf. supr. 65, n.

872. The strict correspondence between the strophe 872—877 and the antistrophe 889—894 should be noticed. Admetus, who has been slowly approaching the palace, now stops, overcome by his grief, and the marching metre (anapaestic) is interrupted. The chorus urge him to advance. **πρόβᾱ**, a shortened form of πρόβαθι: εἴσβα ἔμβα κατάβα ἐπίβα are also found, but not the simple verb: so here when Eurip. uses the uncompounded imperative he writes βᾶθι. βαίνω, βέβηκα are the only parts of the simple verb used in Attic prose. **κεῦθος** = μυχὸν, the inmost, most retired part.

873. **αἰαγμάτων** refers to Admetus' cry, αἰαῖ. Similar formations are ἐλάζω from εἶα, εὐάζειν from εὖα, ἄζειν from ἄ, φεύζειν from φεῦ,

οἴζειν from οἴ, οἰμώζειν from οἴμοι, ὤζειν from ὤ: cf. Valck. Diatr. 21 A.

874. **δι' ὀδύνας ἔβας**, an instance of the very common use of διὰ with verbs of rest or motion to express a state in which one is or with which one is proceeding, e.g. διὰ φιλίας γίγνεσθαι, διὰ πολέμου ἰέναι, δι' ὀργῆς ἥκειν: similar is the use with transitive verbs meaning to keep or consider a person in such and such a state διὰ φυλακῆς, δι' ὀργῆς ἔχειν. Cf. El. 1210 σάφ' οἶδα, δι' ὀδύνας ἔβας.

877. **πάντα**, adverbial with λυπρόν: cf. Soph. O. T. 1197 τοῦ πάντ' εὐδαίμονος: Aj. 911 πάντα κωφός. It is especially common with adjectives. Cf. cr. n.

878. **ἔμνησας**, the simple aorist is very rare: the usual compounds are with ἀνά, ὑπό.

ἥλκωσεν, for the metaphorical use, cf. Supp. 222 λαμπρὸν δὲ θολερῷ δῶμα συμμίξας τὸ σὸν | ἥλκωσας οἴκους.

879. **τί γὰρ ἀνδρὶ κακὸν μεῖζον ἁμαρτεῖν π. ἀλ.**: μεῖζον ἁμ. is for μεῖζον ἢ ἁμαρτεῖν, ἢ being omitted, as it frequently is after πλέον ἔλαττον μεῖον with numerals. Another explanation is that ἀλόχου is genit. after the comparative μεῖζον, 'what is a greater sorrow to lose than a good wife?' For the sentiment, cf. fr. 547 μεγάλη τυραννὶς ἀνδρὶ τέκνα καὶ γυνή | ἴσην γὰρ ἀνδρὶ συμφορὰν εἶναι λέγω | τέκνων θ' ἁμαρτεῖν καὶ πάτρας καὶ χρημάτων | ἀλόχου τε κεδνῆς, ὡς μόνον τῶν χρημάτων | κρεῖσσον τόδ' ἐστὶν ἀνδρί, σώφρον' ἢν λάβῃ.

880. **μὴ ὤφελον κ.τ.λ.** The sentence as a whole is felt to express a wish, and hence μὴ not οὐ (which is strictly correct) is used: cf. Hec. 395 μηδὲ τόνδ' ὠφείλομεν: Med. 1414 οὓς μήποτ' ἐγὼ φύσας ὄφελον | πρὸς σοῦ φθιμένους ἐπιδέσθαι. Hadl. Gr. Gr. § 871, a.

881. **μετὰ τῆσδε**, 'with her my helpmeet.'

882. According to the situation of the speaker this view is either held or opposed by Euripides' characters: with this passage cf. Med. 1090 καί φημι βροτῶν οἵτινές εἰσιν | πάμπαν ἄπειροι μηδ' ἐφύτευσαν | παῖδας, προφέρειν εἰς εὐτυχίαν | τῶν γειναμένων. On the other side, see Ion 488 τὸν ἄπαιδα δ' ἀποστυγῶ | βίον, ᾧ τε δοκεῖ ψέγω. Andr. 419 πᾶσι δ' ἀνθρώποις ἄρ' ἦν | ψυχὴ τέκν'· ὅστις δ' αὖτ' ἄπειρος ὢν ψέγει, | ἧσσον μὲν ἀλγεῖ, δυστυχῶν δ' εὐδαιμονεῖ.

883. Cf. Hipp. 258 τὸ δ' ὑπὲρ δισσῶν μίαν ὠδίνειν | ψυχὴν χαλεπὸν βάρος, ὡς κἀγὼ | τῆσδ' ὑπεραλγῶ.

For **τῆς**=ἧς, cf. infr. 967.

885. It is natural to regard νόσους and θανάτοις as plurals referring

to many instances, though perhaps we may see in θανάτοις an instance of the *allusive* plural : cf. supr. 132, n.; Aesch. Cho. 53 δεσποτῶν θανάτοισι (where both plurals are allusive,='Αγαμέμνονος θανάτῳ). The plural of θάνατος is often used to denote a death which is not natural : Soph. Tr. 1276 μεγάλους μὲν ἰδοῦσα νέους θανάτους (of Deianira's violent death): Aesch. Ag. 1340 (and Paley's n.).

886. **κεραϊζομένας**, not used elsewhere in tragedy : it is a reminiscence of Hom. Il. XXII. 63 κακὰ πόλλ' ἐπιδόντα, | υἷάς τ' ὀλλυμένους ἑλκηθείσας τε θύγατρας | καὶ θαλάμους κεραϊζομένους κ.τ.λ. To Euripides' retentive ear we owe the echo of θαλάμους κ. in θανάτοις κ.

887. **ἐξόν**: the accus. absol. is regularly employed in the case of the partic. of *impersonal* verbs : we find the participles of *personal* verbs too similarly used, but in their case ὡς or ὥσπερ always introduces : cf. Goodw. M. T. §§ 851, 853. Strictly ἀτέκνους and ἀγάμους should be ἀτέκνοις, ἀγάμοις to agree with ἡμῖν understood: for a similar irregularity, cf. Herod. I. 129 παρεὸν αὐτῷ βασιλέα γενέσθαι.

889. **τύχα τύχα**, for the repetition, cf. supr. 328, n.

890. **τιθεῖς**: this (not τίθης) is the correct form of the 2nd sing. pres. indic. of τίθημι. Similar irregular forms (as though from τιθῶ) are 2nd sing. imperat. τίθει, 2nd and 3rd sing. imperf. indic. ἐτίθεις ἐτίθει : cf. Rutherford, N. P. p. 316.

891. The chorus have administered similar comfort supr. 417, and will do so again infr. 931: cf. n. on 417.

895. 'O lasting woe, O pangs of grief for friends (φίλων, obj. genit.) beneath the earth.'

897. These words are addressed to the leader of the chorus. For the constr. of **ῥῖψαι**, cf. supr. 11, n.: this intrans., or rather, middle, sense of ῥῖψαι ('cast myself') is illustrated from Cycl. 166 (but the interpretation of the lines is doubtful), and Hel. 1325 ῥίπτει δ' ἐν πένθει | πέτρινα κατὰ δρία πολυνιφέα: fr. 1055 (probably from the Telephus, a play produced along with the Alcestis) δεῖν δ' ἀγχονῶν τε καὶ πετρῶν ῥίπτειν ἄπο κ.τ.λ.

899. **μέγ' ἀρίστης**, cf. supr. 742, n.

900. **δύο ψυχάς**: we frequently find δύο used with a plural substantive, but δυοῖν requires the noun to be in the dual (except it be an *abstract* noun, Wecklein, Cur. Epig., p. 16).

901. **σὺν ἂν ἔσχεν**, 'would have gotten at once': σύν is adverbial.

902. 'When together they had crossed the nether lake.' The tense of **διαβάντε** must be brought out in translation: the power of Hades

began on the further side of the waters: cf. supr. 870, n. Notice the use of the dual διαβάντε in particularising the two persons, Admetus and Alcestis; the plural ψυχὰς (supr. 900) gave a more general statement, though of course with reference to the two: cf. supr. 735. In the third declension the masc. form of the dual is often used as fem.: cf. Plat. Phaedr. 237 D δύο τινέ ἐστον ἰδέα ἄρχοντε καὶ ἄγοντε: Soph. O. C. 1676 ἰδόντε καὶ παθούσα (where both forms stand together) and Jebb's n. in appendix.

903. It is very possible that Euripides here has in mind his master Anaxagoras, *quem ferunt* (says Cicero, Tusc. III. 30) *nuntiata morte filii dixisse, 'sciebam me genuisse mortalem.'* Anaxagoras was about sixty when the Alcestis was produced, so that ll. 908—910 would not be inappropriate.

904. ἐν γένει κ.τ.λ., 'I had a kinsman': cf. Soph. O. T. 1016 ὁθούνεκ' ἦν σοι Πόλυβος οὐδὲν ἐν γένει. 1430 τοῖς ἐν γένει γὰρ τἀγγενῆ μάλισθ' ὁρᾶν | μόνοις τ' ἀκούειν εὐσεβῶς ἔχει κακά.

906. μονόπαις κ.τ.λ., 'whose son an only child, etc.': cf. supr. 406 n.

ἔμπας, 'nevertheless': a mainly Epic word, which occurs rarely in tragedy (in Eur. here and Cycl. 536).

907. ἅλις, 'enough' in the sense 'not too much,' 'with moderation': the Scholiast explains by μετρίως, a meaning also found Med. 630 εἰ δ' ἅλις ἔλθοι Κύπρις κ.τ.λ., on which line a commentary occurs in Hipp. 443 Κύπρις γὰρ οὐ φορητὸς ἦν πολλὴ ῥυῇ.

909. προπετὴς πολιὰς ἐπὶ χαίτας, 'quick hastening towards hoary age': cf. Hec. 150 (of Polyxena condemned to die) τύμβου προπετῆ.

910. βιότου τε πόρσω, 'far advanced in years': cf. Hipp. 795 πρόσω μὲν ἤδη βίοτος. The construction with a genit. in this sense is a favourite one with Plato, e.g. Prot. 310 C ἔπειτά μοι λίαν πόρρω ἔδοξε τῶν νυκτῶν εἶναι: Apol. 38 C ὁρᾶτε γὰρ δὴ τὴν ἡλικίαν, ὅτι πόρρω ἤδη ἐστὶ τοῦ βίου. Symp. 217 D. It also has the meaning 'far from,' Plat. Phaedo 96 E πόρρω τοῦ οἴεσθαι. The older forms of the word are πρόσω, πρόσσω: later πόρσω, πόρρω: Attic prose uses πόρρω. Euripides prefers πρόσω.

911. ὦ σχῆμα δόμων, 'O sad home': this I believe to be the force of σχῆμα: in phrases like the present it calls attention to some *aspect* of a thing, which aspect we must understand from the context.

912. μεταπίπτοντος δαίμονος, 'now that my life's lot is being cast down from joy to grieving': for μεταπίπτειν of revolutionary change,

cf. Thuc. VIII. 68, 3 τὰ τῶν τετρακοσίων ἐν ὑστέρῳ μεταπεσόντα. δαίμονος, cf. supr. 499.

914. πολὺ γὰρ τὸ μέσον, 'for wide is the difference': cf. Herod. I. 126 οἱ δὲ ἔφασαν πολλὸν εἶναι αὐτῶν (hard work and feasting) τὸ μέσον: IX. 82 ὡς δὲ τῆς θοίνης (Spartan dinner) ποιηθείσης ἦν πολλὸν τὸ μέσον (between its sorry fare and the luxury of a Persian banquet).

915. τότε μέν: μεταπίπτοντος above has suggested the two scenes, one of sorrow, one of joy; πολὺ τὸ μέσον had made the idea still clearer: now he actually depicts them: the scene when in the evening of his wedding-day he brought his bride from her home at Iolcos, amid the glare of torches cut from the pine-woods that overhang her father's city at the foot of Pelion, with glad bridal songs and shouts of congratulation and of welcome from the merry band of friends, all clad in white, who had escorted him, as, with his wife and best man, he was drawn on the marriage-car to the palace at Pherae, which was to receive as its new mistress his hard-won bride; and the scene of lamentation and grief so soon to follow as the same young wife was carried out, shoulder-high, lying dead upon the funeral couch.

917. χέρα βαστάζων, 'lovingly holding my dear wife's hand.' βαστάζω is properly to pick up and carry, but the Attic use, says Suidas s.v., is οὐ τὸ ἆραι, ἀλλὰ ψηλαφῆσαι: cf. Aesch. Ag. 35 γένοιτο δ' οὖν μολόντος εὐφιλῆ χέρα | ἄνακτος οἴκων τῇδε βαστάσαι χερί: Soph. O. C. 1105 σῶμα βαστάσαι ('embrace') δότε.

919. Notice the sad effect of θανοῦσαν, ὀλβίζων so near together; 'counting us happy, her who is dead and me.'

920, 1. ὡς—εἶμεν is oratio obliqua. The reference to their parentage is bitter, considering how discouraging is Admetus' present attitude to his father and mother. εἶμεν for εἴημεν is rare, εἶτε still rarer, εἶεν common.

922. ἀντίπαλος, 'corresponding': a very favourite word with Thucydides: 'the cry of mourning now takes the place of the clamour of gladness of that day, and black robes the place of white: so changed the accompaniment with which I am escorted to my bridal bed, now alas! unpartnered.'

926. παρ', 'at the time of': cf. παρὰ πότον, παρὰ δεῖπνον.

928. By the collocation of the sentences, ἀλλ' ἔσωσας βίοτον καὶ ψυχάν and ἔθανε δάμαρ, ἔλιπε φιλίαν the chorus rouse a train of thought in Admetus, which leads to a frank admission of his own unmanliness, and a recognition of the merited contempt into which he has fallen:

ἄρτι μανθάνω he cries, and were it not for this ὀψιμαθία the little sympathy we have with the poor wretch would disappear. The chorus seem to imagine that they have hit on the right strain of comfort for their king: 'after all remember that you have saved your life: your dear wife is gone, no doubt, but it happens to so many to lose their yoke-fellow.'

930. **φιλίαν** seems = 'those whom she loved and who loved her.'

932. **παρέλυσεν**, 'hath deprived of a yoke-fellow': lit. 'unloose from beside': the word may have been suggested by σύζυγες, supr. 921. Cf. supr. 417, 892.

935. **δαίμονα**, 'destiny': as supr. 499, 914: there is as small an idea of the deity controlling destiny in the use here as in Cycl. 110 τὸν αὐτὸν δαίμον᾽ ἐξαντλεῖς ἐμοί.

937. **τῆς**, cf. supr. 883, 264, n. For the sentiment, cf. Soph. Trach. 1173 τοῖς γὰρ θανοῦσι μόχθος οὐ προσγίγνεται: El. 1170 τοὺς γὰρ θανόντας οὐχ ὁρῶ λυπουμένους: O. C. 955 θανόντων δ᾽ οὐδὲν ἄλγος ἅπτεται.

939. **ὃν οὐ χρῆν ζῆν**, cf. supr. 379, n. **παρεὶς τὸ μόρσιμον**, cf. supr. 695.

940. **ἄρτι μανθάνω**, cf. supr. 531, n., infr. 1069: Bacch. 1295 Διόνυσος ἡμᾶς ὤλεσ᾽· ἄρτι μανθάνω: Or. 254 ταχὺς δὲ μετέθου λύσσαν, ἄρτι σωφρονῶν.

942. 'To whom should I give words of greeting and from whom receive them, that I should have pleasure in entering my home?' Cf. supr. 195, n.

945. **εὖτ᾽ ἂν εἰσίδω**, εὖτε is occasionally used by trag. poets, when metrically convenient, for ὅτε: it is Ionic and poetic, and never occurs in Attic prose.

946. **θρόνους**, sc. κενούς.

947. **αὐχμηρόν** means 'with a dusty uncared-for look.' The word is usually employed of persons, 'squalid,' 'unkempt,' with special reference to their dry and unanointed hair: cf. Or. 387 ὡς ἠγρίωσαι πλόκαμον αὐχμηρὸν τάλας: 223 αὐχμώδη κόμην ἄφελε προσώπου.

ἀμφὶ γούνασι πίπτοντα, 'casting themselves about my knees': for πίπτοντα cf. supr. 175, n.

948. **οἱ δέ**, sc. δοῦλοι, as though οἱ μὲν (παῖδες) had preceded: reference has indirectly been made to the slaves in 947 αὐχμηρὸν οὖδας.

949. **οἵαν κ.τ.λ.** = ὅτι τοίαν: cf. Herod. I. 31 ἐμακάριζον τὴν μητέρα οἵων (i.e. ὅτι τοιούτων) τέκνων ἐκύρησε: Thuc. IV. 26 ἀθυμίαν τε πλείστην

ὁ χρόνος παρεῖχε παρὰ λόγον ἐπιγιγνόμενος, οὓς (i.e. ὅτι αὐτοὺς) ᾤοντο ἡμερῶν ὀλίγων ἐκπολιορκήσειν.

950. ἔξωθεν = 'back into the palace.'

952. οὐ γὰρ ἐξανέξομαι, echo from 941 : the double compound is frequent in this sense.

954. ἐρεῖ δέ με, cf. supr. 658 n. ἐχθρός, *inimicus*)(πολέμιος, *hostis*.

955. The following lines are almost a reproduction of his father's words 694 sqq., which no doubt still tingle in his ears.

957. εἶτα, *indignantis*, cf. supr. 696, whence too ἀψυχίᾳ in the preceding line is echoed.

958. στυγεῖ, the word he himself had used supr. 338.

959. κληδόνα, cf. supr. 315 n. πρός κακοῖσι, cf. supr. 557.

960. κύδιον: this comparative seems to occur only here and Andr. 639 κύδιον (some MSS κύδιστον) βροτοῖς | πένητα χρηστὸν ἢ κακὸν καὶ πλούσιον | γαμβρὸν πεπᾶσθαι καὶ φίλον. Hesychius explains it as αἱρετώτερον. δῆτα, cf. supr. 530, n.

961. κλύοντι, cf. supr. 705, n. πεπραγότι, cf. supr. 246, n.

962 sq. The Scholiast roundly accuses Euripides of an attempt to parade his own learning and culture, δεῖξαι ὅσον μετέσχε παιδεύσεως. We need not go so far as that, but, while admitting that in literature of dramatic form it is difficult for a poet with strongly developed enthusiasms to find suitable *media* on all occasions for their exposition, we cannot acquit Euripides of much misplaced philosophizing. Such reflexions however, when put into the mouth of the chorus, do not strike us as inapposite; the personality or characterization of the chorus is so dim and unreal (strikingly so, when in full possession of the stage they moralise on the lessons of the drama which is passing), that we easily discern the figure of the poet through the thin disguise, which in comedy indeed he boldly throws aside in the Parabasis, and addresses the spectators with his own words direct. (Pollux IV. 3 after speaking of the personal character of the comic parabasis tells us that tragic poets did not avail themselves of this opportunity, but, he adds, Εὐριπίδης αὐτὸ πεποίηκεν ἐν πολλοῖς δράμασιν.) Such a line of defence is not however tenable when criticism is directed against the impropriety of philosophic reflexions placed in the lips of uneducated *persons*, as for instance of the nurse in the Hippolytus (252 sqq.) or the Medea (119 sqq.).

In fatalistic strain the poet dwells on the might of Necessity, without whose help not even the Supreme Power can carry out its own decrees. Let Admetus bow and take consolation from the veneration that will be offered, as at a shrine, at the tomb of Alcestis.

962. 'For myself, I have both ranged through literature and soared aloft in the speculations of science': μοῦσα here=μουσική (literature), μετάρσιος=μετέωρος, referring to the new science of the day abused by Aristophanes in the Clouds (133—253). An age of reason was succeeding to an age of faith in Athens, and the astronomical speculations (τὰ μετέωρα) of Anaxagoras were the especial abhorrence of old-fashioned conservatives, who imagined that such impertinent efforts to get behind Homer could prelude nothing but the subversion of morality and government. μουσική had come to mean 'culture' generally; the old education (γράμματά τε καὶ κιθαρίζειν καὶ παλαίειν, Plat. Theag. 122 E) had developed wider sympathies, and it was in the interpretation of μουσική that this enlargement manifested itself; the Laches (188 D) represents for us the μουσικός as one ἁρμονίαν καλλίστην ἡρμοσμένος οὐ λύραν οὐδὲ παιδιᾶς ὄργανα, ἀλλὰ τῷ ὄντι ζῆν ἡρμοσμένος αὐτὸς αὑτοῦ τὸν βίον σύμφωνον τοῖς λόγοις κ.τ.λ. Still we may see from the present passage that it did not yet at any rate include a training in the natural sciences of that day: then, as now, the methods and matter of scientific training, valuable as they must be acknowledged to be, seemed other than, and supplementary to, the teaching of the humanities.

963. ἧξα suits μετάρσιος only: from it we must supply a verb suited to διὰ μούσας.

965. Cf. El. 1301 μοῖραν ἀνάγκης ἦγεν τὸ χρεών: Hel. 513 λόγος γάρ ἐστιν οὐκ ἐμός, σοφῶν δ' ἔπος, | δεινῆς ἀνάγκης οὐδὲν ἰσχύειν πλέον (the σοφοὶ here referred to are 'Ορφικοί, in whose writings first ἀνάγκη was personified): Phoen. 1763 τὰς γὰρ ἐκ θεῶν ἀνάγκας θνητὸν ὄντα δεῖ φέρειν: fr. 956 ὅστις δ' ἀνάγκῃ συγκεχώρηκεν βροτῶν, | σοφὸς παρ' ἡμῖν καὶ τὰ θεῖ' ἐπίσταται.

967 sq. The Scholiast tells us that certain σανίδες (a curious word to use in this sense: an Athenian would at once think of the public notice-boards) containing records of Orpheus were preserved in a temple of Dionysus on Mount Haemus. Whether this be so or not, a passage from Plato (Rep. 364 E) is worth citing here: βίβλων δὲ ὅμαδον παρέχονται Μουσαίου καὶ 'Ορφέως, καθ' ἅς θυηπολοῦσι, πείθοντες οὐ μόνον ἰδιώτας ἀλλὰ καὶ πόλεις, ὡς ἄρα λύσεις τε καὶ καθαρμοὶ ἀδικημάτων διὰ θυσιῶν καὶ παιδιᾶς εἰσι μὲν ἔτι ζῶσιν, εἰσὶ δὲ καὶ τελευτήσασιν κ.τ.λ. These 'Ορφεοτελεσταί were in bad repute; they no doubt traded on the belief

in the actual existence of the books mentioned above. Pausanias says that the secrets of Orpheus were, at Athens, in the keeping of the family of the Lycomidae. τάς, cf. supr. 883, n.

968. Ὀρφεία γῆρυς, 'the sweet-tongued Orpheus': cf. βίη Ἡρακληείη, 'mighty Heracles.'

970. Ἀσκληπιάδαις: the knowledge of the 'mystery' of medicine was a guild-secret handed down in a caste of priest-physicians, who took their name, and perhaps pretended to derive descent, from Asclepios, son of Apollo. The islands of Cos and Cnidos were their chief seats. Plato (Rep. 406 A) says that the medical science of his day was not that of the early Asclepiadae, certainly not of Asclepios, who gave wounded men inflammatory drinks, but dated from the sickly trainer Herodicos, who ἀπέκναισε πρῶτον μὲν καὶ μάλιστα ἑαυτόν, ἔπειτ' ἄλλους ὕστερον πολλούς.

972. ἀντιτεμών, 'shredding in antidotes': cf. Hom. h. Cer. 229 οἶδα γὰρ ἀντίτομον μέγα φέρτερον οὐδοτόμοιο: Pind. P. IV. 394 σὺν δ' ἐλαίῳ, φαρμακώσαισ' ἀντίτομα στερεᾶν ὀδυνᾶν δῶκε χρίεσθαι: Aesch. Ag. 17 ὕπνον τόδ' ἀντίμολπον ἐντέμνων ἄκος: a metaphor, says a Scholiast, ἀπὸ τῶν ῥιζοτομούντων (those who gather and cut up roots for medicinal purposes).

973. μόνας κ.τ.λ., 'she is the only goddess, who hath neither altar nor holy image that we may approach, she alone hearkeneth not to sacrifice': lit. 'of her alone we can approach neither altar nor image'; notice too the change of subject in l. 975. There is a reference to the cult of ἀνάγκη in conjunction with βία on the slope of Acrocorinthus in Paus. II. 4, 6.

For the position of μόνας and the omission of ἐκείνης or ταύτης, cf. Thuc. III. 43 μόνην τε πόλιν διὰ τὰς περινοίας εὖ ποιῆσαι ἐκ τοῦ προφανοῦς μὴ ἐξαπατήσαντα ἀδύνατον. ('Athens is the only city which one cannot etc.')

974. βρέτας: the poet has in mind those early wooden images (ξόανα), which were the object of the deepest veneration: in the Electra (1254) the ancient wooden statue of Athena Polias in the Parthenon is called Παλλάδος σεμνὸν βρέτας: cf. too Aesch. Eum. 79 ἄγκαθεν λαβὼν βρέτας (of the same image).

976. πότνια, usual term of address to a goddess: cf. infr. 1004.

μείζων ἔλθοις, cf. Hipp. 528 (prayer to Eros) μή μοί ποτε σὺν κακῷ φανείης | μηδ' ἄρρυθμος ἔλθοις.

978. Cf. Hom. Il. I. 527 οὐ γὰρ ἐμὸν παλινάγρετον ('revocable')

οὐδ' ἀπατηλὸν | οὐδ' ἀτελεύτητον, ὅτι κεν κεφαλῇ κατανεύσω: Soph. O. C. 248 νεύσατε τὰν ἀδόκητον χάριν. For the omission of ἄν in the protasis of a conditional relative sentence, cf. supr. 76, n.: Goodw. Gr. Gr. § 234.

979. **σὺν σοί**, 'with thy help': the common Attic use of σύν, e.g. in such phrases as σὺν θεῷ. In Attic prose, except in this sense, σύν with dat. gave way to μετά with genit. (except in Xenophon, whose somewhat eclectic Greek, it must be remembered, is by no means a model of Attic).

980. The Χάλυβες or Χάλυβοι dwelt in the hill-country, south of Trebizond, in the district of Tokat, now famous for copper. According to Strabo their country is referred to by Homer (Il. II. 857) as 'Αλύβη, ὅθεν ἀργύρου ἐστὶ γενέθλη. Xenophon with the Ten Thousand passed through the land of the Chalybes, noting that ὁ βίος ἦν τοῖς πλείστοις αὐτῶν ἀπὸ σιδηρείας. A picturesque description of their life is given by Apollonius Rhodius (II. 1004—1010): no flocks or herds have they ἀλλὰ σιδηροφόρον στυφελὴν χθόνα γατομέοντες, | ὦνον ἀμείβονται βιοτή-σιον, κ.τ.λ.

982. **ἀποτόμου**, cf. supr. 118, n.: Sophocles (O. T. 876) speaks of ἀνάγκη ἀπότομος.

983. **αἰδώς**, cf. supr. 601, n.: consideration for others, especially the weak.

984. **χερῶν δεσμοῖς**, cf. supr. 847 κύκλον δὲ περιβαλῶ χεροῖν ἐμαῖν.

985. Cf. fr. 336, 1 δοκεῖς τὸν "Αιδην σῶν τι φροντίζειν γόων | καὶ παῖδ' ἀνήσειν τὸν σόν, εἰ θέλοις στένειν; Soph. El. 136 ἀλλ' οὔτοι τόν γ' ἐξ 'Αΐδα | παγκοίνου λίμνας πατέρα ἀνστάσεις οὔτε γόοις οὔτε λιταῖσιν. Hom. Il. XXIV. 550 οὐ γάρ τι πρήξεις ἀκαχήμενος υἷος ἑοῖο, | οὐδέ μιν ἀνστήσεις.

ἔνερθεν, never found in strict Attic: κάτω as adverb, ὑπό as preposition, superseded it.

989. **σκότιοι** may mean sons of gods by mortal mothers, 'mighty men which were of old, men of renown' (Genesis vi. 4), like Sarpedon, son of Zeus, slain by Patroclos (Il. XVI. 476): for σκότιος=νόθος, cf. Il. VI. 24 σκότιον δέ ἑ γείνατο μήτηρ. But perhaps we should take it proleptically with φθίνουσι, 'die and go down into darkness,' comparing supr. 125 ἕδρας σκοτίους "Αιδα τε πύλας, a passage we may imagine to have been in the poet's mind from the repetition in 982 of ἀπότομος in 118.

994. **κλισίαις**: 'couch': very rarely used in this sense; cf. I. T. 857 'Αχιλλέως εἰς κλισίαν λέκτρων.

995. **χῶμα**: the earliest form of monument to the dead was a mound of earth heaped up over the grave, a 'barrow,' τάφος χωστός or πολύχωστος: many of these may still be seen on the shores of the Hellespont and elsewhere. on the top of this it became the custom to place a στήλη, with a commemorative inscription, cf. I. T. 702 τύμβον τε χώσον κἀπίθες μνημεῖά μοι. More elaborate monuments, like the ξεστὸς τύμβος here, often in the form of shrines (ἡρῷα), succeeded: 'when the buried person began to be considered as a hero, the grave required an altar' (Guhl and Koner, p. 94 Eng. tr.). No doubt the primitive custom of ancestor-worship made the connexion between 'tomb' and 'temple' an easily-grasped idea; cf. Aesch. Cho. 106 αἰδουμένη σοι βωμὸν ὡς τύμβον πατρὸς λέξω. So Helen betakes herself to the tomb of Proteus as to a sanctuary (Hel. 64, 545).

996. **θεοῖσι δ' ὁμοίως τιμάσθω**: abridged for τιμάσθω ὁ τύμβος σᾶς ἀλόχου ὁμοίως τοῖς βωμοῖς τῶν θεῶν: cf. Goodw. Gr. Gr. § 186, note 2.

999. **σέβας ἐμπόρων**, 'object of wayfarers' veneration.'

1000. **δοχμίαν κέλευθον**, the branch road leading to the temple-grave from the main Larissa road, beside which it was situated: cf. supr. 835.

1003. **δαίμων**: as a mortal, Alcestis could not attain higher rank than this.

1004. **πότνια**, cf. supr. 976, n. **εὖ δὲ δοίης**: cf. Andr. 750 ὦ πρέσβυ, θεοί σοι δοῖεν εὖ καὶ τοῖσι σοῖς.

1005. **φᾶμαι**: cf. the reference to τὸ βωμοειδὲς, which was supposed to be the tomb of Themistocles, quoted by Plutarch (Them. 32, 5) as from Plato Comicus (flor. B.C. 400), ὁ σὸς δὲ τύμβος ἐν καλῷ κεχωσμένος | τοῖς ἐμπόροις πρόσρησις ἔσται πανταχοῦ.

1006. **καὶ μήν**, cf. supr. 105, n., 611. **ὅδ'**, cf. supr. 24, n.

1008. **χρή**, a general rule: had the particular instance been directly referred to χρῆν would have been necessary: cf. supr. 379, n.

1009. **μομφάς**, 'grounds of complaint': cf. Or. 1069 ἐν μὲν πρῶτά σοι μομφὴν ἔχω, εἴ κ.τ.λ.

1010. **ἠξίουν**, 'claimed': cf. supr. 571, n.

1011. **παρεστώς**, cf. supr. 211, n. For τοῖς κακοῖς παρεστώς (for σοὶ ἐν τοῖς κακ. ὄντι παρ.) cf. Aeschin. 78, 3 μὴ βοηθῶν τοῖς τῶν προγόνων ἀτυχήμασι κακῶς ἐπιχειρῇ ποιεῖν τὴν πόλιν. **ἐξετάζεσθαι**, 'to be proved'; a favourite word in this sense with the orators: cf. supr. 15, 640.

1015. **ἐλειψάμην**: the active aorist is found Hom. Il. VII. 481: XXIV. 285; elsewhere the pres. and imperf. only of λείβω or εἴβω are found.

1017. μέμφομαι μὲν μέμφομαι, cf. infr. 1093 αἰνῶ μὲν αἰνῶ: supr. 328, n.

1017, 18. μὲν...οὐ μὴν κ.τ.λ. 'I blame you: I do not however etc.' μὴν is in this rather rare antithesis adversative: cf. Plat. Phaedr. 268 E ἀνάγκη μὲν καὶ ταῦτ' ἐπίστασθαι τὸν μέλλοντα ἁρμονικὸν ἔσεσθαι, οὐδὲν μὴν κωλύει μηδὲ σμικρὸν ἁρμονίας ἐπαΐειν τὸν τὴν σὴν ἕξιν ἔχοντα.

1020. For the absence of a connecting particle, cf. supr. 280, n., 287.

1023. ὃ μὴ τύχοιμι, sc. πράξας: 'but should I fare, as may it not be my lot to fare: for fain would I return.'

1026. Of course the possibilities of time are defied here: that Heracles should leave the palace, find the games, compete and bring back the prize, a considerable interval is required: this point deserves mention only as a warning against an over-refining tendency to examine too closely into statements, which the poet did not intend for strict examination, and with the consistency and possibility of which he probably did not trouble himself. Such a point seems to me to be the precise character of the obsequies of Alcestis. πάνδημον, open to all and therefore worthy of the attention of so renowned a hero.

1027. πόνον in apposition to ἀγῶνα. ἀθληταῖσιν, generally used of boxers: so Lat. athleta. Euripides' views of the Hellenic passion for athletics are interesting: cf. fr. 284 κακῶν γὰρ ὄντων μυρίων καθ' Ἑλλάδα | οὐδὲν κάκιόν ἐστιν ἀθλητῶν γένους......τίς γὰρ παλαίσας εὖ, τίς ὠκύπους ἀνὴρ | ἢ δίσκον ἄρας ἢ γνάθον παίσας καλῶς | πόλει πατρῴᾳ στέφανον ἤρκεσεν λαβών; Euripides is here supposed to be echoing the words of Xenophanes of Colophon.

1028. κομίζω, in the sense of 'winning a prize' more frequently middle: cf. infr. 1030 ἄγεσθαι.

1029. τὰ κοῦφα, cognate accus. after νικῶσιν. From the antithesis of τοῖς τὰ μείζονα νικῶσι we must understand by κοῦφα the somewhat 'trivial' competitions (from the point of view of the great fighter) of running and jumping: possibly there is an intentional play on the two meanings 'trivial' and 'nimble' (cf. κοῦφα βιβάς, and the like).

ἦν = ἐξῆν.

1031. βουφόρβια, 'herd of oxen.' With this list of prizes compare that in Il. XXIII. 259 sq., where γυναῖκα ἄγεσθαι ἀμύμονα ἔργα ἰδυῖαν falls with other prizes to the lot of the victor in the horse-race.

1032. αὐτοῖς, sc. τοῖς βουφορβίοις.

1033. αἰσχρὸν ἦν, 'it would have been shame'; cf. Goodw. M. T. §§ 415, 416, and supr. 379, n.

1035. **κλοπαίαν,** cf. supr. 103, n.: Aesch. P. V. 110 πυρὸς πηγὴν κλοπαίαν.

1037. As Heracles, by the emphatic position of φίλον in l. 1008, had expressed the view that Admetus had not behaved to him as he should to a friend, the latter now hastens to explain that the concealment of his wife's death was prompted by no wish to slight, still less from any feeling of hostility. **ἀτίζων,** a rare poetical word.

1039. Cf. supr. 557 καὶ πρὸς κακοῖσιν ἄλλο τοῦτ᾽ ἂν ἦν κακόν, | δόμους καλεῖσθαι τοὺς ἐμοὺς ἐχθροξένους.

ἦν προσκείμενον, cf. supr. 122, n.

1040. **ὡρμήθης,** 'if you had hurried away etc.,' i.e. in annoyance at a repulse by Admetus.

1042. **αἰτοῦμαί σ᾽,** parenthetic. Admetus' agitation at the thought of the woman is expressed by the short unconnected sentences of 1042—1048: cf. however crit. n.

1044. **ἄνωχθι:** perfect imperative active, only found in perfects with present meaning: Hadl. Gr. Gr. § 456.

1045. **μή μ᾽ ἀναμνήσῃς κακῶν:** similar agitated appeals are 1047 μὴ νοσοῦντί μοι νόσον προσθῇς: 1065 μή μ᾽ ἕλῃς ᾑρημένον.

1048. **ἅλις βαρύνομαι,** 'I am abundantly weighed down': the use of ἅλις with a verb is Homeric.

1049. **ποῦ καὶ κ.τ.λ.,** 'and where, tell me, could etc.?' Cf. supr. 834, n. **δωμάτων,** cf. supr. 9, n.

1050. **πρέπει,** personal use: cf. supr. 512, n.; 'she is clearly marked (i.e. as young) by the dress and adornments of youth.'

1051. The alternatives offered are merely rhetorical: there would be no necessity for the young woman to live in the ἀνδρωνῖτις among the men or in the θάλαμος (see n. on supr. 162), but to suggest the γυναικωνῖτις would have taken away the poet's opportunity. **δῆτα,** *mirantis,* cf. supr. 530, 822.

1052. **καὶ πῶς κ.τ.λ.** introduces (so infr. 1056) a strong objection; cf. supr. 142, n.

1053. **Ἡράκλεις:** the address by name of the not over-strict (cf. supr. 790) hero in the midst of this trite moral is nearly comic.

1055. **ἐσβήσας,** causal: Attic prose does not know this transitive use of βαίνω and its compounds.

τρέφω, delib. subj.

1056. **ἐπεσφρῶ:** the force of this compound seems to be to 'thrust into an improper place': cf. El. 1033 ἀλλ᾽ ἦλθ᾽ ἔχων μοι μαινάδ᾽ ἔνθεον κόρην | λέκτροις τ᾽ ἐπεισέφρησε (a passage similar to this): H. F. 1267 ὄφεις ἐπεισέφρησε σπαργάνοισι τοῖς ἐμοῖς: fr. 781, 46 μή τιν᾽ Ἥφαιστος χόλον | δόμοις ἐπεισφρεὶς μέλαθρα συμφλέξῃ πυρί. εἰσφρέω=merely 'to admit.' The origin of the simple verb φρέω is unknown.

1057. **διπλῆν φοβοῦμαι μέμψιν**: fear of what people may say is a prominent feature in the weak character of Admetus, cf. 558, 959.

ἔκ τε δημοτῶν. The construction changes at l. 1060, where we do not find καὶ ἐκ τῆς θανούσης, but a more suitable form of statement τῆς θαν. πολλὴν πρόνοιαν δεῖ μ᾽ ἔχειν. Apprehensions of one's δημόται are frequently expressed in comedy; cf. Ar. Eq. 320: Lys. 685.

1058. **μ᾽ ἐλέγχῃ...πίτνειν**, the accus. and infin. constr. is rare after ἐλέγχειν.

1059. **πίτνειν**, 'throw myself upon': cf. supr. 175, n.

1060. **ἀξία δέ μοι σέβειν** is parenthetic.

1061. **πρόνοιαν** with τῆς θανούσης, like προμηθίαν supr. 1054.

1062. **ἥτις ποτ᾽ εἶ σύ**, cf. Hom. Od. v. 445 κλῦθι, ἄναξ, ὅτις ἐσσί. **ἔχουσ᾽**, partic. after ἴσθι (verb of knowing). **ταῦτ᾽ Ἀλκήστιδι μέτρα**, cf. supr. 996, n.

1063. **προσήιξαι**: this and similar passive forms, which may be referred to εἴσκω ('make like'), are (with the exception of this passage) confined to epic Greek. These lines afford an example of 'tragic irony.'

1065. **ᾑρημένον**, probably used for the sake of the *paronomasia*, as ἁλίσκομαι is the usual passive of αἱρέω, 'take': cf. however El. 1009 ᾑρημένων δὲ δωμάτων ᾑρήμεθα. In Attic ᾕρημαι has generally a middle sense, except in the meaning 'chosen.' For the phrase, cf. Soph. Ant. 1030 τὸν θανόντ᾽ ἐπικτανεῖν.

1067. **θολοῖ**, 'agitates,' 'confounds': θόλος is the dark fluid emitted by the cuttle-fish (*sepia*) in order to conceal his movements: hence the verb θολόω, 'make turbid' and, metaphorically, 'perturb.' Similarly used is πορφύρω, which is first applied to agitated water, then to mental trouble: cf. Jebb's n. on Soph. Ant. 20.

1068. Cf. Soph. Tr. 852 ἔρρωγεν παγὰ δακρύων: H. F. 449 δακρύων ὡς οὐ δύναμαι κατέχειν | γραίας ὄσσων ἔτι πηγάς. The troubled waters of the soul overflow as it were from the eyes.

1069. **ὡς ἄρτι...γεύομαι**, cf. supr. 940, 531, n. ''Tis but now that I taste the full bitterness of my sorrow.'

1070. It must be remembered that the chorus heard nothing of Heracles' intention to rescue Alcestis, so that they are ignorant of the meaning which the audience will attach to the words θεοῦ δόσιν (Heracles' gift to Admetus of his recovered wife), by which they of course mean 'destiny.'

1071. Cf. crit. n. **καρτερεῖν**, with accus. 'bear up against,' 'endure': cf. I. A. 1370 τὰ δ᾽ ἀδύναθ᾽ ἡμῖν καρτερεῖν οὐ ῥᾴδιον.

1072. **εἰ γὰρ εἶχον κ.τ.λ.**, 'would I had the power etc.': cf. supr. 536, n. The humorous irony of Heracles is noticeable in every line as far as 1120.

1074. **πορσῦναι χάριν**, cf. Supp. 132 δισσοῖσι γαμβροῖς τήνδε πορσύνων χάριν.

1075. **βούλεσθαί σ᾽ ἄν**, indirect for ἂν ἐβούλου: for ἐβουλόμην ἄν, and the like, referring to present time (=*vellem*) cf. Goodw. M. T. § 246. **ποῦ** is often used to denote indignation or sense of absurdity: cf. Ion 528 ποῦ δέ μοι πατὴρ σύ; ταῦτ᾽ οὖν οὐ γέλως κλύειν ἐμοί; Soph. O. T. 390 ποῦ σὺ μάντις εἶ σαφής;

1077. **ἐναισίμως**=μετρίως, an epic adverb found twice in Aesch., here only in Eurip., never in Soph.

1078. When Cicero in banishment was bewailing his misfortunes in unmanly fashion, a friend reproved him: the orator replied that to counsel firmness to another and to display it oneself were very different things; ὅταν πάθημά τι τὴν ψυχὴν καταλάβῃ, θολοῦται (cf. supr. 1067) καὶ σκοτοῦται καὶ οὐδὲν δύναται καίριον ἐννοῆσαι· ὅθεν που πάνυ καλῶς εἴρηται ὅτι ῥᾷον παραινέσαι ἑτέροις ἐστὶν ἢ αὐτὸν παθόντα καρτερῆσαι (Dio Cass. XXXVIII. 18, 2).

1079. **προκόπτοις**, cf. Hec. 961 ἀλλὰ ταῦτα μὲν τί δεῖ | θρηνεῖν προκόπτοντ᾽ οὐδὲν ἐς πρόσθεν κακῶν; Hipp. 23 τὰ πολλὰ δὲ | πάλαι προκόψασ᾽, οὐ πόνου πολλοῦ με δεῖ: the metaphor is from pioneers preparing a way for an army.

1080. **ἔγνωκα καὐτός**, sc. οὐδὲν προκόψων. **ἐξάγει** means 'draws me out of a sensible course.'

ἔρως is a 'yearning for tears': cf. Supp. 79 ἄπληστος ἅδε μ᾽ ἐξάγει χάρις γόων.

1081. **τὸ γὰρ φιλῆσαι κ.τ.λ.**, a general statement, hence the masc. **τὸν θανόντα**. Heracles takes up ἔρως in a different sense.

1082. Cf. Hec. 667 ὦ παντάλαινα κἄτι μᾶλλον ἢ λέγω: 1121 ἀπώλεσ᾽, οὐκ ἀπώλεσ᾽, ἀλλὰ μειζόνως.

1083. **γυναικὸς ἐσθλ. ἤμπλ.**, cf. supr. 242, 418. **τίς ἀντερεῖ;** cf. supr. 152, 615.

1084. **ἄνδρα τόνδε**=ἐμέ: so infr. 1090, 1094, 1128.

1085. χρόνος μαλάξει, cf. supr. 381.

1086. 'Time thou may'st say, if time be to die.'

1088. The short interjectional sentences denote agitation : cf. supr. 1042, n. οἷον εἶπας, the phrase is elliptical : lit. 'to think of such a thing, as you uttered!' Cf. Hom. Od. v. 183 οἷον δὴ τὸν μῦθον ἐπεφράσθης ἀγορεῦσαι. For εἶπας, cf. supr. 58, n.

1089. οὐ γαμεῖς γάρ; γὰρ marks surprise : cf. Soph. Phil. 249 οὐ γὰρ οἶσθα μ' ὅντιν' εἰσορᾷς; λέχος is nominative.

1091. μῶν expects the answer 'no.' ὠφελεῖν τι προσδοκᾷς; 'do you expect that (by so doing) you are conferring a benefit on Alcestis?' For the present infin., cf. Goodw. M. T. § 118.

1092. Notice the irony of ὅπουπέρ ἐστι.

1093. μωρίαν δ' ὀφλισκάνεις : ὀφλισκάνειν means to bring on oneself some disadvantage, e.g. βλάβην, or the reputation for some bad quality (expressed by the name of the quality simply) e.g. μωρίαν, δειλίαν, κακίαν.

1094. With this line supply αἴνει from αἰνῶ 1093. καλῶν, future.

1095. Heracles particularises what he had vaguely stated in 1093 : he also slightly corrects Admetus' last remark 'praise me for my resolve to remain a widower.' 'Nay, not quite that, I praise you for your constancy.' ἐπήνεσ': an action just taking place is often dramatically regarded as already past : cf. Soph. El. 668 ἐδεξάμην τὸ ῥηθέν, 'I welcome the omen.' Ar. Eq. 696 ἥσθην ἀπειλαῖς, 'your threats amuse me.' Goodw. M. T. § 60.

1097. Notice the irony of the connexion : 'you say you would die rather than desert Alcestis : well then, receive this lady.'

1098. μή, πρός σε κ.τ.λ. Cf. supr. 275, n.

1099. καὶ μὴν ἅμ. γε, 'and yet you will be doing amiss, etc.'

1100. καρδίαν δηχθήσομαι, cf. Hec. 235 μὴ λυπρὰ μηδὲ καρδίας δηκτήρια | ἐξιστορῆσαι : Ar. Ach. 1 ὅσα δὴ δέδηγμαι τὴν ἐμαυτοῦ καρδίαν.

1101. This word-fencing would be greatly to Euripides' liking, and no doubt popular too with Athenian audiences. πέσοι, metaphor from dicing.

1102. εἴθε μὴ ἔλαβες, cf. supr. 1072, 536, n.

1103. 'And yet a friend's victory is in some sense your own' is the meaning in which Admetus takes these words : a remark which he conceives to have the greater point, as he is practically to receive the prize of his friend's victory ; this he politely refuses with the formula καλῶς ἔλεξας.

1107. κἀγώ, 'I, as well as you, am somewhat insistent': εἰδώς τι, 'with reason': the irony is of course manifest. ἔχω προθυμίαν, cf. 1054.

1108. Another instance of Admetus' weakness of character: he dares not offend.

μήν, cf. supr. 1018, n.

1110. κομίζετ', addressed to the servants: εἰ χρὴ echoes 1105.

1111. προσπόλοις receives the emphasis: 'not into the hands of servants, but thine own, will I entrust her.'

1112. σὺ δ' αὐτὸς κ.τ.λ. Admetus' last feeble attempt to save himself from complete surrender.

1113. μὲν οὖν corrects a previous statement: 'nay, into thine own hands will I deliver her.' Cf. supr. 821, n. The middle τίθεσθαι is used of 'depositing' one's property, e.g. in a bank. Cf. χερσὶν ἐνθεῖναι, supr. 854.

1115. ''Tis thy right hand alone whose pledge I trust.'

1118. καὶ δή, often used thus in answer to a command: cf. Soph. El. 1436 *Electra.* ᾗ νοεῖς ἔπειγέ νυν. *Orestes.* καὶ δὴ βέβηκα.
Γοργόν' ὡς καρατομῶν, 'with averted gaze, like Perseus cutting off the head of Medusa'; cf. crit. n.

1119. ἔχεις; Heracles asks, as he places Alcestis' hand in her husband's: ἔχω replies Admetus. 'Aye, keep her then,' adding as he removes the veil which had concealed the features of the rescued wife, 'and you will say that the son of Zeus is no ill guest.' For the break in the line, cf. supr. 390, n.

1121. πρέπειν, with dative='resemble': cf. Bacch. 917 πρέπεις δὲ Κάδμου θυγατέρων μορφὴν μιᾷ.

1123. τί λέξω; the use of the future implies that the surprise is so great that the speaker cannot at once find words to express his wonder: very similar in origin is the formula τί λέξεις; on the receipt of bad news; cf. supr. 262, n.; Hec. 511, n.

1125. κέρτομος, 'delusive': cf. Anth. Pal. VII. 191, 4 κέρτομον ἀντῳδοῖς χείλεσιν ἁρμονίαν (of Echo): I. A. 849 ἴσως ἐκερτόμησε κἀμὲ καὶ σέ τις (says Achilles to Clytaemnestra of Iphigeneia's pretended marriage to the former).

1126. 'Nay, not so; in her thou see'st thy wife.'

1128. 'No wizard is the man thou mad'st thy friend.' οὐ ψυχαγωγόν, perhaps implying σωματαγωγός. Cf. Aesch. Pers. 687, where the ghost of Dareius addresses the chorus of elders ὑμεῖς δὲ θρηνεῖτ' ἐγγὺς ἐστῶτες τάφου, | καὶ ψυχαγωγοῖς ὀρθιάζοντες γόοις | οἰκτρῶς καλεῖσθέ μ'.

1131. **θίγω, προσείπω κ.τ.λ.;** interrogative subjunctives: in this construction a man may either *deliberate* with himself, or appeal to another: instances of the former are found supr. 863: of the latter, here.

1133. ' Dear wife, who again dost see and breathe.' **ὄμμα,** of one who αὐγὰς ἠλίου βλέπει : cf. supr. **122, n.**

δέμας, of the living body, cf. supr. 348, n.

1135. **ἔχεις** following ἔχω 1134 reminds us of 1119 ἔχεις; ἔχω. The idea of the θεόθεν φθόνος, which attended great prosperity, was familiar to the older religion : cf. Or. 974 (of the house of Pelops) φθόνος νιν εἷλε θεόθεν : I. A. 1097 μή τις θεῶν φθόνος ἔλθῃ : Herod. III. 40 ἐμοὶ δὲ αἱ σαὶ μεγάλαι εὐτυχίαι οὐκ ἀρέσκουσιν (said Amasis to Polycrates of Samos), ἐπισταμένῳ τὸ θεῖον, ὡς ἔστι φθονερόν.

1137. **ὁ φιτύσας** (poet. for φυτεύσας) **πατήρ,** Zeus, as opposed to Amphitryon, his putative father.

1139. **ἔπεμψας,** 'didst thou bring?' lit. 'escort.' So Hermes is νεκροπομπός, but in the opposite direction.

1140. **δαιμόνων :** the Schol. notes φασὶ γὰρ καὶ τοὺς νεκροὺς δαίμονας : this is doubtless true of later Greek : cf. crit. n.

1142. Cf. supr. 845 sq.

1143. **γὰρ** marks surprise : cf. supr. 1089, n. The silence of Alcestis is a fine stroke of the poet.

1146. **ἀφαγνίσηται κ.τ.λ.,** 'offer expiatory sacrifice to,' i.e. 'free herself from (ἀφ-) the consecration to the nether gods,' described supr. 76. For a cognate force of ἀπο- in compounds, cf. supr. 768, n. It would be interesting to know why a term of three days is chosen for the purification : possibly there may be some connexion with τὰ τρίτα, so called ἐπειδὴ τῇ τρίτῃ τὸ τῶν νεκρῶν ἄριστον ἐφέρετο (Schol. Ar. Lys. 611).

1147. **δίκαιος ὤν,** prob. 'as you ought,' considering what benefits you have received from a ξένος. For this (somewhat prosy) use, cf. Thuc. IV. 17 δίκαιοί εἰσι ἀπιστότατοι εἶναι, 'they have good reason to be most suspicious.'

1150. **πορσυνῶ,** 'will carry out': cf. Soph. El. 670 πρᾶγμα πορσύνων μέγα, 'in furtherance of an important matter.' **τυράννῳ,** adjective, as Med. 1125 ἡ τύραννος κόρη.

1151. **συνέστιος :** so (El. 785) Aegisthus says to the pretended Thessalians—Pylades and Orestes, on their mission of blood—νῦν μὲν παρ' ἡμῖν χρὴ συνεστίους ἐμοὶ | θοίνῃ γενέσθαι. No doubt there would be many a sacrifice and feast in the palace at Pherae.

1152. αὖθις, 'in the future': cf. Or. 910 ὅσοι δὲ σὺν νῷ χρηστὰ βουλεύουσ᾽ ἀεὶ | κἂν μὴ παραυτίκ᾽ αὖθίς εἰσι χρήσιμοι: Hipp. 312 τοῦδ᾽ ἀνδρὸς αὖθις λίσσομαι σιγᾶν πέρι.

1153. νόστιμον δ᾽ ἔλθοις πόδα, 'may'st thou come on homeward foot': for the accus., cf. supr. 869, n.

1154. A contrast to his former contemplated edict, cf. supr. 425. In the time of Euripides, Thessaly was divided into four tetrarchies Thessaliotis, Pelasgiotis (in which was Pherae), Histiaeotis and Phthiotis, all nominally subject, at any rate in war-time, to a supreme Tagus: this theoretical unity was rarely a fact, and Thessalian politics were notorious, even among the στάσις-loving Hellenes, for their centrifugal character. From supr. 590 sq. we may gather that Euripides, if he thought of the matter at all, supposed Admetus to have ruled the τετραρχία of Pelasgiotis.

1155. χοροὺς ἱστάναι βωμούς τε κνισᾶν were familiar words of ritual to the Athenians; cf. Ar. Av. 1230 πρὸς ἀνθρώπους πέτομαι παρὰ τοῦ πατρὸς | φράσουσα θύειν τοῖς Ὀλυμπίοις θεοῖς | μηλοσφαγεῖν τε βουθύτοις ἐπ᾽ ἐσχάραις | κνισᾶν τ᾽ ἀγυιάς: orac. ap. Dem. 1072 Ἀπόλλωνι Ἀγυιεῖ Λητοῖ Ἀρτέμιδι καὶ τὰς ἀγυιὰς κνισσῆν καὶ κρατῆρας ἱστάμεν καὶ χοροὺς κ.τ.λ. κνῖσα is the 'reek of burnt sacrifice.'

1157. μεθηρμ. βελτ. βίον, 'have changed our lot of life for a better than of late.'

1158. ἀρνήσομαι with a participle occurs also Or. 1581 ἀρνεῖ κατακτάς, κἀφ᾽ ὕβρει λέγεις τάδε;

1159—1163. This 'tag' is found at the end of the Medea, Andromache, Bacchae and Helen: perhaps we owe it to the actors. I cannot forbear to give Prof. Gildersleeve's rendering of what he calls a 'wretched tail-piece' (quoted in Mr Earle's edition):

> "How many the forms of these devilish storms!
> And much that is odd 's fulfilled by the gods;
> That comes not about for which you look out;
> What you don't expect that God doth effect,
> And such was the course of this story."

CRITICAL NOTES.

THE text of the Alcestis has been preserved for us in the following manuscripts :

B, Codex Vaticanus 909, of the xiith or xiiith century ; it is preserved in the Vatican library at Rome, and contains scholia and glosses : it has been corrected by two hands at least.

C, Codex Hauniensis, now at Copenhagen : of no great value.

a, Codex Parisinus 2713 : of the xiiith century : it gives a text derived from the same archetype as BC, but has been edited and emended by a Byzantine grammarian in accordance with the scholarship of the period.

b, c, d are Florentine manuscripts of the same class as *a* : I have not cited them, as they are of little independent value.

The above belong to the first family of Euripidean manuscripts, to which Kirchhoff in his critical edition of the plays (larger edition 1855, smaller edition 1867) assigns very great weight, unduly disregarding the authority of the manuscripts of the second family, which found a champion in Nauck shortly after the appearance of Kirchhoff's great work. These manuscripts are :

Flor. (in the Laurentian library at Florence) of the xivth century, and

Pal. (in the Vatican library), also of the xivth century, though probably of later date than Flor. Scholars are now unanimous in respecting the readings in which these two manuscripts agree, considering their agreement as evidence of the reading of a common archetype (represented in the following critical notes by S). This archetype was probably of the xiith century, and, though by no means free from interpolations and blunders, is of the greatest value for the construction of the text, as it provides us with an independent recension which we may compare with the tradition of the first family of manuscripts. The latter part of the play, from line 1029 onwards, is also found in a manuscript (Harleianus 5743) now in the British Museum, one of the thousands collected by Robert Harley, first earl of Oxford, and his son Edward, second earl, and sold by the widow of the latter in 1753 to the nation for £10,000. It is of the same character as Pal. and Flor.

---

16. Monk would emend πατέρα τε γραῖάν θ' on the ground of the absurdity of explaining πάντας φίλους as merely his father and mother: by his emendation he would make three possible substitutes for Admetus, a friend, his father and his mother. Nauck rejects the line, but if it were retained would read καὶ πατέρα γραῖάν θ'. Dr Verrall however points out ('Euripides the Rationalist,' pp. 27, 28) that the Fates' bargain was to take in exchange for Admetus one of his family, that is, either father, mother or wife. 'The death of a person of another family, who would be buried with *his* loved ones in a different burying-place, and worshipped with other and alien rites, would be no compensation at all.'

17. MSS ἥτις, an early mis-correction due to the neighbouring γυναικός; Reiske corrected to ὅστις.

18. We may read either θανὼν...μηκέτ' or θανεῖν...μηδ' ἔτ'.

25. ἱερέα must be written, not ἱερῆ of the MSS, as Attic never contracts -εα to -η in the accus. of nouns in -ευς: Meist. Gr. Att. Inschr.² § 55 with note 1008.

31. ἀφοριζόμενος καὶ καταπαύων. Nauck condemns as a gloss; for insufficient reasons, I think: cf. n. in Commentary.

37. I have put a mark of interrogation after παῖς. See n. on 32 in Commentary.

55. γέρας. S has κλέος, no doubt an adscribed interpretation, which has ousted the original.

57. τιθεῖς. This, the correct form of the 2nd sing. (cf. Cobet, Var. Lect. p. 221; Nov. Lect. p. 699), is preserved (as τιθεῖς) in Pal.: the rest have τίθης.

59. ὤνοιντ' Pal., ὠνοῖντ' Flor., ὄνοιντ' BC; the latter preferred by Kirch. and Prinz in the corrected form ὄναιντ', the stages of corruption being ὄναιντ', ὄνοιντ', ὠνοῖντ'; both traditions are recognized by the scholiasts: as I understand the passage (cf. n. on 50 in Commentary),

the reading preserved in Pal. and Flor. (including οἷς for οὕς) is to be preferred. I also read γηραιοὶ for MSS γηραιούς, with W. Dindorf and Hermann.

64. πείσει F. W. Schmidt for MSS παύσει. The sarcastic reference to the 'persuasiveness' of Heracles is well in accord with the tone of the passage.

70, 71. Condemned by W. Dindorf, Kirch. (ed. min.), Prinz.

79. Following Monk, I have inserted ἔστ' after πέλας for metrical considerations.

81. The order of the words is due to Blomfield.

82. Nauck transferred τόδε to follow Πελίου; in the MSS it follows φῶς.

94. MSS οὐ γὰρ δὴ φροῦδός γ' ἐξ οἴκων νέκυς ἤδη. The arrangement in the text is due to Kirchhoff.

96. After this line an anapaestic monometer has fallen out, corresponding to line 110 of the antistrophe; στείλας ἄξια seems to me to represent what is required by the context; cf. n. in Commentary.

100. φθιτῶν S: φθιμένων the rest of the MSS, unmetrically.

103. MSS οὐδὲ, corrected (by Musurus probably) in the Aldine edition to οὐ. Dindorf meets the metrical difficulty by reading οὐδὲ νεαλής: the latter word he would also introduce into Soph. O. C. 475, where Jebb points out that its meaning is not 'young,' but 'untired': the same objection holds here too, though perhaps not so strongly.

114. Λυκίαν Monk for MSS Λυκίας.

115. MSS εἴτ' ἐπὶ τὰς ἀνύδρους | Ἀμμωνιάδας ἕδρας κ.τ.λ. Nauck's restoration, given in the text, brings the passage into correspondence with the antistrophe.

117. I have printed παραλύσει for the MSS παραλύσαι. Objection may be taken to the reading of the MSS, both on the ground of the omission of ἄν (cf. n. on supr. 52 in Commentary), and the form of the word: 'the evidence is simply overwhelming, and proves to certainty that optative forms ending in -αι were quite unknown to the Athenians.' Rutherford, N. P. p. 436, who admits its occurrence in Aesch., while denying it in Soph. and Eurip. Prinz also reads παραλύσει, noting it as a conjecture of Gilbert Wakefield.

119. ἐσχάραν Reiske for MSS ἐσχάραις.

120. For ἐπὶ of the MSS I have written ἔτι. The same confusion occurs in the antistrophe, l. 130, where BC give τίν' ἔτι βίου, Pal. and Flor. τίν' ἐπὶ βίου.

131. προσδέχωμαι Musgrave for MSS προσδέχομαι.

132, 3. I have printed these lines as the MSS give them, though they are clearly wrong as they stand. Kirch. thought that the two lines are made up of the beginnings of five lines of an anapaestic system, the latter part of each verse being lost. Dindorf regards 132—136 as metrically correspondent with 105—111, a view which involves the supposition of a loss of the two lines which should answer 109, 110. If in a system of mixed lyrics and anapaests it might be permissible to write the lines as follows πάντα γὰρ ἤδη τετέλεσται βασιλ|εῦσι, θεῶν δ᾽ ἐπὶ βωμοῖς πάντων κ.τ.λ., one could understand the reason for the endeavour to correct what would appear to the copyist unmetrical lines, which resulted, however, only in the production of an impossible paroemiac.

135. οὐδ᾽ ἔστι κ.τ.λ. S; the other MSS read (unmetrically) ἀλλ᾽ οὐδ᾽ ἔστι κ.τ.λ.

177, 178. It is very probable that Nauck is right in condemning line 178: κορεύματ᾽ is ἅπαξ λεγόμενον, and πέρι is most unusual: cf. n. in Commentary.

197. For τ᾽ ἄν I have written τἄν: cf. n. in Commentary.

198. οὔποθ᾽ οὖ is Nauck's correction of the MSS οὔποτ᾽ οὐ or οὖ ποτ᾽ οὐ.

200. εἰ...σφε S; ἦς...γε B; a is nearly right with ἦι...σφε.

204. Between 204 and 205 a verse has been lost completing the sentence commenced in 204: Elmsley first noted the lacuna.

207. As a rough adjustment of the loss of a line at 204, two verses from the Hecuba (411, 412) were introduced here, but expelled by Valckenaer: ὡς οὔποτ᾽ αὖθις, ἀλλὰ νῦν πανύστατον | ἀκτῖνα κύκλον θ᾽ ἡλίου προσόψεται (προσόψομαι in Hec.).

213. In the words of Prinz, '*quomodo* 213, 214 *et antistrophici* 226, 227 *corrigendi sint, prorsus incertum.*' I have kept as near to the MSS as possible, giving preference to the tradition of S in the order of interjections in 226, reading πάρεστιν for πάρεστι in 214, and accepting Monk's στερεὶς for MSS στερηθεὶς in 227: see n. infr. on 226.

219. εὐχόμεθα Pal., εὐχώμεθα Flor., ἐχωμεθα B, εὐχώμεσθα a: I have given εὐχόμεσθα, which corresponds metrically with κατθανοῦσαν in 232. The neighbouring subjunctives τέμω, ἀμφιβαλώμεθ᾽ would account for the corruption. I have assigned 218—225 to the chorus, thinking that the prayer should be the offering of all, not of a semi-chorus only: similarly 231—237: there is of course a natural break at 219 and 232,

but not necessarily a change of speaker. Flor. assigns 218—225 to the attendant, thus affording some slight support to my arrangement, inasmuch as it regards the eight lines as spoken uninterruptedly and by a speaker other than that of the preceding lines. The usual division is to assign 213, 214: 215—217: 218, 219: 220—225 each to a semichorus, and similarly in the antistrophe.

223. . Not only metrical difficulties but difficulties of construction meet us here and in the corresponding passage of the antistrophe 235 sq. τοῦδ' ἐφηῦρες, καὶ νῦν is the reading of the MSS (though C has τοῦτ'), and in the antistrophe χθὼν τὰν ἀρίσταν. Apart from the entire lack of metrical antiphony, as the passage stands in the MSS it is hard to give a satisfactory construction for τοῦδ', while in the antistrophe μαραινομέναν παρ' Ἅιδαν, 'wasting away to Hades,' is most harsh. I have ventured to emend the passage by reading in 223 τοῦτ' ἐφηῦρες τῷδε, believing that τοῦτ' was first corrupted to τοῦδ', perhaps owing to the influence of πάρος preceding (mistaken for a preposition), and that, τοῦδ' being established in the text, τῷδε was regarded as an error and removed; and in 235 χθών, ἰοῦσαν τὰν ἀρίσταν κ.τ.λ., thus providing a natural construction for the passage. Dindorf thinks τοῦδ' ἐφηῦρες an interpolation which has taken the place of the original word (he suggests παρῆσθα). Hermann's τῷδ' ἐφηῦρες τοῦτο and repeated στέναξον (after χθών) in 235 are adopted by Mr Earle.

226. παῖ παῖ φεῦ φεῦ ἰὼ ἰώ S: cp. supr. n. on 213.

228. ἆρ' Hermann for MSS αἲ αἲ.

232. εἰν Dindorf for MSS ἐν.

252 sqq. The reading of this strophe and antistrophe is most uncertain. If we assume that strict syllabic correspondence is not necessary in an agitated passage like the present, largely made up of short interjectional sentences, then by the transference of μέθες με found in the MSS (with the exception of S) before τί ῥέξεις in 262, where it causes excess, to follow οὐχ ὁρᾷς in 259, where it remedies defect, we have a very tolerable metrical equivalence, and an improved sense: see n. in Commentary on 259. There is no need, then, to excise (with Dindorf, Nauck, Prinz, following the Aldine ed.) ἐν λίμνᾳ in 252.

262. τί ῥέξεις; B has πράξεις: the corruption would arise from ΤΙ of τί ῥέξεις being read Π, whence πρέξεις, corrected to πράξεις.

275. μὴ πρός σε θεῶν, σε was added by Porson.

294. φιτύσειν B and corrected in a: the rest by a common error φυτεύσειν: cf. infr. 1137, n.

295. ἔξων B and corrected in Flor., the rest ἔξην; cf. n. in Commentary.

304. 'ἐμῶν suspectum' is Prinz's note: a suspicion which in my opinion is worse than baseless: surely the point of the passage lies in ἐμῶν, 'in the house where once I was honoured mistress, let not *my* children be slighted.'

311. Here follows in the MSS a line made up from supr. 195 ὃν καὶ προσεῖπε καὶ προσερρήθη πάλιν.

318. The reading in the text is due to S: the rest give τοῖσι σοῖσι θαρσυνεῖ.

321. Prinz remarks 'μηνός vitiosum.' To me the entire line seems 'vicious,' and probably due to an interpolator who did not see that καὶ τόδ' in 320 needs no verb, and was anxious perhaps to parade his knowledge of the Athenian custom of 'days of grace'; cf. n. in Commentary. ἐς τρίτην is rarely found in Attic without ἡμέραν added; cf. Pierson on Moeris, p. 152.

326. οὐχ ἄζομαι Ba; οὐ χάζομαι S and correctors of a. The scholiast no doubt found the former, as he quotes in illustration μηδ' ἄζεο θοῦρον Ἄρηα (Hom. Il. V. 830), but there is, I think, something to be said for οὐ χάζομαι. ἄζομαι always implies 'religious awe' of gods, parents or the like, a meaning unsuited to the passages in Eurip. where the rival readings are ἄζομαι and χάζομαι, here, that is, and Or. 1116, καὶ μὴν τόδ' ἔρξας δὶς θανεῖν οὐχ ἄζομαι, where the sense is 'I do not mind dying twice.' That χάζομαι, which is common in Homer, remained in the language is proved by ἀναχάζεσθαι, Xen. Cyrop. VII. 1, 34: Anab. IV. 1, 16; IV. 7, 10: διαχάζεσθαι Cyrop. VII. 1, 31: Anab. IV. 8, 13. An objection is that χάζομαι is always constructed with the genitive, never, so far as I can find, with the infin., while an infin. is found with ἄζομαι. Eurip. then either uses ἄζομαι in a new sense, or χάζομαι in a new construction.

332, 333. Condemned by Nauck. The MSS give οὐκ ἔστιν οὕτως οὔτε πατρὸς εὐγενοῦς | οὔτ' εἶδος ἄλλως εὐπρεπεστάτη (ἐκπρεπεστάτη S) γυνή. Many corrections have been proposed. I have printed a conjecture of my own, which involves little change, gives a good sense (cf. n. in Commentary on 332, 333), and does not violate the canon that *facili lectioni praestat ardua*, as changes of ἄλλως to ἄλλων and εὐπρεπεστάτη to εὐπρεπεστέρα seem to me to do.

356. τρόπον Prinz for MSS χρόνον.

378. μ' Monk for MSS γ'.

409 sq. The lacunas were marked by Hermann.

427. μελαγχίμοις πέπλοις B; μελαμπέπλῳ στολῇ S and a corrector of *a* : the latter may be right.

434. For τιμᾶν S gives τιμῆς. The last word in the line is given variously; μόνην B, μόνη S, λίαν Ca : Kirch. points out that the divergence is due to the loss of the original disyllabic ending : Nauck emends τέτληκεν...θανεῖν.

449. I have kept the reading of the MSS ὥρα, which has been altered by editors to ὥρας, on the strength of Hesych. περι(ν)ίσσεται ὥρας· περιέρχεται τὰς ὥρας: and for κύκλος I read κύκλον, 'when the season of the Carneian month cometh round on circling course.' This gives the required sense easily, κύκλος K. μηνὸς περινίσσεται ὥρας harshly, when we remember that it is the time of *arrival* of the festival, and not the period *occupied in the coming*, which is referred to. The use of the accus. (cognate or extension over) of κύκλος in this sense is frequent in Eur., cf. Phœn. 477, 544 : Or. 1645 : Hel. 112.

463. A corrector of Flor. for πέσοι writes πέσειε, probably to bring the line into correspondence with 474, where he read τοῦτο γὰρ. The 1st aor. ἔπεσα, though common in Alexandrine and Byzantine Greek, has been banished from Attic; it is found in Pal. and the Harleian (in the British Museum) at Tro. 291.

468. A line has fallen out here : κατθανεῖν σύ γ᾽ ἐτόλμας may represent the sense ; cf. n. in Commentary.

473. τὸ Erfurdt's correction of MSS τοῦτο ; cf. supr. 463, n.

482. S preserves the right reading συνέξευξαι: the rest have προσέζευξαι, a compound which is not found till Lucian.

487. Again the reading of S τοὺς πόνους is preferable to τοῖς πόνοις of the rest.

501. For the MSS παισὶν I have read πᾶσιν ; cf. n. in Commentary; the enumeration of first, second and third makes the exaggeration natural : παισὶν seems pointless.

520. πέρι S : ἔτι the rest, which I prefer. πέρι would seem to a copyist, ignorant of the usage illustrated in the Commentary, a natural correction.

526. τόδ᾽ MSS, τότ᾽ Wakefield. ἀμβαλοῦ, Nauck for ἀναβαλοῦ.

527. B*a* give the reading in the text. S is strangely uncouth ; Pal. gives τέθνηκεν ὁ μέλλων καὶ ὁ θανὼν οὐκέτ᾽ ἐστιν, improved in Flor. to τέθνηκε (-χ᾽ ὁ, first hand) μελλων χὠ θανὼν οὐκ ἔστ᾽ ἔτι.

542. Elmsley (followed by several editors) reads αἰσχρόν τι παρὰ

κλαίουσι to avoid the lengthening of a naturally short vowel before κλ- ; cf. n. in Commentary.

551. προσκειμένης Wakefield for MSS προκειμένης : the corruption is a common one: cf. infr. 833.

558. ἐχθροξένους S : κακοξένους the rest.

565. τῷ μέν. I see no reason to alter this, the reading of the MSS ; cf. n. in Commentary. Prinz reads τῷ.

569. MSS give ὦ πολύξεινος καὶ ἐλεύθερος κ.τ.λ., which I keep : for the explanation, cf. n. in Commentary. Prinz adopts πολυξείνου καὶ ἐλευθέρου.

578. Possibly for σὺν we should read σῶν.

594. Either a word has slipped out here, or ἄγαμαι in 602 is an importation : the former alternative is the most likely, as ἄγαμαι is found in all MSS except Flor., where a corrector has struck it out.

617. δύσφορα S ; δυσμενῆ the rest.

635. ἀποιμώζεις B : S has ἀποιμώξεις, which is late : Attic uses fut. ἀποιμώξομαι.

636. After this line the MSS have οὐδ' ἡ τεκεῖν φάσκουσα καὶ κεκλη-μένη | μήτηρ μ' ἔτικτε· δουλίου δ' ἀφ' αἵματος | μαστῷ γυναικὸς σῆς ὑπε-βλήθην λάθρᾳ. Editors vie with one another in condemning lines 636—642 either wholly or in part : to me it seems probable that 636 is genuine, and provided the peg on which an interpolator, who thought that the equally culpable mother should get her share of abuse too, hung his unlucky triplet, wherein the king stolidly suggests the lowest of origins for himself. Line 640 follows naturally enough on line 636, nor does the repetition contained in 641 disturb me : repetition is common in excited speech, nor is Eurip. at pains to avoid it even in level passages.

645—647. Very probably Badham was right in condemning these lines : the solitary intrusion of the plural εἰάσατε is suspicious.

647. μόνην S ; ἐμόν B.

650. Two lines—κἀγώ τ' ἂν ἔζων χἤδε τὸν λοιπὸν χρόνον, | κοὐκ ἂν μονωθεὶς ἔστενον κακοῖς ἐμοῖς—made up from supr. 295, 296, follow in the MSS. They interrupt the argument here, which deals with Pheres only : ' You had but a short time to live, and (653 sqq.) your life had been a happy one : so why should you grudge so small a sacrifice ?'

657. διαρπάσαι S ; διαρπάσειν the rest.

658. S seems wrong here in reading ἀτιμάζοντα σὸν...προύδωκας : the person represented in the accus. (μ') should be the subject of the ὡς-sentence.

660. ἦ : MSS ἦν, but ἦ *eram*, ἦν *erat* is the rule.

666—668 are bracketed by Badham and Prinz : 668 by Nauck. I see no reason for the condemnation ; cf. n. in Commentary.

674. ὦ παῖ : wrongly inserted here from confusion with the next line (Elmsley).

697. λέγεις MSS ; ψέγεις Cobet.

706. τὸ Wakefield for MSS τά.

708. λέξαντος MSS ; Hermann's 'λέγξοντος is tempting.

713. μείζονα Schaefer for MSS μείζον' ἄν.

734. ἔρρων restored from the scholiast τινὲς δὲ ἔρρων γράφουσι σὺν τῷ ν : ἔρροις Ba ; ἔρρου S. The tense of the MSS ξυνοικήσασα seems wrong : I have written ξύνοικος οὖσα.

736. τῷδ' ἔτ' Elmsley : τῷδέ γ' Ba, τῷδ' ἴτ' S.

777. Nauck would alter to συνωφρυωμένος.

780. οἶδας MSS, οἶσθας Nauck : cf. n. in Commentary.

792. πιθοῦ Monk after Pal. : the rest have πείθου.

795. τύχας : the scholiast notes an old variant πύλας ; the same variation occurs infr. 829, where *a* gives both words, but a corrector has struck out τύχας. In that passage πύλας seems right. I cannot help thinking that the words here are corrupt, as ὑπερβαλὼν τύχας (which the scholiast explains καταφρονήσας) is a very strange expression, to which I can find no parallel. Mekler thinks the words τάσδ' ὑπερβαλὼν τύχας, στεφάνοις πυκασθεὶς '*e vv.* 829, 832 *huc retracta esse*.'

797. φρενῶν S, κακοῦ the rest. Kirchhoff, disliking S, remarks that the variations are the result of early conjectural remedies for a missing word, and so Nauck, who suggests τρόπου. I regard φρενῶν as the true reading, which was lost or corrupted in the other family of MSS.

810. οὔκουν S wrongly for οὐ χρῆν μ'. οὕνεκ' : Prinz writes the preposition εἵνεκ', but cf. Meisterhans Gr. Att. Inschr.[2], p. 177. Nauck transposes 810, 811 to follow 813, thus bringing out an effective contrast between οἰκεῖος and θυραίων : Prinz condemns the two lines.

811. οἰκεῖος : *a* has θυραῖος, which may be a gloss on ὀθνεῖος.

817 sqq. In the MSS follow these three lines :

πένθος γὰρ ἡμῖν ἐστι· καὶ κουρὰν βλέπεις
μελαμπέπλους στολμούς τε. HP. τίς δ' ὁ κατθανών ;
μῶν ἢ τέκνων τι φροῦδον ἢ πατὴρ γέρων ;

It hardly needs the authority of the scholiast (ταῦτα τὰ τρία ἔν τισιν οὐκ ἔγκειται) to assure us that some interpolation is present in the text. The interruption of the στιχομυθία by weak lines, which break the progress of Heracles' gradual enlightenment just before the climax, to say nothing of the *fractus versus* 819 (cf. Wilam. Moell., Anal. Eurip. p. 195 sq.), is intolerable. Most editors expel the three lines, though Dindorf and Mr Earle retain them. I have kept 820 for what seem to me imperative reasons. It will be well to consider the steps in the process of discovery. The first hint is given by the servant in 807 τί ζῶσιν; 'how say you "alive"?' The impression of the existence of some great hidden sorrow grows in the mind of Heracles, till in 812 he cries μῶν ξυμφοράν τιν' (observe the strong word inapplicable to a *stranger's* death) οὖσαν οὐκ ἔφραζέ μοι; In 814 he feels sure that there is some *domestic* trouble : the belief deepens with the assenting reply of the chorus (815) into complete certainty (816). In 820 he asks, thus leading to the climax of the following line, 'is it a child or perchance the father?' 'Nay (μὲν οὖν) no child, no parent : 'tis his wife.' The μὲν οὖν of 821 tells us that, if the line printed in the text is not the line Eurip. wrote, at any rate it gives what must have been its meaning. The amputative Nauck spares 820, though to compensate for his mercy in this direction he removes both 816 and 817, as well as the guilty couplet 818, 819 (altering also the τρία of the scholiast to τέσσαρα).

829. Cf. supr. 795 n.

832. τὸ μή: F. W. Schmidt conjectures τόδ' ἦν, not improbably.

833. προσκειμένου Scaliger for MSS προκειμένου: cf. supr. 551.

845. πεινῶντα is F. W. Schmidt's unconvincing conjecture (approved by Prinz) for πίνοντα.

846. λοχαίας (the MSS give λοχήσας) was conjectured by Hartung on the strength of the schol. γράφεται λοχίας (Schwartz λοχαίας), with Dindorf's approval. Prinz now cites in further support from Etym. M. (cod. Flor.) κἄν περ λόχαια σαυτὸν (*sic*) ἐξέδρας (*sic*): it is worthy of mention that this quotation is there adduced in illustration of Eurip.'s use of the word λοχαῖος in the Telephus, a play produced along with the Alcestis : cf. fr. 727 b (where Dindorf gives the passage from the Etym. M.). Cf. n. in Commentary.

877. MSS give πρόσωπον ἄντα λυπρόν, which does not correspond with the antistrophe πιέζει φανεῖσα θανῶν (894) : moreover ἄντα never occurs in trag. Hartung conjectured σ' ἔναντα. Musgrave τιν' ἄντα. Dindorf condemns ἄντα λυπρὸν as an interpolation. I have printed σε πάντα λυπρόν : cf. n. in Commentary. The corruption may have arisen from the similarity of προСΩΠΟΝ СΕΠΑΝτα, together with the recollection of the common Homeric ἄντα ἰδεῖν.

890. τιθεῖς BS : τίθης a : cf. supr. 57, n.

910. πόρσω Gaisford for MSS πρόσω, which, though Eurip.'s favourite form (cf. n. in Commentary), is unmetrical here.

921. εἶμεν Heath from εἰ μὲν in Pa : ἦμεν the rest.

939. χρῆν Elmsley for MSS χρή.

974, 975. ἔστιν...ἐλθεῖν, transposed by G. A. Wagner : MSS have ἐλθεῖν...ἔστιν.

978. νεύσῃ S, νεύσει the rest.

992. θανοῦσ᾽ ἔτ᾽ ἔσται is Prinz's emendation for the unmetrical θανοῦσ᾽ ἔσται of the MSS. Nauck for ἔσται reads ἐς ἀεί.

1009. μομφὰς Flor. a ; (schol. μέμψεις) : μορφὰς the rest.

1014. Condemned by Prinz, Nauck and others, following Lachmann.

1019. οὕνεχ᾽ : Prinz εἵνεχ᾽ : cf. supr. 810, n.

1029. From this point we have the assistance of the Codex Harleianus 5743, preserved in the British Museum.

1037. ἀτίζων Harl. : ἀτιμάζων the rest.

1045. μή μ᾽ ἀναμνήσῃς κακῶν S : but B has μή με μιμνήσκεις, a μή με μι*μνήσῃς, which are hard to explain if the straightforward μή μ᾽ ἀναμνήσῃς was in the archetype. I believe the original to have been μηδέ με μνήσῃς : cf. supr. 878 for the use of the active aorist, which is rare, and would naturally be corrupted ; or possibly μηδέ μ᾽ ἀμμνήσῃς, which would better account for a. I cannot think that the punctuation ἄλλον τιν᾽...σώζειν ἄνωχθι...μὴ ᾽μέ᾽ μιμνήσκεις κακῶν· is right.

1059. ἄλλης S : ἄλλοις the rest.

1062. ταῦτ᾽ Aemilius Portus (who taught Greek at Heidelberg at the end of the xvith century, son of a Cretan who was Greek professor at Ferrara) for MSS ταῦτ᾽.

1071. ὅστις εἶ σύ MSS. If this reading is right, the chorus are speaking in general terms : Lat. *quisquis es.* Hermann emends ὅστις εἶσι, 'whatever god shall come' (cf. 976 μή μοι, πότνια, μείζων ἔλθοις ἢ τὸ πρίν). Monk ἥτις ἐστί (sc. δόσις). Perhaps χρὴ δ᾽, ὅστις εἶ, σε κ.τ.λ. might be suggested, or ὅστις ἧκε (sc. θεός), as κ and ιϲ are frequently confused : cf. Cobet V. L. p. 124.

1077. ὑπέρβαλλ᾽ Monk following a (ὑπέρβαλ᾽) : ὑπέρβαιν᾽ the rest.

1087. νέου γάμου πόθος Flor. : πόθοι the rest. Prinz gives a conjecture of J. Guttentag νέος γάμος πόθου, which is plausible.

1097. γενναίως Lenting : γενναίαν S : γενναίων the rest.

1108. This verse is omitted in B, but added by a later hand.

1114.   δῶμα δ' S : δώματ' the rest.

1118.   καρατομῶν Lobeck's emendation of the MSS καρατόμῳ, which would involve the elision of the ι of the dative Γοργόνι.   On this elision in tragedy, see Appendix to Jebb's Soph. O. C. p. 285, 286 : the alleged instances have all been emended by Lobeck and others.

1123.   λέξω S : λεύσσω the rest, taken by error from the next line.
θαῦμ' MSS : Nauck's correction φάσμα is accepted by most editors.

1130.   τύχῃ Reiske for MSS τύχην.

1137.   φιτύσας B, φυτεύσας the rest ; cf. supr. 294.

1140.   κυρίῳ a, κοιράνῳ the rest.   I take δαιμόνων κυρίῳ as = 'with that one of the δαίμονες (θάνατος is a δαίμων, cf. 62, n. in Commentary) who had charge of her.'   If κοιράνῳ be retained, we should read (with Jacobs) νερτέρων for δαιμόνων : it is unlikely that in Eurip.'s time Thanatos could be called δαιμόνων κοίρανος : cf. n. in Commentary.

1153.   πόδα a : ὁδόν B : δόμον S : the three variants are of ancient date.   Wilamowitz-Moellendorff suggests δρόμον.

INDICES.

I. GREEK.

The figures refer to the line-numbering of the notes.
Verbs, except in special forms and phrases, are placed below in the
Infinitive.

ἄνωχθι, 1044
ἀξιοῦν, 571, 1010
ἀοιδός with gen., 453
ἀπαντλεῖν, 354
ἀπειπεῖν, 487, 737
ἀπλακών, form of, 242
ἀπό, force of, in compounds, 768, 1146
ἀποιμώζειν, 768
ἄποινα, construction of, 7
Ἀπόλλων ἀγυιεύς, 170
ἀπομνήσασθαι χάριν, 299
ἀποστερεῖν, 384
ἀπότομος, 118, 982
ἆρα, = ἆρ᾽ οὔ, 228, 341, 477, 771
ἆρα, 636, 669
ἄρδην, 608
ἄρματα, = 'chariot-horses,' 483
ἀρνεῖσθαι, with partic., 1158
ἄροτοι γυᾶν, 590
ἀρταμεῖν, 494
ἄρτι, ἀρτίως, 531
ἀσκεῖσθαι, 161
ἀσπάζεσθαι, 191
ἄσπονδος, 424
ἀστένακτος, 173
ἀτίζειν, 1037
αὖ, 30
αὖθις, = 'in the future,' 1152
αὐλός, 346
αὑτοῦ for ἑαυτοῦ, as indirect reflexive, 18
αὐχεῖν, 675
αὐχμηρός, 947
ἀφαγνίζεσθαι, 1146
ἀφορίζεσθαι, 31

βαλών, 680
βάρβιτος, 345
βαστάζειν, 724, 917
βίᾳ θυμοῦ, 829
βλέπειν, with accus. not tragic, 773
βλέφαρον, 398
βουφορβεῖν, 8
βουφόρβια, 1031
βρέτας, 974
βωμός, 119

γάμος, γάμοι, meanings of, 316

γάρ, 3, 163, 179, 279
  ,, prefatory, 158
  ,, marking surprise, 1089, 1143
  ,, implying assent, 42, 715
  ,,   ,,   dissent, 147
γε, of assent, 47, 62
  ,, after καὶ μήν, emphasizing single word, 369, 713
γε μήν, 516
γεγενῆσθαι, 85
γέρας, 55
γνησίως, 678
γοῦν, 694
γύης, 590

δαίμων, of superhuman being, 62, 1003, 1140 (with cr. n.)
δαίμων = 'fortune,' 499, 561, 935
δαίμων = 'fortune' individualized, 384
δάκνεσθαι καρδίαν, 1100
δάπεδον, 590
δαφοινός, 581
δεδορκὼς ἦν, 123
δεικνύναι with partic., 763
δέμας)(σῶμα, 348, 468, 1133
δέμνιον, in singular, 183
δεξιὰν προτείνειν, 194
δή, after ἐνταῦθα, 176
δῆλα (ἐστί) = δῆλον (ἐστί), 218
δῆτα, strengthening appeal, 308
δῆτα, marking consequence, without impatience, 380
δῆτα, showing impatience, 530, 689, 960, 1051
δι᾽ ὀδύνας ἔβας, 874
διακναίεσθαι, 109
διαλλάσσειν, 14
διαμάχεσθαι, followed by accus. (infinitival), 694
διαπρέπειν, 642
διεξελθεῖν, 15
δίκαιος)(ὅσιος, 10
δίκαιος ὤν, 1147
δίνη, δῖνος, 244
δίψιον Ἄργος, 560
δμαθέντες, 127
δόμος, curious use of, 160
δ᾽ οὖν, 73
δραμεῖν ἀγῶνα, 489

II. ENGLISH.

𝕮𝖆𝖒𝖇𝖗𝖎𝖉𝖌𝖊:

PRINTED BY JOHN CLAY, M.A.

AT THE UNIVERSITY PRESS.